Ted Williams,
My Father

Ted Williams,
My Father

CLAUDIA WILLIAMS

ecco
An Imprint of HarperCollins*Publishers*

HarperCollins books may be purchased for educational, business, or sales promotional use. For information please e-mail the Special Markets Department at SPsales@harpercollins.com.

FIRST EDITION

All photographs with the exception of those otherwise noted and page 11 (top left and right, and bottom right) and page 12 (top) are © by Ted Williams Family Enterprises, Ltd.

Library of Congress Cataloging-in-Publication Data has been applied for.

ISBN 978-0-06-225956-1

14 15 16 17 18   OV/RRD   10 9 8 7 6 5 4 3 2 1

*In memory of my beloved father and my beloved brother.
I miss you every day, always.*

*For my mom, who is the great woman who stood behind
the great man. I love you.*

*For my husband, Eric, thank you for being by my side
throughout this journey; I love you dearly. And to his
three beautiful, smart, and sensitive daughters: Emma,
Erin, and Elise, I hope you always cherish and love the
wonderful father that you have.*

For Courtney, my dear friend, whom I love like family.

Contents

Contents

Ted Williams,
My Father

Prologue

From the beginning of my life, I knew Ted Williams as my father first and a fisherman second. Baseball player might not even have been third. I knew nothing specific about what he'd done on the field or over his career. I only vaguely knew he had played baseball, and that was long before I was born.

On September 28, 1960, a cold, overcast day, Ted Williams stood at home plate for the last time. The stands were only partially full. Very few people realized this would be the last time they would ever see the Splendid Splinter play.

Twenty-two years later I saw my father in a baseball uniform for the first and only time in my life; I was ten years old and my father was sixty-three. It was May 1, 1982, at an Old-Timers' Game in Fenway Park—a perfect spring day with the stands packed. I didn't have a clue what I was about to experience. From where I sat, it was almost as exciting that my big brother, John-Henry, was on the field as an honorary bat boy, and the fact that he was going to pick up the bats after the hitters went to the plate was thrilling.

As my mom and I sat in the stands, I knew I was going to see my dad at any moment. The announcer's voice echoed through the stadium. Before the game began, he introduced each player as he took the field, but the announcer never said their names first. As if teasing the crowd to guess which player it was, he would only mention some of the player's statistics and maybe a small bit of his history—almost testing the crowd to see if they knew the player about to emerge from the dugout before actually hearing his name. When the announcer began each introduction, I'd tug on my mom's jacket.

"Is that Dad?"

Then the name would be said, and the announcer would start again with stats of another player.

"Is that Dad?" Followed by another. "Is that Dad?" *When is Dad coming?*

"Bobby Doerr" . . . "Dom DiMaggio" . . . "Johnny Pesky" . . .

Finally, the announcer started highlighting a player whose career had big numbers, records that still stood, and how this player had served two "hitches" in the Marines. Those were the last words I heard. The crowd came alive. A wave of excitement swept over me as my senses responded to the people's reactions all around me. Something was building, something was happening. The claps and the cheers were so loud I could feel the vibration of the whole stadium and the electric energy racing through the air. Whoever this next player was, he was surely good. I couldn't even see my dad as he walked out on the field because everyone was standing up. I was swallowed up by a sea of people. I wouldn't have thought it possible, but the uproar grew even louder, and through the deafening noise I felt only emotion. My skin tingled and the rippling sensation traveled right up my back and behind my ears. The intensity was so great. I strained to see him, to catch even a glimpse. I was looking up and around and trying to weave my eyes through the crowd to see him. I so wanted to see him. It was then that my mom looked down at me.

"*That's* Daddy."

It was at that moment that I first realized that my dad had done something very special on a baseball field. I stood lost in the middle of the stadium among thousands of people, and I was proud. I was stunned by the roar of the crowd and the reaction to my father. I suddenly knew, as I looked at the backs of so many people standing in front of me, that Dad was more than a phenomenal fisherman. My mom reached down to pick me up and hold me above her shoulders. I saw my dad. He seemed so far away. As his little girl, I felt like he was now completely out of reach. He stood tall next to the other players on the baseball field, but now he was even larger than before. *My dad is something else,* I thought. Over the coming years I came to have a much better understanding of just what that was.

FIVE YEARS AFTER TED WILLIAMS WAS INDUCTED INTO THE National Baseball Hall of Fame, I was born. I learned his complexities long before I learned his statistics. My parents divorced when I was young, and while my brother and I were largely raised by our mother, our relationship with our father grew and changed over time. We spent weekends and summers with him and eventually much more time than that. We saw him not just as a figure who existed between the lines of a diamond but as the very human person that he was. My relationship with him was not defined or shaped by the game. It was shaped by him, it was shaped by me, and it was shaped by my brother. Together the three of us were a team. Together we formed our own little family.

Even after my parents divorced, they remained close. Throughout her life, Mom's memories of her relationship with him have been some of her most treasured. In January 2008, my mom suffered a stroke. She had to move from the hills of Vermont to Florida, just down the road from where I live, so that I could better care for her. Since the day she started her recovery, all she has longed for is to be better and to return to her home on the hill in the woods of Vermont. The funny thing with my mom's stroke is that she remembers what she wants to remember, and as I help her through her therapy and recovery I start to realize how precious memories are. Slowly, she is forgetting them, one by one.

I promised my mom that I would not let her forget Dad or John-Henry, despite her progressive dementia. I promised her that I would preserve as much as I could by writing down the memories of our family. She wants to remember the moments in life when Ted Williams was like a man no one else knew. She wants people to know who her son really was, and I want to tell the story. I want to share for the first time in my life what it was like to have these incredible people as part of my family. I want to share with women and men, sons and daughters, the importance of a father and the lessons one can always learn from him regardless of any family dynamic. No one knows my family like I do. And no one else knows these stories.

Mom wants to remember her life on the hill. She wants to remember the family inside the house that stares out over a vast and beautiful view of New England. Her children are laughing and playing and enjoying every bit of life. Her husband, a fisherman, a Marine, an American hero, and a baseball player, is the only man she will ever marry, and she loves him every day. She wants to return to her house of memories, sit by the fireplace, and have me sit beside her and tell these stories.

I decided to write this book as a testament to what it was really like to grow up with Ted Williams, my father. I have read a lot of what has been written about my father. People have been quoted saying they were my father's best friend, or a lifelong acquaintance, or a longtime girlfriend, and I have never even heard their names before. Some of the statements I have read are absolutely delusional, but still they have been presented as credible by many journalists and biographers. It's been very hard to believe and difficult to accept. I am the only person still living who can tell you what it was truly like within the walls of the Williams family.

This is not a report of "he said/she said"—this is a story of the family who surrounded a great man, how he influenced us, and how we were ultimately molded by who he was. This book presents only the facts. All our actions and decisions have been reflections of the love, the hate, the joy, the pain, but most importantly the impenetrable bond and trust within our family. I am a product of two fantastic parents, and I am honored to embrace every part of my family.

I invite you to just read and hear my story. Your opinion is your right, and when you have reached the last page of this book you will surely have another one. I ask only that you try to imagine what you would do if you were in a similar situation.

How does one weigh whether something merits explanation or is worthy of discussion? If I didn't write about it, it is because it did not deserve it. I have nothing to lose, and I have chosen to expose myself and my family so that at least you, the reader, will have a firsthand and intimate account of the truth. No one else knows these stories, though some may know bits and pieces. I hope these written memories allow you to understand better than any news article or media snippet what really mattered.

Motivated by a promise and a sense of urgency, I began this journey by writing all that I could, as fast as I could, before memories fade and the past seem so far away that I can no longer light the fire that burns to tell you something.

Chapter One

I'T'S LIKE A FLASHBACK . . . LIGHT IS TWINKLING OFF THE WATER like diamonds, and the rippling of the river rushes by me sitting on the bank. I can still hear the water and see the sparkles. He stood so tall in the middle of the river. The rising sun illuminated his figure, creating a silhouette of a man in deliberate motion—rhythmically lifting a rod and throwing a line back and forth, then whipping it through the air like a whip glazed with water. You could hear it just by seeing it.

These are the images that reside in my mind, preserving the first memories of my father. I was not yet eight years old.

This man was so good at whatever he was doing. He was so exact. The handmade fly at the end of his line looked just like a real exotic insect, and he could cast the disguised hook precisely where he wanted, leaving only the slightest ripple where it landed. Every few minutes the whole motion would start again, and then again, for countless hours. Surely a man with this conviction and determination would possess the same amount of patience and diligence in all that he did.

Whether it was on the Miramichi River in Canada or on a nineteen-foot boat off the Keys in Islamorada, Florida, my first memories of my father are of a fisherman—*the greatest fisherman in the world* as far as I was concerned, because he could make it look like the most beautiful display of art and craftsmanship one had ever seen.

After baseball, Dad lived for fishing. Every free moment he had, he was fishing. I grew up knowing him specifically as a fly fisherman. He had fished all waters with all gear, but his heart was with the Atlantic salmon. He said that what he loved the most about salmon fishing was the buildup, from the relentless pursuit to the ultimate fight and the challenging capture. He reveled in the constant fine-tuning of his gear, the adjustments to his line and tackle, and the study of every aspect of fishing. He was a scientific angler.

"I dream of catching salmon," he'd say. "I can't get enough of it. It's my favorite fish."

Dad traveled to almost every continent in the world and fished in close to a hundred rivers, but he always returned to the Miramichi. He wrote in his fishing journal that he was certain that he was the only person in the world who had caught more than a thousand salmon, a feat he accomplished by 1976, nearly twenty years before he stopped fishing. Ted Williams was inducted into the International Game Fish Association Hall of Fame in 2000, one of only three athletes to be inducted into the Halls of Fame of more than one professional sport.

Even though the attention span of a child is usually limited, I could sit patiently on a big river rock watching my father, mesmerized by his grace and skill. His eyes never left the water—his passion clear from his focus and body language. He knew exactly where his fly was, and he was keenly aware of any water disturbance around it.

I learned at a very young age that no matter what I did in life, it had better meet the highest standards and be driven by the hardest of work, laced with enthusiasm and passion. But how would I ever find some light behind this huge shadow of excellence? As a young child, I felt safe with my mom. She was proud of whatever I did—it didn't matter what it was. My position was not as secure with the man standing in the middle of the river. There was always a foreboding sense that if I did anything wrong or did not meet his standards or gain his approval, I would never make him proud.

ELEVEN YEARS AFTER MY FATHER HIT HIS LAST HOME RUN, I WAS a baby girl in his arms. I wouldn't truly understand or appreciate what my father had accomplished on a green diamond for many years after those first memories of him fishing. Little did I know at the time, as I played by the river, watching my father, that he was so much more than a great fisherman. He had also accomplished a lot more than just home runs and baseball batting records. Only time and the display of history would reveal to me the truly incomparable feats my father owned in his lifetime.

I believe a daughter's love for her father is innate. For years, however, I did not know how to approach this intimidating man. I first *learned* to love him and know him through observing the relationship that my big brother, my protector, had with him. It was just four days before Dad's fiftieth birthday when John-Henry was born, on August 26, 1968. Three years later I came along, on October 8, 1971.

John-Henry was the son Dad always wanted. He loved John-Henry enormously, and I could see it, feel it, and I knew it at a very young age. I did not resent it. Rather, I empathized with my sibling, worried for him and felt the pressure on him. Everything Dad hadn't accomplished in life John-Henry was to excel at, fulfilling all of our father's expectations. Ted Williams was a champion, and champions, regardless of their field—sports, business, the arts, politics, whatever—can be very demanding. They challenge the people around them to rise to their level. A champion is a tough act to follow.

Unfortunately, divorce presents even more challenges for a dad and his son. Sadly, my parents were divorced by the time I was three and John-Henry was six. I am certain the uncontrollable circumstances of being apart from John-Henry frustrated Dad to no end. And Dad did not handle frustration with grace or dignity. It challenged his world, and he did not like to be challenged without finding a successful resolution.

It took me many years to finally put together the puzzle of my father, and it was a very, very difficult puzzle. Never knowing him as an at-home parent was an added challenge; visits were like condensed sweets, full of highfalutin sugar and spice. Throughout our childhood, my brother and I saw our father only at specific times of the year—in the summer at his fishing camp in New Brunswick, and over the Christmas holidays at his Islamorada home in the Florida Keys. But sometimes, on special unannounced occasions when Dad was in New England or Boston, we were there together, somewhere nearby.

Our visits were a roller coaster of excitement and expectations, and never dull. My brother and I craved being around our dad. All three of us made the most of every visit, and visits were never void of emotion. Dad was larger than life. At almost six-four, he seemed like a giant to me; this huge booming man trouncing around was overwhelming, intense, and fascinating all at once. He was hard to figure out. One minute he was laughing with us, making turkey calls, endearingly calling us "little shits," and playfully giving us big "whooping potches" on our bottoms. Only seconds later, the smallest disturbance—a phone ringing, a door slamming, a raised voice— would set off a chain of internal reactions in him that would bloom into a full-on outburst. He could become a beast, snarling and cursing the skies so badly you could only wonder in amazement whether you would survive the imminent wrath of any higher being.

Dad couldn't wait to see his son during the holidays or summers. The two buddies were always off to do something together. They would go to the ballpark together or play catch or hit. I wanted so badly to be part of their special union. I had a huge disadvantage, though. I was a girl. *Girls aren't allowed in the dugout. Girls can't play baseball, and girls don't want to hunt or fish.* But worst of all, there was already a girl—a daughter from a previous marriage—who had sorely disappointed Dad. There were already two strikes against me. The last thing I wanted to do was disappoint or anger my father and hear him talk about me the way he did his first daughter.

"*As long as I have a hair in my ass she will be a pain in it!*"

You wouldn't believe how many times during my young years I wished I had been born a boy.

Chapter Two

FOR MANY PEOPLE THE LEGEND OF MY FATHER BIASES THEM from the start. They know Ted Williams from his accomplishments alone, which is to say, they don't know him very well. Whether as a ballplayer or a war hero, it's true that my father was exceptional, but he was also exceptionally complex. He did things on the field that few have done, and that clouds people's perception of him, often causing them to overlook the fact that, for a man who guarded his privacy fiercely, the difference between the public and the personal could be striking.

All too often we expect our heroes to be perfect. Often only a single facet of the diamond is revealed—because that's all the general public can take in and comprehend. But even diamonds can have flaws. Ted Williams was quickly criticized and sometimes despised because that was easier than finding the patience to try to figure him out. People who did not understand him commonly described him as arrogant and stubborn, but my father did not apologize for that. In Dad's opinion, he had earned the right to be that way. He had done everything possible to justify being that confident.

As he said in his book *My Life in Pictures:* "What's wrong with wanting to be better. . . . What's wrong with being the best? If you go out trying not to be the best, well . . . I don't know what the point is."

He was not always understood or liked. His language alone could alienate most anyone.

"Whenever I get afraid or upset about something, I swear something awful."

Dad was also fully aware of the mistakes he had made in his life and felt regret that he could not do anything about them. He also knew, however, how genuine and caring a person he could be, especially toward those less fortunate and in need of help.

"It's awful easy to find something wrong with someone and sometimes hard to find something good. I just hope I'm not in the latter category."

My father was born Teddy Samuel Williams in 1918 in San Diego. His brother, Danny, came along in 1920. They lived in a one-story wood-frame bungalow in a working-class neighborhood. In Dad's description of his childhood, it was almost as if he was a lost boy. It did not sound or feel warm in his family. His father, Samuel Williams, of Welsh descent, was a US marshal and rarely at home. His mother, May Venzor, of French descent, seemed to have traded her own family of two boys for a Salvation Army family. Dad would describe her as "strictly Salvation Army, and, as a result, strictly nonfamily." She spent more time out on the streets converting sinners and preaching against liquor than she did raising her two boys.

Sometimes she'd take Dad along, and he'd cringe behind the big bass drum, mortified as she banged away on it, marching down the streets of San Diego. Ironically, I believe that seeing his mom so devoted to religious salvation, and not to her two sons, is where my father's resentment of religion was born. Often he and Danny would come home from school to sit on the porch, locked out until their mother came home past ten o'clock. She had little time for cooking or housecleaning, and my father grew up ashamed of the shabby, 1,200-square-foot house on Utah Street, the stuffed chair in the living room with a hole in it because the mice had eaten through it. Still, Dad was closer to his mother than his father. His favorite picture of his mom hung above the dresser. It was a photo of May playing the guitar. He described her as "a very kind and empathetic woman." He described his dad as never being interested in him, a man who didn't even follow baseball but did enjoy photography. He was a quiet man, and he eventually drifted out of their lives.

With both parents effectively absent, the boys didn't learn appropriate boundaries and were not shown discipline. Their mother wasn't there to teach them how to be "good boys," and their father wasn't there to give them consequences. As two lost boys would, Teddy and Danny responded to their largely unsupervised upbringing in different ways. Dad described his childhood as an experience that would make you or break you. Danny went bad, becoming a juvenile delinquent and growing up to be a petty thief and crook, always in and out of jail. Teddy went good, becoming a disciplined ballplayer who practiced every day at the ball field, only two blocks from his San Diego home. He saved his money and bought his first car before he was eighteen. He came home one day, however, to find it up on blocks: Danny had stripped the tires and sold them. Danny would finally settle down, marry, and raise kids. But in 1960, at the young age of thirty-nine, Dad's brother died of acute myelogenous leukemia.

I used to ask my father about his childhood and my grandparents. He didn't seem to like talking about it.

"Read my book," he would say.

Still, he'd let bits and pieces out. Despite his family hardships, Dad was determined to fill the voids in his life. He was resourceful and associated himself with people who took a liking to him. His next-door neighbor taught him to fish and bought him his first reel.

The high school baseball coach would meet him at the ball field and toss the ball around with him. And Rod Luscomb, who managed the nearby playground and had pitched in the minor leagues, taught him baseball. He would become the hitting sensation at Hoover High School. At the age of seventeen, the New York Yankees made him an offer, but his mom didn't want him to move so far away. So instead, he signed with the San Diego Padres, a Pacific Coast League team.

Baseball and fishing became my father's two lifelong passions. They became his salvation and his sanctuary. Like a trained soldier, he carried his bat and glove to school and spent every second he could perfecting his swing. When he needed a break or found some free time, he went fishing.

I remember when I found Dad's high school yearbook tucked away in his library among his many books. Next to the seniors' pictures were always a few words about what they studied, what they wanted to follow as a career, or things they enjoyed as a hobby. Next to Dad's picture was only one word, the word that would identify him for the rest of his life as one of the best. It simply read, "Baseball."

Dad learned everything he knew about communication skills from the gang of boys with whom he played baseball. Coaches, managers, and fellow ballplayers became his new family. I would describe Dad as a kid who *acted* cocky and tough but in reality was simply craving attention. He wanted someone to praise him and acknowledge how good he was at hitting a baseball. "Compliments would only push me to improve." He learned a little bit from all the players around him, and whenever someone paid a compliment to someone else, Dad wanted to know what it was for, so that he could adopt it. *Oh yeah?* he'd think. *I can do that too—just watch me do it better!*

It was that attitude that led him, at age nineteen, to say, "All I want out of life is that when I walk down the street folks will say, 'There goes the greatest hitter who ever lived.'"

Dad would explain that he'd say that because he was a cocky kid who needed the motivation, the constant reminder to stay focused on his goal. He explained his success as coming from the stubbornness of a young man and his determination to be successful, even if it was at just one thing. As he admitted to us many times, he'd always hoped that statement made by a young nineteen-year-old would come true. In a 1995 interview on ESPN with Peter Gammons, however, my father made this remarkable statement: "When the announcer actually introduces me as such, and I'm sitting there about to stand up, I actually really want to sit down a little lower, sink down in my seat, and not be recognized as the greatest. I can honestly say I was not better than Babe Ruth, Lou Gehrig, Jimmie Foxx, Rogers Hornsby. I think I belong in the company of some of them, but to say I was the best—I don't think so. I'm satisfied just knowing I am in the company of some of the greatest hitters in history—that's the greatest honor."

Dad would also say, "I think, more importantly than that though, I was a helluva guy. I had compassion, and I was always interested in trying to help people that needed help."

FOR NINETEEN YEARS MY FATHER WORE THE #9 FOR THE RED SOX. Dad was eligible for the batting title twelve years in his career. Of those twelve opportunities, he won six times, came in second three times, and finished third one time. At the age of twenty-three he won his first batting title and his last at the age of forty. He won the Triple Crown in 1942 and 1947 at twenty-four and twenty-nine and narrowly missed winning it a third time in 1949 (when he was second in batting average by 0.00015). He won the American League Most Valuable Player Award (MVP) in 1946 and 1949 and narrowly missed winning it a third time in 1947. (It was reported that a Boston sportswriter purposely left Dad completely off the ballot, causing him to lose the award by one point. This is not true: it was a Midwestern writer who did not put him on the ballot.) He also won the American League home run championship four times. And at the age of forty-two, he recorded his best display of power, averaging a home run every 10.69

at-bats. To this day he remains the leader in career on-bases with a percentage of .4817. The Red Sox retired his number in 1984.

Teddy Ballgame did not master everything, though. He absolutely fell victim to the fickle love of the crowd and the criticism of the press. Kids are all about emotion and feelings; they thrive on attention and being liked. Their feelings are hurt if you criticize them, and they'll do anything to please you, especially if they get positive feedback. Dad wasn't immediately accepted as the new kid in baseball, because he was so good. Expectations were high, and in only his second year in the major leagues some fans and the press began to ride him for disappointing them—they wanted more—the start of what would be a career-long battle. Some players might have shrugged it off, but Dad was too driven, too intensely focused on being the best and wanting to impress. When he lashed out at sportswriters, he earned new nicknames like "Terrible Ted" and the "Problem Child." Even when he hit a home run and the whole crowd cheered, he was still angry with them for criticizing him and refused to tip his cap as he rounded the bases. When he was rejected, it angered him, hurt his feelings, but it also made him even more determined to prove them wrong. The following year he showed everyone, becoming the last batter in the game (so far) to hit a phenomenal .406 average.

"I WAS AND AM TOO COMPLEX A PERSONALITY, TOO MUCH OF A confusion of boyish enthusiasm and bitter experience to be completely understood by everybody, so forget that." From the way my father spoke and the words he used, "The Kid" emerged. The way he verbalized as an adult was a mix of playground expressions and childlike wonderment, beaten and aged with rough-guy sarcasm and dugout swearing. I invite you to watch the YouTube clip of Ted Williams on *What's My Line* in 1954. He is thirty-six years old, and if you don't see exactly what I'm talking about, then I don't know my father. You can just see his excitement and playfulness despite his age. It's as if his life was played out on a big playground.

Dad hated the press because they were his punishers, the bullies on his playground, and, as he would put it, "They were always trying to blow things out of proportion, stir things up, and rip you." The knights of the keyboard took control and manipulated a lot of Dad's career just by choosing what they did or didn't write about. In 1931 baseball writers began voting to determine who would receive the Most Valuable Player Award. Dad's MVPs were won and lost based on whether a writer wanted to recognize him. Ted Williams is the only player ever to win the American League Triple Crown (leading the league in batting average, home runs, and runs batted in) and *not* win the MVP Award that same year. Astoundingly, the writers did this to him twice, in 1942 and 1947.

No wonder Dad held a grudge against the press for his entire life and taught his children to be just as wary of the media as he was. Despite great mentors and fellow athletes who tried to pass on their nuggets of wisdom about handling the press, Dad was stubborn and would not let go. The great Jim Thorpe told Dad once that he had to get a grip on the press because they could make you or break you. Dad didn't listen; he was going to die fighting. "Never let them break you," he'd say.

IF IT HADN'T BEEN FOR THE WAY THE CROWDS AND THEIR LOVING cheers counterbalanced the negativity of the media, our father told us, he probably would have quit baseball in 1954. He had even announced to the *Saturday Evening Post,* "This is my last year in baseball." For starters, he was going through a divorce from his first wife, Doris. To make things worse, on the first day of spring training he broke his collarbone, which required surgery. But the wonderful cheers and applause of the thousands of fans in the stands nourished and revived him, and he was inspired to play on. Remarkably, despite this being a tough season for him in several respects, he would have won another batting title if he hadn't missed so many games because of his injury—and he still led the league with a .345 batting average.

He hit twenty-nine home runs, beating Mickey Mantle and Ernie Banks that year. Later, he would win the American League batting championship in 1957 at the age of thirty-nine, and then win it *again* the next season, making him the oldest player ever to win a batting title.

Dad's performance was directly linked to the way the crowd received him. That is a very unhealthy relationship, though: it is unrealistic and severely fluctuating. Adulation was Dad's lifeline, driving him to keep going, keep persevering, keep fighting. Even at death's door during his last public appearance, Dad was able to acknowledge the crowd when they stood and applauded for him. The crowd, however, does not show allegiance through good and bad; it shows only a shallow, performance-based affection and is heavily influenced by what everyone in the crowd reads, and chooses to believe, in the papers. Healthy relationship or not, it was what drove Dad, made him even more determined to excel. He was always trying to make up for some shortcoming the press had written about or make up for a poor performance on the field.

What I believe made Ted Williams great at home plate was his ability to take all his anger, all his hurt, and channel it with supreme discipline and control right into his wrists, the grip, the bat, the precise connection with the ball, blasting it exactly where he wanted it to go, shoving it right down the throats of sportswriters.

If I can just do something good at bat, the fans will love me again and I can make those reporters eat a hell of a lot of crow.

At spring training and later at the Ted Williams Baseball Camp, he would explain to the students of the sport how to become better.

"To do anything well in sports, you have to practice. Hitting a baseball is no different. You just have to take the time and work at it, and this means practice and more practice and more practice. Get better if you want to be a hitter. Hitting a baseball with a bat is the toughest thing to do in sports."

Clearly, as evidenced by his baseball stats, he was skilled at it, and he honed those skills with endless hours of practice, swinging the bat until his hands bled. He was so disciplined that before he even walked up to the plate, he had studied the pitcher and knew what pitches he threw. Knowing what ball was best for him to hit, he would watch the ball carefully and was rarely fooled by the pitcher.

"You got to get a good ball to hit. I'll preach it for the rest of my life. Get a good ball to hit."

Our father loved baseball. Baseball wasn't just a paycheck for him, it was the venue in which he was able to release all his passion and become great. Dad would be the first one, however, to be the most critical of himself. If he didn't play up to his own standards, he was not happy.

In 1959, as he turned forty-one, Dad suffered a pinched nerve in his neck. As a result, he played in only 103 games and had the worst batting season of his career. "I had a lousy year, the worst I ever had. I don't deserve what I made last year. I've gone from nothing on this club to making $125,000 a year. I want to take the biggest cut ever given a player."

The season was not up to his standards. So he gave himself a severe pay cut, signing a contract for $90,000.

"Standards aren't any good unless you live up to them."

WHEN HE WAS AT HIS PEAK, THE ONLY THING THAT GOT IN THE way of my father's career was war. Dad served in the Marine Corps in two wars, World War II and the Korean War. The Japanese bombed Pearl Harbor in December after Dad's .406 season. Many ballplayers were drafted or had enlisted by the start of the 1942 spring season. Dad got a deferment as his mother's sole supporter (she'd divorced his father by then) and because he was helping out his brother, Danny. The press howled about it. "You'd have thought Teddy Ballgame bombed Pearl Harbor himself," he later wrote. "Unpatriotic. Yellow. Those were some of the milder epithets." In May 1942, he enlisted in the Navy and became a pilot and instructor at Pensacola for the duration of the war. Later, in May 1944, he was commissioned as a second lieutenant and naval aviator in the US Marine Corps.

While on active duty in Korea, Ted Williams was given an offer to play on the Navy baseball team but declined. He did not think it was proper to abandon his duty as a Marine and his service to his country as a naval aviator. He fought in active combat and publicly supported the Marine Corps in deeds, words, and advertising campaigns.

"The greatest achievement that I ever really did other than play baseball was become a Navy Marine pilot. Jesus, they are the greatest bunch of guys I ever met."

In February 1953 in Korea, when his plane was shot by enemy fire and was burning, instead of ejecting, he was courageous and chose to crash-land his plane on its belly. He chose to risk dying in the plane rather than eject. He was afraid he'd leave his knee caps in the cockpit, being six-four, and ruin his chance of ever playing baseball again. It has been projected that if wartime service had not made Dad miss 727 games—five seasons of baseball—he would have produced 2,301 runs, 2,242 runs batted in, and 686 home runs, stats that would have ranked him first, second, and third, respectively. In 2001 Dad was also inducted into the Marine Corps Sports Hall of Fame.

Beyond his wartime accolades, Dad was also quite generous. This was one of the greatest things that Dad ended up learning from his mother. Despite how much he resented all the time she spent with the Salvation Army, he learned generosity and charity.

"Christ, my whole family dates back to charity, and I like that. I think about that, and I certainly like that. It certainly taught me to be a very sympathetic person and a forgiving person."

In 1948 he became the spokesman for the Jimmy Fund, a fund-raising division of the Dana-Farber Cancer Institute in Boston. I have been told by Mike Andrews, former chairman of the Jimmy

Fund, that Dad was the single most influential person in helping to raise funds and making it the best-loved charity in New England. He helped to raise money for the Jimmy Fund his whole life. Before he died, he asked that people remember him by making a donation in his name to the Fund.

In 1953, when Dad returned from the Korean War, he insisted that guests at a "Welcome Home, Ted" dinner at Boston's Hotel Statler pay $100 a head—with all proceeds benefiting the Jimmy Fund. Close to $130,000 was raised that evening.

A little-known fact: The night before Dad's last at-bat, he drove from Boston to Rhode Island to make four separate Jimmy Fund appearances. Before the night was over, he also visited a terminally ill boy at the Jimmy Fund Clinic. As many know, the next day he hit a home run in his last at-bat.

So why is Ted Williams great? That is an easy question to answer if you are a fan. It's a lot more complex when he is your father. My father's courage did not end at the painted lines of the outfield or when he climbed out of the cockpit of his plane. For the rest of his life he remained principled and courageous; unafraid to ask questions, he never hesitated to defend another person. He drilled into John-Henry and me a very basic principle.

"A person has a responsibility and a duty to speak up when they see a wrong."

Dad seemed to have a natural sense and intuition of what was right and what was wrong.

In 1966, during his induction speech into the National Baseball Hall of Fame, just three years after Martin Luther King's "I Have a Dream Speech," Dad played a very integral part in getting players from the segregated Negro Leagues recognized and admitted into the Hall of Fame. Dad, on his own, decided to bring up the importance of these players. "The other day Willie Mays hit his 522nd home run," Dad said in his speech. "He has gone past me, and he is pushing, and I say to him, 'Go get 'em, Willie.' Baseball gives every American boy a chance to excel," Dad said. "Not just to be as good as someone else, but to be better than someone else. This is the nature of Man and the name of the game. I hope that someday the names of Satchel Paige and Josh Gibson in some way can be added as a symbol of the great Negro players that are not here only because they're not given a chance." Dad was principled and felt a duty to help rectify the fact that the "great Negro players" were not being recognized for their achievements and abilities but rather had long been ignored solely because of the color of their skin.

It was well known that Dad's enormous respect for his fellow ballplayers extended to Negro League players. There are numerous stories about him insisting that his Negro fellow ballplayers be treated as equal to him. Jim "Mudcat" Grant, a two-time All-Star pitcher and an African American, played for the Cleveland Indians in the late 1950s. Just recently, Mudcat told me a story about when he and Dad crossed paths. The Indians were playing the Red Sox in an exhibition game in New Orleans. The black ballplayers were required to stay at a separate hotel, but for some reason their luggage was delivered to the "white" hotel. Mudcat was designated to retrieve the luggage, but the bellman refused to help or even allow a black man in the lobby to retrieve their luggage. After nearly three hours of futility, Mudcat says, my father arrived in a taxi. Dad walked right over to Mudcat, shook his hand, and asked him how he was doing.

"I'm not doing too good. You know I can't stay here."

"I know. It is a shame you can't stay here."

Then Mudcat pointed to the white bellman.

"That fella says I am not allowed to get our bags."

Dad turned with purpose, walked straight up to the bellman, faced him squarely, and said something to him. When Dad returned, there was a sense of accomplishment in his stride.

"He's right, Mud, *you* cannot get your bags . . . because that bellman is going to get the bags for you."

Then Dad stood there beside him, watching while that bellman loaded every piece of luggage into the vehicle for Mr. Grant.

Dad did not flinch when comparing himself to a black player. His clear vision transcended race and recognized humans for who they really were as people, for their abilities and their character, not for their color. Even on July 25, 1966, in Cooperstown, a day devoted to him and his achievements, he did not miss an opportunity to stand up for what was right.

TWO YEARS BEFORE I WAS BORN, DAD'S MEMOIR *MY TURN AT BAT* came out. It begins with a remarkable statement: "I'm glad it's over. Before anything else, understand that I am glad it's over. I'm so grateful for baseball—and so grateful I'm the hell out of it as a player. . . . I mean, I wouldn't go back to being eighteen or nineteen years old, knowing what was in store, the sourness and the bitterness, knowing how I thought the weight of the damn world was always on my neck, grinding on me. . . . I'm grateful that part of my life is over."

Dad had a single-track mind. He was unable to multitask. He focused on one thing and did it to exhaustion and to the exclusion of everything else. He compartmentalized and mastered one thing at a time—but only if he thought he could be successful at it. This aspect of what made him exceptional at baseball is also what made him so difficult for the public to understand—particularly after his retirement from the game. When Dad was "finished" with something, he turned the page and never looked back.

When he finally left baseball behind, he had invested all the emotional energy and focus into it that he could. The only way he could regain his strength was to excuse himself from the relentless pursuit of perfection. He was and always will be associated with baseball, but emotionally he was done with playing the game and the stress it caused him long before I was born.

He didn't sever all of his ties with the game, however. In 1969 he became the manager of the Washington Senators. He led the team to their only winning season and was voted Manager of the Year. In later years he managed the Texas Rangers and went on to become a hitting instructor for the Red Sox, helping out during spring training and throughout the season. He and his longtime friend Al Cassidy founded the Ted Williams Baseball Camp. His book *The Science of Hitting,* still the definitive text on the subject, came out in 1971, the year I was born.

He continued to love watching baseball on TV and kept up with all the current players. And when he thought he could use his affiliation with baseball to have an influence or help a friend—whether it was granting an interview, appearing on a sports special, or making a public appearance—he didn't hesitate. Dad was relentless, for instance, in supporting the induction of his friend and teammate Bobby Doerr into the Hall of Fame in 1986. He gave one of his best in-depth interviews to *Sports Illustrated,* but only after the magazine agreed to donate $10,000 to a handicapped friend. Later he provided priceless advertisement and promotion for his son's companies, Green Diamond Sports and Hitter.net.

Nevertheless, when he stopped playing baseball, Dad was finally free to pursue his other love, fishing. *This* was the person I first came to know. Baseball was minimal in his life—as was I until he finally started developing a relationship with me in his midsixties. At that point, he had been retired from baseball for over twenty years. As a child, I knew almost nothing about Ted Williams; instead, I tried to learn everything I could about my dad "The Kid."

Chapter Three

You have to know the past to understand the present.
—CARL SAGAN

I F DAD HAD STUDIED WOMEN THE WAY HE MASTERED HITTING a baseball, this book would be about a completely different man.

For much of his life, women were difficult for him to understand—he found them too dynamic and complicated, too sensitive, too damn emotional. Dad didn't have the patience for something he could not perfect, let alone understand. He didn't have much luck with women, and he didn't know how to raise children.

I don't think Dad had much respect for women. He once wrote a note to John-Henry that said, "Always be proud of what you do," but a major flaw that Dad developed throughout his life was disrespect for women. I don't believe that Dad was proud of the way he treated women, but he also couldn't help himself. I think this stemmed from his mother's abandonment of him and his brother at a very young age to spend all her time with the Salvation Army. At the time, Dad found appropriate ways to cope to deal with her absence, but he did not come out of the experience unscathed. His view of women and the sanctity of marriage and family was significantly warped. As if this weren't enough, he also learned from his father to abandon women, especially if they did not provide what a man expected.

These views and expectations played out in his life, especially in his early relationships. From the age of sixteen on, The Kid was one of the boys, and the boys' club is not where you learn how to treat women. As a handsome star baseball player, his first relationships were with groupies. He had a weakness for their attention, their fawning and words of praise. He craved words of affirmation and acceptance, regardless of his flaws and intense emotional outbursts, and it seemed that every woman who came along was able to convince him that she would be the one to love him unconditionally. I also believe that he was aware of his weakness for this kind of persuasion and that it angered him that he would succumb to it so many times—once again, an area he seemed not to be able to control. So Dad lost respect for women. My father hated what he saw as their manipulative ways, their allure, the way they expressed their sexual power. To him, when women were like that, they were only good for one thing.

Women were often throwing themselves at him, often drooling (literally drooling) over him. These expressions of sexual appetite and temptation were Dad's Achilles' heel—women could lure him away and become his kryptonite. He hated it, hated that he fell for it every time. In his mind, women's demeanor warranted his worst behavior.

As a grown man, Dad's first real opportunity to develop a meaningful relationship with a woman came after he left San Diego and married a woman named Doris Soule. He met Doris in 1938 during a hunting and fishing trip in Minnesota. She was the daughter of a fishing guide. After a long, sporadic courtship, they married in 1944, on the same day he received his second lieutenant's wings as a Marine pilot and instructor in Pensacola. At ten years, it was his longest marriage on paper, but in truth it wasn't a happy one. He soon discovered that she didn't like baseball or the Florida fishing scene, his two passions. He was away for long stretches that got longer over the years. When their daughter, Barbara Joyce (nicknamed Bobby-Jo), was born in Boston in January 1948, he was fishing in Florida. Even though Bobby-Jo was born two weeks early, the hostile Boston press crucified him for not being there—and for taking five days to get to Boston after he heard the news. "You are not a nice fellow, Brother Williams," one of them wrote. "I do believe that baseball and the sports pages would be better off without you."

The marriage continued to deteriorate. Doris had a serious drinking problem, and Ted, an extremely disciplined man, lost all respect for her. She filed for divorce in 1954, citing continual mistreatment and verbal abuse. She retained custody of Bobby-Jo.

Next was Lee Howard. She was a model, a tall and shapely blonde. She could put up with his tirades and long absences for only two years.

Then he met another model, Dolores Wettach. She was on a flight back from a photo shoot in Australia. When the plane stopped in New Zealand, Dad walked on and sat across the aisle from her. He'd been on a fishing trip. When he saw this beautiful woman across the aisle, he wrote a little note and tossed it at her. He'd written, "Who are you?" She laughed, wrote, "Who are *you*?" and tossed it back. She wasn't being coy. She had no idea who he was. She knew absolutely nothing about baseball. He scribbled, "I am Mr. Williams, a fisherman who would like to meet you."

She was my mom.

MY MOTHER WAS BORN IN NEW YORK CITY IN 1934. HER FATHER, Charles Jean Wettach, was Swiss German and immigrated to the United States at the age of eighteen. According to family accounts, he moved out to Montana, where he was a gaucho cowboy and worked on a sheep farm. Her mother, born Ethel Elizabeth Erikson, grew up in Minnesota. Mom was the oldest of four children: herself, Pauline, Heidi, and Joseph. When she was a child, they moved to Flushing, Queens, to start a mink farm. During World War II, as Mom recalls, neighbors harassed her father, suspecting he was a German spy because he had a heavy accent and listened to German broadcasts on a shortwave radio. Mom also remembers police investigating the neighbors' reports. Around that time the mink farm needed more land. A family friend, Hans Schumbachler, had described Vermont as "little Switzerland," so around 1942 the family moved to Putney, a village of maybe two thousand residents nestled among apple orchards and sugar maples, not far from Brattleboro.

As the oldest child, Mom was the first to learn how to work on the mink farm and how to dress an animal. This was where my mother learned the knife skills that would later impress her animal husbandry instructor at the University of Vermont (UVM)—and eventually my father. In fact, the instructor was so impressed that he asked her to demonstrate to the class of mostly men how to skin an animal, carve its carcass, and trim the fat. She was an absolute master at using a knife and a sharpening steel. When they married, she taught my father. For the rest of his life, even after he and Mom divorced and he was living with another woman, Dad always had his antique sharpening steel that looked like an ancient dagger hanging in his kitchen. Mom had given it to him for his birthday in 1971. I think it was symbolic and telling that the first thing he did when he went to work in the kitchen was to use that steel to sharpen his knife just the way Mom had taught him. He would pick up the steel and start sharpening the knife, pulling the blade down one side and then the other, and say, "I'm just putting a little eephus on the eiphus," almost as if he were giving Mom a nod while in the kitchen, acknowledging her complex knife skills. It was one of his favorite expressions, and I never knew why until I did some research: One of Dad's most famous home runs was one he hit at the 1946 All-Star Game, played at Fenway Park, off Rip Sewell. He was the only player ever to hit a home run off of Sewell's eephus pitch.

Mom was a great cook. Dad liked her poached eggs so much that he called them "college-educated eggs." The only way her eggs could be better than his, he figured, was because she had gone to college. Whenever he made eggs for us kids, he'd ask, "How do these compare to your mother's college-educated eggs?"

Mom was a student at UVM when she was first noticed for her beauty, and she won the Miss Vermont USA competition in 1956. After she graduated from the School of Nursing, she was in New York City on a nursing rotation when two photographers spotted her on the street. They approached her, told her she should be a model, and asked if they could please take pictures of her. She innocently followed them back to their apartment. Luckily for Mom, they were true photographers and happened to be partners. Before she knew it, she was meeting Diana Vreeland at *Vogue*.

Her modeling career took off like a rocket. The great fashion photographers of that time, like Milton Greene, Norman Parkinson, Helmut Newton, and Art Kane, loved working with her. Greene called her the most dewy-eyed model of 1961. Parkinson wrote, "I was always looking for the unusual undiscovered loner. Wettach was exactly that—a lovely girl but never alone."

By all accounts, Mom was a fantastic model. Her face and her features jumped off the pages of *Vogue*. She was described as having hands and feet that went on forever. Her fingers were long and thin, and her feet were a size 11AAA. Comfortable in many different surroundings and circumstances, she was willing to do whatever the photographers wanted or needed for a great shot—even if it included bending into contorted positions for poses and making them appear easy. When other girls refused to get into cold water or interact with wild animals, Mom was the first to step up. A beautiful picture was taken of her on that photo shoot in Australia that would end in her meeting Dad on the flight home. She's walking down a beach holding the paw of a kangaroo. The other girls were afraid of the animal—

one swift kick of its hind legs could have ripped your skin open—but my mother was not. She enjoyed being around animals. She calmly and kindly asked the animal for its paw and then led it down the beach. She was always willing and able to put in the extra effort, and it showed in her photographs.

Carlo Ponti, the film producer and Sophia Loren's husband, spotted Mom in *Vogue* and decided he had to have her in his next movie. He flew her to Italy—she didn't speak a word of Italian—and put her in his movie *Controsesso* (*Countersex* in English). The film is actually three short films by three different Italian directors, all comedies about what men will go through to have sex. She was the female lead in the one called "Una donna d'affari," about a musician who wants to make love to a beautiful and mysterious businesswoman (Mom). It came out in 1964.

You can find a clip of her on YouTube and see for yourself how gorgeous she was. After she started getting international attention, she was hand-selected to play the role of Pussy Galore in the James Bond movie *Goldfinger*. Ultimately, she ended up losing the part, though, because they decided Mom was too sexy for the role; they wanted someone more "severe-looking."

For his part, Dad continued to flirt with her on that flight from Australia until they landed in California. Since he was staying in San Diego and she was continuing on to New York, they would have parted there if her flight had not been delayed. He decided to stay around.

He was persistent in asking for her phone number, and eventually she gave him her address. He kept writing her, telling her he was coming to New York and wanted to see her, and he did. It wasn't until their third date, out for dinner at a restaurant called the Marquis, that she began to realize how famous Mr. Williams the fisherman actually was, no doubt because of the way everyone around them treated him. In Dad's book *My Turn at Bat,* which came out while they were still together, he marvels at finding a model who would just as soon tramp around the woods or sit in a boat with a rod in her hands. "She loves the outdoors almost as much as I do."

They were married in 1968. Mom was thirty-four, and Dad was forty-nine. They moved into a farmhouse in Putney, Vermont, just down Pine Banks Road from where she was raised. Her parents still lived there, and they helped raise their grandchildren. John-Henry had just been born, and as my mom describes it, Dad was thrilled to have a son. Surely he would be able to relate to a boy.

As with his daughter Bobby-Jo, Dad wasn't there when my brother was born, and once again the press ate him up for it. In truth, it didn't really bother my mom or dad. In the 1960s, men still were not often involved in the birthing process, and quite frankly, Mom didn't want him around during the struggle of labor. Honestly, I don't think Dad could have handled childbirth. Not to mention that Mom didn't want the added stress of having the great Ted Williams in the waiting room. His presence always ended with a crowd, lots of commotion, and his frustration. She was a nurse and knew what was ahead of her.

Dad described John-Henry as the most beautiful baby he had ever seen. I suppose many parents say that about their own children, but a look at the photos makes it clear that Dad believed it. Dad was a bit of a camera buff and took many, many photos of his baby boy. Their connection was mutual. According to Mom and Dad, little John-Henry, when he was only a few hours old, picked up his head the first time he saw his father.

When it came to choosing a name, Dad was very involved. For whatever reason, he thought John was a fitting and strong name that would describe his son. Mom couldn't stand it. They went on to consider Henry, which was also a solid name in Dad's opinion, but Mom cringed at that as well. Mom was looking for something a bit more original, befitting the first son of Ted Williams. She tried to think of a name that would honor the physical strength that Dad was referencing, and then she found it. She combined John and Henry and gave the name John-Henry (as in the Steel-Driving Man) to my brother. Dad loved it. He always referred to John-Henry by his full name, no abbreviations, no nicknames.

Dad's first encounter with the press after the birth of his son was rough. First, the media grilled him on where he was at the time of his son's birth. (Answer: fishing for Atlantic salmon in Canada.) Then a snide reporter broke through the swarm of inquiries with this question: "What are you doing giving your son a nigger's name?"

There were a few chuckles from the crowd, and then Mom describes Dad's response as this: "Oh yeah? You think that's funny? I happen to really like the name John-Henry. And what about Williams, what do you think about that name?"

Mom has always believed that Dad was referring to all the African Americans who had the last name of Williams. Either way, Dad snuffed that line of questioning instantly and the conference was over.

Mom described John-Henry as a perfect baby who slept all the time and hardly cried. He was always eating, often with two bottles, one in each hand. Dad was eager to be involved with his little man and played with John-Henry right away. He didn't hesitate to hold his son, and Mom remarked on Dad's patience and attentiveness to his male creation. For someone so rough and loud on the outside, Ted Williams seemed to melt around his baby son. Mom describes Dad as holding John-Henry as gently and lovingly as possible, playing peek-a-boo (the favorite game) and horsey, then taking walks and going to the ballpark.

When Dad started taking him to the ballpark, he bought John-Henry special wing-tipped shoes to wear. Everywhere Dad went, John-Henry followed. This was more like it. This was what Dad expected from a child, especially a son. John-Henry was given his own set of baseball gear, and Dad taught him to swing right away. John-Henry, at least for a while, was a miniature Ted Williams. My brother could do no wrong in his father's eyes. Dad understood his son, and his son loved being around him.

Everything about his approach to John-Henry was different from how my dad had been with his older daughter, Bobby-Jo. Up until John-Henry's birth, his experience as a father had been disappointing; simply put, he had failed at being a father to Bobby-Jo.

The roots of this failure went to the heart of Dad's personality. He was the most determined and focused person I have ever known. Everything he did, he did to perfection. Where most people are content with 100 percent, Dad didn't even start until he was well beyond what was considered great, and then he was further fueled by his drive and passion to become an expert. Nothing was worth doing if it wasn't done to perfection and complete domination. Whatever the discipline, he zoned in on it and refined it to perfection.

Dad believed perfection was attainable in any pursuit if there was a scientific method behind it. Dad always did his research; he was always designing cerebral hypotheses and doing small experiments. He observed and studied his subject relentlessly—whether it was the fish he was trying to catch or the pitch he was trying to crush. He analyzed everything that fish or that pitcher did, and when and why they did it. If he could not prove his hypothesis through consistent, concrete evidence and the support of statistical probability, the whole cycle would start again until some pattern revealed itself. I saw this in everything he did. Only when his experiments and observations proved his theory time and time again and produced the same result did Dad believe in his hard work and trust his chances.

That was Dad's approach to everything—everything. He hated it when people said he was "a natural-born hitter" or "the greatest natural hitter since Shoeless Joe Jackson." Or when they exaggerated how good his eyesight was, as though that explained his excellence at the plate. He knew they meant well, but to him these were not compliments.

"All the talent in the world won't get you anywhere if you don't work your ass off."

Every performance tested whether he had actually done enough work. Could he do better? Did he need to go back and review every detail again? He was obsessed with proving his theories.

"If you don't approach something with the intent of being the best, what's the point?"

Perfectionism, however, has its downsides. One of the short-comings of Dad's relentless pursuit of perfection was that if he couldn't be successful at something, if he couldn't manipulate it and control it, he was likely to walk away from it. This was what he did to Bobby-Jo early on, and it haunted both of them in very different ways. Bobby-Jo was a troubled child who grew up with an inattentive alcoholic mother. As a father, he supported Bobby-Jo financially, but he was distant, seeing her only at intervals and becoming highly critical of the careless way her mother was raising her. Some of his instincts about her proved to be right: by her teen years, Bobby-Jo was making some poor decisions. Sexually pro-miscuous, she got pregnant at seventeen, and when her mother said she'd have to ask her father to pay for an abortion, she slit her wrists. He got her placed in a psychiatric hospital, and she had the abortion. At eighteen, pregnant again, she eloped with a man. It was a rough marriage. According to her first husband, she drank, took drugs, was in and out of psychiatric care, and continued to be promiscuous. Whenever she wanted money for anything, she asked "Daddy" for it—a new car, plastic surgery, money for her kids' education. These things were blemishes on Dad's profile, and he didn't want anyone to know about them.

All of Bobby-Jo's mistakes caused him a lot of grief, reminding him of all the frustrations of being a parent, the mistakes he had made as a parent. These memories angered him, and whenever he talked about her, that anger and disappointment—directed not only at her but at himself as well—spilled over. Bobby-Jo was an embar-rassment to Dad, a reminder of his own failures, and while he wished her the very best, he also wished she would quietly disappear.

When I asked him one time about his regrets, Dad admitted he would have liked to have made his marriages work so that he could have spent more time with his children. One might wonder why Ted Williams couldn't use some of his conviction and determination to become a better father. To me the answer is obvious. He never learned how. Between his two parents, he was never shown a good example. I think my father earnestly tried to be a good parent, but children don't come with an instruction manual you can study until you know it by heart. Children are loaded with unpredictable behaviors and emotions. Most importantly, though, children are small reflections of their parents—both good and bad. You wish and hope to see only the good, but they will have flaws. They won't be perfect—no one is. Sadly, if Dad could not be successful at something or master it to perfection, there had to be something wrong with it. It wasn't for lack of trying or effort; it was a lack of patience and flexibility.

Despite the fact that she was sixteen years younger, Dad trusted Mom and confided in her regarding his troubles with his first daughter. He admired Mom's parenting skills and thought she was a wonderful mother. He respected her nursing background and asked for her guidance and assistance when problems arose with Bobby-Jo. Mom attempted to help out but knew instantly that there was no simple fix for Bobby-Jo's issues. Her promiscuous behavior led Mom to suspect that she had manic depression and possibly borderline personality disorder. It was clear to Mom that she also had an alcohol addiction, and she suggested to Bobby-Jo and her first husband that they seek psychiatric help for her.

So little man John-Henry was like a clean slate, a new beginning. Where he might have gone wrong with his daughter, Dad was going to do everything right with his son. Unlike during his previous marriage, he was done playing baseball, so he had time for his young family. Plus, his new wife, intelligent and beautiful, was not an embarrassment. She was an international model, a *Vogue* model, a former Miss Vermont, an actress, and a lady. If anything, she stole some of the limelight from him. Their son was the apple of his eye and was adored by all. Everything was looking up. This was the happiest time during my parents' marriage.

Then Mom became pregnant with me. It was 1971, and Dad did not want another child. He did not want to disrupt the perfect thing they had going. Mom wanted to make Dad happy. She tells me that she was actually on her way to terminate her pregnancy when she bumped into her acting and modeling coach. I guess I owe my life to this lady, because Claudia Franck convinced my mom to keep me.

"That might be a very special child one day."

I WAS BORN ON OCTOBER 8, 1971, AND AGAIN MY FATHER WAS NOT there to witness the birth. I know there was much ado made by the press over the years about my father not being present at the births of his children, but the fact that he wasn't there does not offend me. I hold no resentment. Like those billions of children born under similar circumstances before me, I feel no less or more loved by my father knowing that he was or was not present at the time of my birth. I wouldn't even mention it here if the press hadn't been so critical of my father—after all, it's not like I can remember it.

When Dad did arrive at the hospital, my mom explained that I was born, surprisingly, with strawberry-blonde hair. "A *red*head?" Dad exclaimed. "Well, where is she?" Impatient as always, Dad kept moving forward, "Never mind . . . I'll find her . . . ol' Teddy Ballgame will find her!"

Dad called me his butterball. According to Mom, though, when she brought me home, everyone said, "Now *that* is Mr. Williams." I would later be described as a vanilla Ted and adopted the nickname the Blonde Bomber as I matured. (Turns out that's a name of a dry fly that is long, round, made of the undercoat of the hollow deer hair, and floats on the water.)

Early on I understood the closeness between Dad and John-Henry, and I tried to grow up quickly in an attempt to be worthy of their company. But I was very naive and young for my age, and for the first several years my father did not include me as completely in his life as he had with John-Henry. It did not take me long to understand that I had the disadvantage of being a girl, which felt like an inferior species.

Coming from the generation he did limited my father's expectations of me. He always wanted to see me become a teacher. He wanted me to "be sweet," get a "good job," "save my money," and hopefully, he would imply, find a nice man to take care of me. Humph! That was the last thing I had on my mind.

I had to make a choice either to respect and embrace the great relationship my brother had with Dad or to continue to fight for my father's attention. My attention-getters were also limited: they had better not get *negative* attention. There were definitely a number of years when I resented the relationship between Dad and John-Henry, but more than anything I wanted my father to be happy, I wanted my brother to be happy, and I wanted everyone to get along. John-Henry got to do everything with Dad, and I seemed to be the only one to notice the inequality. If I complained at all, I was dismissed and criticized as a whiner. I had to find a way to distinguish myself from my brother in Dad's eyes and exceed the expectations that had already been set in place by the mistakes Bobby-Jo had made. It was up to me to prove to him I was worthy. His mind was already made up, and I had a big hill to climb.

I resolved that I would never ask my father for anything and would never be a burden of any sort. John-Henry was incredibly smart. He was the kid who could look at the book the night before the test and get an A. I was the kid who read the book the whole week prior to the test, took notes, made flash cards, read the chapter again, and still only got a B. When I realized that my brother did not have my work ethic, I worked even harder. Dad started noticing the difference in our report cards and my good grades compared to John-Henry's. From about the fifth grade on, Dad started rewarding us for our grades. An A was worth $25, a B was worth $5, and a C wiped out all Bs. I started making more money than my brother, and my father used this as motivation for his son to get a little serious about his education. Dad would tease him.

"How come your sister is making more money than you are?"

The friendly competition was another way for Dad to stay connected and for us to brag and boast when we saw him.

There was one difference between us that Dad took notice of. John-Henry was always spending all his allowance money and would even borrow from me at times. When I realized that John-Henry didn't save money, I became a miser. I saved every penny I could. It became a ritual for Dad to ask me how much money I had saved. I couldn't wait to tell him the latest sum, and from there my father started instructing me on financial strategies. I think I was twelve when I opened my first CD at a bank. My father would encourage me through sarcasm. He would jokingly ask, "Are you sure you don't have a little Jew in you?" I had a savings account, and I just kept saving. Whenever my father asked me if I needed anything, it was always, "Nope, I don't need anything—thank you, though." Dad very seldom bought us presents; it was always a check or money in a birthday card. Those funds went right into the bank. John-Henry begged for a brand-new car when he turned eighteen, and Dad bought him a Pontiac Grand Am. I decided I would ride a bike. I took the bus to school when everyone else was driving a car. I was unwavering.

Even when I tried to relate to my mom, I was not an equal. Our house had pictures on the walls from my mother's *Vogue* and *Harper's Bazaar* modeling days. Through puberty and my adolescent years, I likened my looks to those of a troll in comparison. My brother, on the other hand, was gorgeous. As he grew up everyone— and I mean absolutely everyone—would remark on how handsome he was and say that he belonged in Hollywood.

Having two kids to raise did little to slow down my mother. In the early fall of 1971, the year I was born, Mom decided to create an even better home in the secluded hills of Vermont. She soon discovered the value of privacy and what it would mean to her husband. My father often complained about everybody driving by his home just to peek at where the Splendid Splinter lived.

"We get more drive-bys than Carter has pills," he'd say, referring to an old saying from the '40s, about a pill-producing company called Carter.

Wanting to make her new husband happy, Mom decided to surprise him while he was away and fix the privacy issue by simply moving the house to a more secluded area on the property. How hard could it be?

Mrs. Ted Williams got help from a local covered-bridge genius, Milton Graton, to move the whole house approximately four hundred yards straight up a hill that loomed behind the house. As the foliage changed color, the house began to move. With the assistance of local friends, a team of oxen, trucks, tractors, and Mr. Graton, the farmhouse finally found its new resting spot on top of a mountain far removed from sight. The new resting spot now provided a million-dollar view of Vermont, New Hampshire, and the Connecticut River. The view was awesome, but the secluded location, hidden from inquiring neighbors, was priceless. Mom was sure her new husband would be impressed not only by the spectacular view but also by having the privacy he so desired.

When my father came home, he drove into the driveway only to discover that his residence was gone. He sat in the car for a while, wondering if he had pulled into the wrong place. Wasn't this the road? He was bewildered, baffled, and bothered. Anger crept into his face, and his jaw started clenching.

"Where the hell is the goddamned house?"

Tearing out of the driveway, he drove up the road, where he parked and fumed for a while. He didn't know what else to do. He sat in the car desperately hunting for explanations. He already knew Dolores had something to do with this new development.

"What the hell has Dolores done now? What in Christ's name is going on?"

His new wife was something of an enigma to him. She was a dark-haired, hardworking farm girl, but also a gorgeous *Vogue* model. She was a caring registered nurse, but she could fish like a pro. She was a sultry actress, but she was strong like a bull. She was constant competition for him, but he loved the challenge. She could make his mouth melt in anticipation of her meals, turn up every dial to his emotions, hold his heart in her hand . . . and now, somehow, she had made the house disappear. She was magic.

But this was reality. Surely if he just drove back down the road and into the driveway, the house would be there. Now Mom's words, "I have a surprise for you," flooded his thoughts. *Jesus Christ!* Dad couldn't believe what was about to be confirmed as he pulled onto the dirt road of his humble Vermont abode again. His stunning, shocking, and unpredictable wife had moved the whole damned house. Jesus Christ! There, look up, past the trees, on the hill. . . . There stood Mom, waving like a wild woman.

"Here I am, Ted! Come on up!"

When Dad recalled the event, he would shake his head every time.

"Jesus Christ! What a woman!"

Now, I was just a baby in Mom's arms, and so this story is not mine. But it has been told many times by my father and my mother. This funny moment in their lives together encapsulates what their marriage was like. Every moment was energized, full of passion and a frenzy of excitement.

I asked my dad one time what he thought when he realized that Mom had moved the entire house. He shook his head in disbelief as he relived the moment.

"Your mother doesn't just move furniture, she moves houses! Jesus, I hope you're not like your mother! I hope you have *my* genes!"

Mom always laughs mischievously when telling her version. She says that Dad's biggest concern was whether or not the water was turned on, and if it was hot. "Is the plumbing working? Are you sure the water is hot?"

Dad would often describe Mom as a pain in the ass, but in the next breath he would ask, "How is the Queen?" About five years before Dad died, Mom received a package around Christmas. It is one of the most famous pictures of Dad. On the top of the photo was inscribed, "To the Queen, who did a super job on two beautiful kids. Thank you."

Dad would describe Mom as "a hell of a woman, never a dull moment with that woman!" I would learn that, said in the right context, "pain in the ass" could actually be a term of endearment from him.

Chapter Four

WHEN SHE MARRIED MY DAD, MOM STOPPED MODELING, put her nursing career on hold, stopped everything. Very much like my dad, she believed in marriage and had an idealistic view of family. Unfortunately for the four of us, their marriage was not to last.

It did not take long for my mother to see that the qualities that made Ted Williams great at so many things also made it difficult for him as a father. Dad's life revolved around how much he could manipulate and control. I don't mean that in a bad way, but there was always a need to limit aggravations and frustrations. Control meant the power and ability to rectify a wrong, eliminate problems, prevent pain. It's interesting to note that the term "control freak" comes from the 1960s, the era in which Dad's display of perfection at home plate would come to an end. It didn't matter who you were, man or woman, old or young, Dad would never change his ways for you, and having kids with him made this incredibly clear to my mother.

Dad never talked. He boomed. His voice was loud, demanding, and sometimes sarcastic. His voice was often compared to John Wayne's, but that was on good days. The only time he lowered his voice would be to ask sarcastically, "Are you all right?" He would look at you sideways, giving you the "froggy" look. You know Kermit on *The Muppet Show*? Remember when he would purse his lips and lower his head? That's how Dad looked when he was quietly speaking to you. You might hear, "The jury is still out on you," or, "Isn't it funny, but old Ted Williams isn't so sure about you yet," or, "Are you all right? Jeeesuuss."

Dad had the ability to ask the simplest of questions and evoke the most nervous and convoluted answers. Maybe it was a touch of hero intimidation, but you would sense that Dad already knew some underlying secret answer when he asked you the question. Naturally, it put you on the defensive right away, and you would end up second-guessing your own ingrained knowledge. My brother and I saw this happen to a lot of guests who would come over, and it was always the simple questions that seemed the hardest.

"So, where did you go to school?" Dad would ask a newcomer, in a voice like John Wayne talking to a pilgrim.

"Well, uh . . . I went to school in New England . . . in Vermont actually . . . the University of Vermont, to be exact."

Dad would simply look at them, focus, and say, "Are you *sure*?"

And if there was a Hall of Fame for swearing, I am certain my dad would be an inductee. As a swearer, Dad was gifted. His chosen words, on their own, could be shocking and breathtaking, but his ability to *deliver* the words was worthy of admiration. Even people with the most sensitive ears were left conflicted—hating the words, but admiring the art. It was remarkable how Dad could identify and deliver, in midstream, the proper profanity missing in an expression or phrase and put it in its proper place. It was so wrong it was just right. He made swearing sound like poetry. Somehow Dad's swearing wasn't common; it wasn't crude, rude, vulgar, or foul. He combined words and turned them into swears that sounded as though they had always existed.

How does swearing become a term of endearment? I don't know, but I loved it when Dad called me his "little shit." I loved it when he described the flies that he and I would tie as "grabby little bastards." And when he described my mom as a "pain in his ass," I knew he still loved her.

But even artists know you can turn those moments of art into atrocity and really wound with words. Just as a knife can have a jagged edge and a smooth edge, a simple change in Dad's delivery could make his words cut—deeply and harshly. This was where he separated the wheat from the chaff. If you had the strength of character to withstand the initial blow, you would understand and even appreciate the passion that lay behind his words—even if they were meant to hurt. I saw my dad transform into a monster when his swearing was coupled with feelings of rage and frustration about things he could not control. But in the end a relieved man would emerge, and if you were still present after the storm, your allegiance would be rewarded and never forgotten. Dad found that allegiance in John-Henry and me. We let the swearing roll right off, like water off a duck's back. Only the good ones stuck.

I hesitate even to write down what he would say, because no matter how one tries to describe his words, they just don't read well. His magic was in the composition, the music, and the voice. Hearing the live performance was mesmerizing in the way it made you think and rethink the statement, which served his ultimate goal of getting you to feel and appreciate his passion for the matter being discussed. There was his go-to opening line, "As long as I have a hair in my ass. . . ." That right there tells you that it's going to be a long time and that he must really mean it and feel it to get that personal.

I can tell you this: every time my dad swore he did so from the depths of his soul, filled with passion and expressing every injustice he felt and the agony of every wrong he couldn't make right. Everyone needs an outlet, a coping strategy. For Dad it came in the form of verbal expression laced with expletives few have heard. Ted Williams needed to swear. Without his swearing, he would have never been able to express himself with the emphasis that he demanded. For Ted Williams to repress his emotions would have been dangerous to his health and his psyche. It was my father's heartfelt form of prayer. As odd as this may sound, his anger and ability to swear and curse the skies were what allowed him to be great at so many things. Dad was all about control. He would lose control to gain perspective on what he could and couldn't do about a situation. The things in life that Dad could not control put him into orbit, and he would obsess about them and worry himself to exhaustion.

My brother and I witnessed our father's emotional rollercoaster rides firsthand. To us it was just scary. I referred to him as the "Beast" when he got angry, threw things around, and swore and cursed the skies. Dad had no patience when John-Henry or I would cry—and I cried a lot. He called me the "Yowler." He would shout, "Jesus Christ, shut that Yowler up!" But he was never violent toward us or our mother. The one and only time my dad ever spanked me, I deserved it. It was on the banks of the Miramichi. He had told me to sit on a specific rock right by the shore. Just a few feet away, however, was a huge boulder sitting in the shallow water. I thought that rock would be a much better perch from which to watch my father. He came charging toward me and gave me a swift, hard spank. I was too young to understand why he was so angry. I had jumped from the shore to the big rock in the river. The current was very fast and strong there. If I had slipped and fallen, I could easily have been swept away. That was the only time he ever spanked me.

As quickly as he got upset, he would literally turn the other cheek and ask for a peck, right here, for your old dad. But we were kids—our well-being depended on his emotions. We weren't ready and didn't know how to snap back so quickly. It took time for us to realize that we couldn't let his flashes of anger bother us. His anger truly wasn't about us, but about something personal to him. Something inside of him would set him off, and the Beast would rear its ugly head. So my brother and I learned to become constants in his life. Eventually, we were able to replace Dad's fair-weather fans without conditions. Maybe we didn't completely replace his beloved Boston fans, but we loved our father and everything about him, and we became his most loyal supporters. John-Henry and I had our own touch of hero-worship, but we weathered every storm together. When Dad had an outburst, we would try to soothe rather than respond or escalate; he'd be back around anytime now—he was only temporarily out of order.

This need to control the world around him played a big role in his moods and was exhausting for all of us. I witnessed Dad's fatigue every time he endured something he could not change or control. Even a simple cold in one of his kids could get him mad.

"Well, what the hell do you want me to do about it? Why did you have to go and get sick?"

That's not exactly the response you're looking for when you're a sick child. He was angry that he couldn't just fix it.

According to psychologists, becoming a "control freak" can be caused by feelings of separation from, or fear of abandonment by, something or someone you love. The control freak also fears that things will go wrong if he can't be instrumental in every aspect. And he has an overwhelming desire to prove something. The result of this for Dad was that he was constantly defending the very area where he knew he was vulnerable: the terrible childhood angst of being alone remained with him throughout his life. Ted Williams hated to be alone, and as I'd come to see years later, that feeling came from an emptiness inside him that only my brother and I would be able to fill.

Of course, back when we were kids, my brother and I didn't

understand any of this. Mom, however, was a different story. With all of her intuitive wisdom, she recognized that keeping us with our father was a losing battle, and she decided, for our sake, to do something about it. My mom was sensitive and fiercely protective of her children. When she saw how verbally aggressive Dad could be, she feared for us—not for herself, but for her children. She was afraid we were too impressionable and that it would be impossible for our brains to comprehend our sometimes scary father.

And so, in 1974, three years after my birth, my parents divorced and our separated lives began. When the marriage didn't work out, Mom was extremely disappointed and felt as if she had failed as a woman and a wife. My mom was a lady—intelligent and independent. She didn't even know who Ted Williams was when she met him. She didn't need Dad—she wanted him. "He was easy to love," she'd later say. She fell in love with a man who exuded passion in everything he did. She fell in love with a man who loved adventure and loved nature and had traveled all over the world, just as she had. She loved his fortitude and determination to succeed at whatever he put his mind to. Dad hated mediocrity; he always said, "Don't do anything half-assed. Act like you give a damn." She encouraged him and believed in him. She admired his enthusiasm for whatever he wanted to learn.

Ultimately, the decision she made, she made for us. Without children, I believe their relationship would have survived both their strong characters, but she was afraid of the long-term effect the emotional turbulence would have on us. She made the decision she felt was right, in spite of the love she felt for her husband. In the end, I think she finally said, "I can't do this anymore."

THE FIRST COUPLE OF SUMMERS AFTER MY PARENTS' DIVORCE, Dad came to pick up John-Henry and me on his way to Canada. He was on his way to fish for Atlantic salmon at his cabin in Blackville, New Brunswick. While I was invited to go those first summers, it seemed I was always suffering from some ailment—usually ear infections, affecting my equilibrium.

As John-Henry and Dad would drive away in the station wagon to go fishing, I'd cry and chase after them, wishing Dad would reconsider, and I'd often lose my balance and fall as I tried to run down the hill of our driveway. But Dad couldn't take care of a sick daughter and still go fishing—he couldn't leave me alone in the cabin—so I frequently stayed home with Mom while my brother and Dad got to go fishing.

I got lucky during those summers, though, because it was then that Mom taught me invaluable lessons in how to understand Ted Williams as a father and a man. She slowly gave me the tools to handle each situation, outburst, and character flaw. Mom knew that it would be difficult for her children, especially a daughter, to understand this intense, intimidating man. She made it very clear to me that I would never fix him. I had only two options. Accept him and embrace him, or walk away. Sometimes, as the summer came to an end, my mom and I would drive up to the fishing camp in Blackville so I could spend a few summer days with my brother and Dad. It was as if the master was testing the student. She was giving me small trials to see if I had learned from my summer sessions with her in Vermont. In just a three-day visit, I could try out all my new skills, and my mother could test my resolve and fortitude.

Despite loving Dad enormously, Mom didn't have enough time to figure out Ted Williams during their marriage. It was only after they separated that she could begin to teach her children how to navigate this man and find the best father we could within his huge persona. It was our mother who was able to help me and my brother understand a father who was absent quite a bit in our lives. Without our mother's help and guidance, my brother and I would have never grown to appreciate and love our father the way we did. It was because of our mother's enduring respect for and adoration of our father that her children formed an impenetrable bond with him.

In the end, Ted Williams knew that Dolores Williams had given him the greatest gift he could have received—two children who accepted, respected, and loved him unconditionally, no matter what. Above anything else, I give my mom and dad a ton of credit for maintaining admiration and respect for each other through their divorce. I believe that they never stopped caring for or supporting each other as parents. I know that Mom continued to love him despite their divorce and still loves him today.

Even when he was at his worst, what my mother never forgot was that my father could be the most caring person. He had a heart that seemed to bleed compassion for his fellow man. He was extremely empathetic, but his emotional displays and outbursts would make any observer question his heart or love if they didn't know the man. It was easy to label Ted Williams a misogynist bastard, but that's a bit too hasty. Understanding him required a patient ability to comprehend the depths from which he had come.

Mom understood all this instinctively. She would always be supportive and balanced in her explanations of Dad's behavior, especially during the confusing times when our dad would lash out with his swearing, with cruel humor, or with rampages of frustration toward someone or something out of his control. I can't remember my mother ever being manipulative or trying to turn our allegiance away from our father because of his occasionally tumultuous ways. She could have easily poisoned our devotion to our father by bad-mouthing her ex-husband or demeaning the importance of his role in our lives, but she never did. She never forgot the fact that he was the father of her children and that his presence in our lives was of critical importance to us. I guess it's a lot different dealing with Ted Williams as a wife than as the mother of his children.

When Mom talked about him, she would portray Dad as someone who would *always* be difficult to understand, around whom there was bound to be a lot of "bad weather." Mom told us that we would have to be quick in discovering what the weather was like, whether it was a hurricane brewing or just a tropical storm. If the former, get the hell out of the way and wait on the beach for his return. To her, Ted Williams was someone you had to study and figure out. If not, you could be wounded, permanently scarred, and never able to enjoy the larger-than-life man he was.

"Greatness is not easily understood," she would say.

Chapter Five

After they divorced, Mom became restless. She returned to New York to rekindle her modeling career, but a lot had changed in five years. Mom was pushing forty now, though she still looked thirty.

She was not happy with any of our babysitters. When she realized she could not be both a mom and a model and do either to the standards she expected of herself, she chose motherhood. Mom moved us back to Putney, where she raised us on the farm. She knew Ted Williams would return to the house on the hill every so often, however briefly, to visit his son and daughter. On our sixty-acre farm, he was safe and no one bothered him. There he could relax and enjoy the visits that, despite being short and sweet, made for an easier transition from married life to divorced life. Mom saw Dad only a bit less than she did when they were married, and for a couple of summers after their divorce Mom would still follow Dad up to Canada so that John-Henry could spend some additional time with his father.

Dad returned to Islamorada in the Florida Keys, where he'd had a house since he started fishing there in the late 1940s. When I was in third grade, Mom realized that John-Henry missed his father terribly. So, she moved us to Islamorada. We lived in a little beach cottage just down the road from his house, and all three of us spent time with him there. There was a moment when Mom thought they might get back together, but unfortunately there was already another woman who had been waiting patiently to be in Dad's life. Sadly, it didn't work out, and Mom moved us back to Putney just a year later.

The surrounding towns of Putney, Westminster, and Bellows Falls knew that the former Mrs. Ted Williams had returned to her house on the hill. It seemed that while John-Henry and I were at school, Mom would work all day attempting to transform her country home into a well-groomed Green Mountain estate with a million-dollar view. She learned how to use a chainsaw and started cutting down trees for better views of the rolling landscape. She got a wood splitter and started preparing for the long, cold New England winters in the late spring. She planted a garden, and we lived off our own fresh vegetables and various types of melons. She purchased chickens for eggs. Aside from the occasional steak or fish purchased in a store, we were sustained by the earth our mother cultivated and the animals we raised. We were wholesome and all-natural. Sugar was poison, while bee pollen and raw honey were staples in our diet. Mom cared for her land every day, and her beautiful long thin fingers grew tough and calloused.

In the wooded hills of Putney, Mom's glamorous life slowly crumbled away. She went from a rapidly growing fish in a big pond to an oversized fish in a tiny pond. She fully invested herself in being the best mother she could be. Dad would forever describe her as "a great mother—tough as nails, but a hell of a mother."

The driveway was about a quarter of a mile long, but you could cut straight up the hill if you were in a hurry. When the school bus dropped me off at the bottom of the driveway, I had a choice of either walking straight up the hill or taking the long, rocky, winding driveway. I preferred to take the long way. As I started up the driveway, I would look up at where the house stood to see if there was any smoke coming out of the chimney. It was like deciphering a signal. I learned that if there was a lot of smoke, Mom was probably busy cooking or cleaning and I would have extra chores to do. If there was little smoke, either she was not home or she had gotten distracted reading something or lost track of the day and was always surprised to see me home.

Just past our crooked iron gate, a pond over to the right was hidden by tall grass and overgrown shrubs, but on hot summer days it was easy to find. The cement pad for the foundation where the house used to stand can still be found if you stomp through the tall wild rhubarb that Mom would harvest to make her pies. She decorated them with the dandelion flowers that could be found throughout the fields. There was a pine tree a bit farther up on the left that was so large you could live in it if you wanted, and John-Henry and I practically did. My brother and I would climb it and teach our geese to fly by tossing them into the air, or we would take a break from chores and look out into the back field to watch for deer.

A little farther up the road was an area of driveway that seemed to be purposely sprinkled with white birch trees. I always wondered why we did not plant more; they were very pretty and made that area of our driveway seem special. As you approached the second small hill of the driveway there was another field to the right and on the bend sat the sugarhouse. Almost every spring we would make maple syrup with our grandparents and share it with the rest of the family or sell it. Even Dad helped us gather sap and boil it down to make maple syrup one early spring. He loved maple syrup and couldn't believe it took forty-three gallons of sap to make one gallon of syrup. "No wonder it's so damn expensive! Jesus!"

Way up in the woods off the road was a barn. This was where we kept our animals at night. Our chickens, geese, a sheep, and my horse Bella Nina all slept in the barn. Sometimes I did too, in the top loft, to keep my animals company.

As the house would come into view, it was partially blocked by the beginnings of a stone wall. It was built over many years, including my childhood, and each section represents a different time in our family life. Each stone could tell a story. It's about five feet tall, and it clearly shows the improvement over time in our building skills. The rocks seem to fit better as the wall wraps around the front yard of the house along the final stretch of the driveway. One of our chores was to get rocks from the garden, pile them in the 1962 Jeep Willys truck, and bring them to Mom, who would place them where she saw fit. If a rock was really large, she would use a plank to roll it into the best place she could find.

I ended up getting a hernia at a very young age from lifting rocks that were way too large, trying to show my mom how strong I was. She called my dad and said, "Well, it's official. Your daughter has your genes." Dad suffered three or four hernias during his career. That was the start of a friendly banter they kept up from then on. Whenever John-Henry or I did anything good, our mom or dad would say, "Well, those are my genes." If we did something wrong, it would be, "Well, we know where you got those genes from."

There are stones in that wall that were placed there with the help of the mailman, the UPS man, Ted Williams, former Mr. Universe Franco Columbu, models, actors, doctors, children, friends, family, and complete strangers. Mom had moved a house to build her king a castle and protected it with a barrier of stones, all in the hopes of providing a place of privacy and security for the ones she loved. Every summer when Dad would come to get us, he praised Mom for the growing wall and for how nice the place was starting to look. It was an endless job. If it hadn't been for a stroke, she would still be placing rocks.

The house itself is old. I don't know how old for sure, but my mom would often tell me that it was from the late 1800s. The floorboards average thirteen inches in width. My brother and I would play on the exposed overhead beams that helped hold up the house. Every

Christmas we were convinced that Santa really did exist because the slate roof allowed the ice and snow to slide off, making a sound just like a sleigh and a team of reindeer. My mom installed very large glass-paned French doors, approximately six-by-twelve feet, to give the house four huge windows facing the rolling hills. There are hidden charms in every nook and cranny throughout the house: soapstone sinks, exposed copper pipes, and even a spiral staircase. Each room has a secret. In one room exotic animal heads, right out of an African safari, stare at you. In another, a small Miss Vermont trophy sits on the fireplace mantel. You can find evidence of lives filled with experiences that are second to none. It is something to discover.

ABOUT A YEAR OR TWO AFTER WE RETURNED TO PUTNEY, DAD convinced Mom to allow his children to travel to Florida over the Christmas holidays. It was exciting. We were unaccompanied minors traveling in a big jet plane, an adventure in itself, and we were going to see our dad. We ached to run and play with him.

Reunions were always the best—but the thrill of being back together seemed to last only a few days. Being without Mom was intimidating. She protected us when Dad got grumpy or impatient with us little kids squealing, running around, and fighting. She would sense before we could when the Beast was getting irritated. Our gauges were not yet that well calibrated, and before we knew it we would upset him somehow.

That first time I made the trip with John-Henry I was eight or nine and John-Henry was eleven or twelve. Unaccompanied minors had to wait until all the other passengers de-boarded before we were allowed to exit the plane. John-Henry reminded me to be on my best behavior, not to cry or whine, and told me I better go to the bathroom before we left the airport because it was a two-hour drive before we'd get to Islamorada. Then John-Henry shared with me the best part of airport pickups.

"We're going to have to find Dad."

"What do you mean, find Dad?"

"Dad will be hiding in the airport somewhere, and we have to find him. He'll probably see us before we see him, but keep a look-out anyway."

It sounded just like hide-and-seek—how fun. As we walked up the ramp from the plane I wondered who would find him first. I didn't really want to leave my brother's side, so instead of running around to search, I just thought of good places Dad might hide. There were a lot of people in the terminal, but no one who resembled my dad. Six-foot-four is hard to conceal, but Dad seemed to have found a way to hide himself well. I started looking behind chairs, thinking maybe he was crouched down, or hiding behind the check-in counter. My brother said impatiently, "He's not going to be there. Come on."

It was so exciting that our dad was willing to play hide-and-seek in this huge airport. John-Henry had experienced this before. Being three years older, he'd been allowed to venture out on his own to Florida without his little sister. He knew the game—and he knew the hiding spots.

"Do you see him?" I asked.

"Yup, over there. See him?"

"Where? I don't see him."

John-Henry stopped and pointed. All the way against a far wall, in front of large windows, a man in an old-looking fishing hat with sunglasses propped on the rim stood behind a pillar. He was just poking his head around the pillar's edge. I squealed with joy and giggled, then took off running. Dad was just like us. He was a big kid and so fun to be around. At first.

I grabbed his waist and squeezed as hard as I could.

"We found you!"

"Really? *You* didn't see me. Your brother had to point me out. What do you think of your old dad? He can hide pretty damned well, can't he?"

What I believed at the time was a game was actually Dad's way of life in public. He *had* to hide. We were swamped with people as soon as we emerged from our secluded corner.

"Ted! Can I have your autograph?" someone yelled. Four or five people rushed up to surround us. I found the pocket on Dad's loose khaki fishing pants and held on tight. Dad kept walking as he signed, and kept talking about how he had to get home and get his kids to bed. All the way to the baggage claim we were flocked by people who came out of nowhere asking for his autograph and picture. People stepped on my feet and tried to push me out of the way. I looked for my brother. He was walking three steps behind. He knew the drill.

It seemed to take our bag forever to come around on the belt. It was like a feeding frenzy. The more people noticed the school of people around us, the more showed up. Dad finally had enough and turned and walked away.

"I'll get the damned car. John-Henry, get the bag."

We stood there watching our father stride away. Our moment of joy had been obliterated by the swarm of people who wanted a piece of our dad.

"Your dad's the greatest!" someone yelled. "You kids need any help?" asked someone else. "You know where you all are parked?"

I just wanted to get out of there and get back with my dad. These people were crazy. Didn't they see he was with his kids? Didn't they know he hadn't seen us in a while and missed us?

Yes, reunions were the best, but our time was limited.

Dad pulled up along the curb. Sure enough, some strange guy grabbed our little duffel bag and brought it out with us. My brother kept saying, "I got it, I got it," but this guy was not going to be denied possibly his last chance to get an autograph from Ted Williams. What a silly man. He was rude and very pushy, I thought.

"Get in the car!" Dad yelled as he opened the back of the mustard yellow Suburban and signed yet another autograph. This didn't sound like fun anymore. I started to feel fear as I climbed into the backseat. When I turned to look behind me, I only saw more people coming out of the airport toward us. John-Henry was in the front seat hurrying to put his seat belt on. "Put your seat belt on, quickly," he said to me. I fumbled with my buckle as I sensed the urgency to flee.

"I have *got* to leave," Dad was telling the man. "The kids' mother will be upset if I don't get them to bed soon." And with that, Dad was in the driver's seat. He slammed the car into drive and pushed the accelerator to the floor.

I didn't dare say a word. I sat quietly, looking at the back of my brother's head, waiting for him to turn around so that I could mouth to him that I had to *go.* I'd forgotten to use the bathroom.

As time went on and I got older, I became more aware of the response Dad evoked from a crowd. When we were with him in public, it would be only a matter of time before someone recognized Ted Williams and we were engulfed.

The first time I ever saw a Red Sox baseball game was at Fenway Park, in April 1983. Interestingly enough, I was not with my father. Instead, I was eleven years old and with my fifth-grade class on a school trip to see an afternoon game. We rode our familiar school bus all the way from the little town of Westminster to Boston's crowded Yawkey Way. Our chaperones led the way as we shuffled along through the unfamiliar shaded tunnels that smelled musty and stale. With our buddies, hand in hand, we made our way to our seats. We arrived just as the park was beginning to get crowded. Our eyes and ears soaked in every oddity. People were loud, and the Boston accents sounded like a foreign language. Men were walking up and down the aisles selling *hot daawgs, cawtton candy,* and something called *beahr.* We must have been sitting in the smoking section, but it was the most unusual-smelling smoke I had ever smelled.

Soon after we nestled into our seats and impatiently waited a few minutes for the game to start, someone spotted a unique seat that seemed not to belong. Way off in the right-field bleachers was a red seat. It really stood out, even though it was so far away. We all wondered why it was red. The cynic in our group guessed that someone had died in that seat and now no one was to sit there. Another little girl thought it was the best seat in the house and only very special people were allowed to sit there. I secretly wondered if it had anything to do with my dad. I still had only vague knowledge of Dad's baseball career and had heard others speak about how well he hit the ball. Whenever we spent time with Dad, it was away from the public. Only a select few of Dad's close friends were around him when his children were too. Even in grade school, my relationship with Ted Williams was not well known among my peers. To me, he was just Dad, and I wasn't about to say anything. I didn't want the attention.

Finally, someone found the courage to ask Mr. Murphy why the seat was red. All the tiny heads turned toward our homeroom teacher. He looked at us and said, "That seat identifies the longest home run ever hit in this stadium."

"Whoa," remarked one of the boys. "That's really far!"

"See," said the smartest girl in class, "I *told* you it was the best seat."

That seat is 502 feet from home plate. My father hit it on June 9, 1946, off Detroit pitcher Fred Hutchinson. I don't believe any of my classmates knew or understood who my father was, but the teachers and chaperones must have talked among themselves about the little blonde whose father was Ted Williams.

More and more, as these moments began to occur they led me to realize that having the father I did influenced the way people treated me. A few weeks later, our teacher assigned us to do a science project that would demonstrate combustion. I made a cannon that shot tennis balls. A pilot friend of my mother's taught my brother and me how to make it. I drafted the tennis ball cannon with graphs and pictures, then constructed it from used tennis ball cans. For a final fifth-grade project, it was rather sophisticated and pretty cool. I shot off the tennis balls during class, and it seemed that everyone was impressed. I was happy and proud of what I had done and felt recognized when I got an A. Dad knew nothing about it and had nothing to do with it.

The day after we received our grades, one of my classmates came up to me and said, "My mom said that the only reason you got an A on your project is because your dad is Ted Williams."

I thought to myself, *Well, that is my dad's name, but why would that get me an A?* My dad did not even know of the project. What a silly thing to say. By the time I got home I had worked myself into a tearful frenzy. I was confused and bothered, and I had to have an answer.

"Mom, did I get an A on my science project because of my dad's name?"

Mom knew right away what was going on. I did not and could not appreciate my father's impact on the little town of Westminster. He was certainly adored in Boston, that much I saw. But what did that have to do with me and getting an A on a science project? Ted Williams was just the name of my father, and I knew he liked to fish, had played some baseball in Boston, loved to eat, and had a very short temper.

Now, at eleven, I was learning about resentment and jealousy. I realized that people would be quick to judge me because of who my parents were and would simply ignore who I was as a person. It was my first lesson in how hard it is, if not impossible, to avoid people's preconceived ideas about you if you're famous or related to someone famous. From then on, I was labeled, my identity directly linked to my father. I was "Ted Williams's Daughter." In my presence, people would talk about me and around me, all speaking to me as the daughter of Ted Williams and never stopping to ask *my* name.

"This is Ted's daughter." "Do you know who her father is?" "I'm a big fan of your father."

People would seem too lost in reminiscing about their hero to think to ask my name. Over the years I would meet many people who walked away never knowing what my first name was. There would also be many people I *never* even met who talked about me and criticized me without ever getting to know me. This continues to amaze me.

I realize this may sound naive, but it took my brother and me a long time to understand the magnitude of Dad's celebrity. Our mother did not want us to be exposed to or spoiled by fame. Our mother wanted to be sure that we valued hard work, respected others, and appreciated everything life had to offer. My brother and I had more chores than most children our age, and I know for a fact that we were not given or allowed the same luxuries as our friends. Mom believed that television was bad for the brain and hard work was a good form of exercise. Movies were only a once-in-a-while treat. She was also a believer in the book *Sugar Blues,* which warned parents that sugar was poison. We got our desserts only if we finished our dinner, and even then they were made with honey as a natural sweetener instead of refined sugar. We knew we had better say "please" and "thank you," and we didn't dare speak back to Mom or we could get our mouths washed out with soap. She spanked us with a wooden spoon and would send us to the cellar to pile wood if we misbehaved.

She wanted to be sure that we would be humble and not ever feel entitled just because of who our father was. To John-Henry and me, Ted Williams was Dad and that was it. That was more than enough. We respected him greatly as our father, and we loved him. He was not a celebrity. He was human. He played with us, he joked with us, he taught us many things, he hugged us, he scolded us, and he loved us.

Mom was tough, but I would not change a thing about the first thirteen years of my life.

Chapter Six

Richard Ben Cramer said it so very well in the June 1986 issue of *Esquire:* "Ted Williams wanted fame, and wanted it with a pure, hot eagerness that would have been embarrassing in a smaller man. But he could not stand celebrity. This is a bitch of a line to draw in America's dust."

Dad wanted to be The Greatest Hitter Who Ever Lived. He never wanted much else, and he most certainly did not want the burden of celebrity. He was never rich by the standards of today's best ballplayers. In his own words, "I've always had a way to make some money, but I've always managed to find a way to spend it." He enjoyed the special benefits that his fame brought him, but only in their simplest form. The attention everywhere he went, the lack of privacy in public places—none of that was to his taste.

As I got older I came to see how much Dad truly enjoyed the bare necessities of life—they were the simple things he lived for. He never wanted a Mercedes, or jewelry, or fancy clothes. He loathed pretension and all other kinds of "bullshit." Dad found real peace and comfort in the basics of food, shelter, and clothing. Taking care of the basics centered him and genuinely made him happy. He didn't want to worry about not having them. I don't know whether that desire grew in him as a result of being deprived in some ways during his childhood, of having lived through the era of the Great Depression, or whether he just wanted to avoid having to constantly worry about how he was going to get through tomorrow.

In all of my years with Dad, he drove either a station wagon or a Suburban. He never went for the flashy stuff. In 1952, just before he went to serve in the Korean War, the Red Sox held a Ted Williams Day at Fenway and presented Dad with a brand-new Cadillac. He thought it was prestigious. He also said he got more speeding tickets in that car than any other. Dad got rid of it rather quickly because, as he figured, the police "were just looking for Cadillacs so they could nab 'em for speeding."

Regardless of his personal experience with the coveted vehicle, he certainly used it as bait and a motivational tool. Growing up, we'd occasionally hear Dad say something like, "Boy, if you can do that I'll give you a Cadillac." Part of what made that statement so memorable was the delivery: he'd say it in a voice that let you know it couldn't be done but dared you to try anyway.

After Dad's death, John-Henry and I needed to go through many items in our father's home. We saw an old home video in Dad's library. It had to have been shot in the mid- to late 1970s, so Dad was nearly sixty years old. He was in a Red Sox uniform at spring training, helping the next wave of Red Sox players sharpen their skills. He was overweight and clearly not in his best shape. He was playing a game of pepper—tossing a baseball into the air and hitting it out to outfielders working on their fielding skills. Dad held the bat in one hand as he tossed a baseball into the air with the other. Before the ball hit the ground, Dad would grip the bat, swing, and hit the ball every time. Only he didn't just hit it—he hit it squarely and directly to the outfielder he had chosen.

At one point he turned the discussion to Cadillacs, motivating and teasing the players one after the other. He tossed the ball up and yelled, "Three in a row and you get a Cadillac. Field three in a row, and I'll *buy* you a Cadillac."

First, he hit one to the left fielder to bring him toward the infield. It was hit just where you'd place it for a young player to be able to get it.

"Great grab! Next one's coming. Remember, three in a row and I'll buy you a Cadillac."

Dad hit the second ball just far enough over the left fielder's head to make him move backward, but not so far that it couldn't be caught.

"Great job! Next one's coming. Remember now, three in a row and you get a Cadillac. This is it." Dad tossed the third ball up, swung, and hit it over the left fielder's head. It didn't look like Dad swung at this ball any harder, but it went soaring out of the ballpark. Not a chance.

Dad did the same thing to the right fielder and the center fielder.

You could see the smiles on the young outfielders' faces. John-Henry and I laughed as we watched. I believe Dad was having as much fun showcasing his own talents as the young players had dreaming of winning a Cadillac from The Greatest Hitter Who Ever Lived.

I was so impressed by the fact that Dad could make contact with every ball and place it right where he intended. John-Henry explained to me the added difficulty that Dad faced by tossing his own ball. The speed of a pitched ball would have generated some of the power in his hitting motion, but tossing the ball required that he generate all the power on his own to hit the ball over the fence. At near sixty years of age, he tossed the ball, hit the ball, placed it precisely with every swing, and sometimes knocked it over the fence. He did it all confidently, while torquing each young player just right. Dad always impressed us.

For shelter and clothing, function was always paramount over form. Dad's houses were never grandiose or opulent. For a house to be his home, it only needed a functioning roof, hot water, working toilets, a kitchen, and a comfortable bed. He loved his cabin on the river in Canada as much as his two-story home in the Florida Keys. For a shirt to be his favorite, it only needed to be comfortable. Dad did not like the task of shopping. He had no patience for such a trivial activity. When he found a comfortable article of clothing, he bought a dozen. Fashion was the least of his concerns. It was customary to see Dad in the same clothes for three or four consecutive days. Don't get me wrong, they were clean each day. But comfort was king, and he saw no reason to change his look for the sake of someone else. If he had to appear at a public event and needed to be presentable, someone very persuasive, with an easy, relaxed style, had to be sent in to help him dress. Otherwise, Dad might show up wearing a '70s-style velour shirt or his favorite Hanes V-neck tee and his baggy khaki fishing pants.

As children, we would follow our father around like puppies, learning how these simple pleasures in his life worked. He had so many unique rituals that were curious and humorous all at the same time. Dad was very neat and clean, maybe to the point of being a little compulsive about it. We would sit on the bathroom sink counter and watch our father shave with his three-headed Remington shaver. He loved Aqua Velva. There were about a dozen bottles of it in his medicine cabinet. He would splash so much aftershave on his face that the cool alcohol splatter would reach us. He explained that you had to make sure you had enough to get it all over your face and neck.

"You can't get enough of this stuff—you never want to smell."

There was no dabbing. More like aggressive slapping until his cheeks, neck, and chest were all pink. He probably went through a bottle a week. When he was done, he'd place a towel around his neck.

"You want to make sure you don't get any hair on your shoulders," he would explain.

There was nothing worse than loose hair hanging off your shoulders he would say with a disgusted look on his face. Then he would take out this comb that looked like a horse curry grooming comb and explain that you should brush each side of your scalp twenty-five times. It actually was a massage comb, and he would attack his scalp vigorously. After rinsing his comb, he would slick his hair back with just the wetness of his hands. Then, ever so carefully, he would step away from the towel, lifting it away as if it were a contaminated cape. He would fold it to prevent any damned dirty hairs from escaping and then chuck it to the floor, never to be touched again.

Oral hygiene may have been the most explicit lesson we learned. Dad believed in hard-bristle brushes. Didn't matter what the dentist said, the harder the better. Dad had all his teeth when he died, so he must have been doing something right. He would brush his teeth like he was mad at them. Also a counting ceremony on each side of his mouth and on all sides of his teeth. He would then stick out his tongue, hold it with a washcloth, and brush it until he gagged. The first time I heard my father brush his teeth I was concerned: it sounded like he was very sick and throwing up. I went to find my brother and told him I thought Dad was ill. I brought him to the outside of the bathroom door so that he could listen to what I had heard. My brother smiled and said, "Oh, that's just Dad brushing his teeth."

And then there was the Listerine. He loved Listerine—only the original, harsh-tasting version. Someone once gave him a beautiful crystal liquor decanter. Dad was not much of a drinker, so he filled this lovely decanter with Listerine and kept it in the bathroom. Every morning he'd pour a crystal glass half full of Listerine to gargle. He threw his head back for a deep gargle lasting at least a minute. I think he may have even drunk a little, just to make sure he killed every last germ. After he finally spit it out and rinsed with water, he would look at himself in the mirror, smile, cock his head slightly, point at his reflection emphatically, and then wink.

"You handsome son of a bitch."

We found this very humorous.

"What do you think of your ol' dad now?" he would ask.

Mesmerizing.

"Thorough" came to mind for starters. My mother would tell us that Dad was the cleanest person she ever met. Coming from a nurse, that said a lot. Dad was always very conscientious about how he smelled. I can't remember my father ever smelling of body odor or having bad breath.

When we were kids he was always checking us out, asking us to give him a huff for his approval. Eventually we were all going through our morning cleaning rituals together. The first time Listerine hit my sensitive mouth I thought my mouth was on fire.

"That's good, that way you know it's working," Dad would say encouragingly. "You always want to be kissing sweet."

Ironically, I never saw my father kiss anyone on the lips—never, not even Mom. He would always turn his cheek.

OF THE THREE BASIC NECESSITIES, DAD LOVED FOOD THE MOST, and it held his attention like nothing else. To know Ted Williams was to know him around what my brother and I would refer to as "feeding time."

He *loved* good food. It didn't need to be rich, sweet, or hifalutin; he wasn't interested in using his celebrity to get into five-star restaurants. He appreciated a great steak on the grill and all kinds of fish, pork, and lamb. Corn on the cob, potatoes, Swiss chard (à la Dolores), or most any kind of beans were more than sufficient to complement the meal. Dessert was best when it was simple: chocolate cake, Key lime pie, or just Oreos and cold milk. Milkshakes and root beer floats were the best treats.

His love for food was infectious. He could make you salivate with hunger over the simplest dish just by sharing his passion and enthusiasm. He might ask his guests, "D'ya like chicken? Yeah, well, I know this *grrreat* chicken place right down the road. You're gonna love it!" The visitors would be all wound up, the first ones in the car. Then Dad would take them to the local fried chicken joint, the Chicken King restaurant. They were always blatantly disappointed over the commonness of the place, but once served, they were convinced that this plain ol' fried chicken was in fact the best fried chicken ever.

Spicy food was a particular passion for him. I have fond memories of my dad and grandfather, my mom's dad, eating hot peppers together. My grandfather loved hot peppers, and when Dad drove up in the summer to pick us up to go to Canada, Grumpa would be waiting. Our grandfather was affectionately called Grumpa because he was often grumpy and would yell at John-Henry and me in German if we did not close the front door. He was from St. Galen, Switzerland. Our grandfather was very important to my brother and me in our upbringing, filling in as the male role model we desperately needed. Dad knew this and appreciated our grandfather. He would visit Grumpa just across the way from Mom's house every time he was in town. They'd sit at the kitchen table and together sample an assortment of Grumpa's garden-grown radishes and peppers. Then Grumpa would bring out the pickled jalapeño peppers and accompanying pigs' feet and head cheese. Dad thoroughly enjoyed those afternoon snacks. I think one of the reasons he loved my mother's cooking so much was that it was loaded with flavor and tons of spices, just like her father had taught her.

At restaurants, when Dad ordered a salad and the waiter came over with the pepper mill, Dad would say, "Look, I'm not trying to be funny, but I love pepper. Go ahead and put a lot on." The waiter would grind away as Dad kept motioning him on for a minute or more, until his salad was frosted with black grounds. Tabasco was also a staple at almost every meal. Asked once how much he enjoyed Tabasco, Dad shook the bottle into a tablespoon until it was full to the brim and downed the sauce with pleasure.

Dad believed in the medicinal properties of spice and fresh vegetables. I once saw him eat a whole baked garlic clove with salad and bread. Once, while watching a baseball game, he remarked that the players needed more garlic in their diet. A garlic company heard about this and sent the team a bushel of fresh garlic.

Dad had a voracious appetite. Breakfast and dinner were the biggest meals. Lunch, snacks, and the occasional root beer float were standard ways to bridge the gap. All time was measured by the next meal, and houseguests were invited to "sit and eat," "come to breakfast," or "stay for dinner." Feeding time acquired even more purpose when Dad threw down food challenges to find the best dish or the best cook. If he had a dish he really liked and a friend bragged about his own version, there was always a cook-off. Dad would instruct his chef just how to make his dish, and then there would be a blind tasting and voting by the family or anyone else who wanted to participate.

There were some things Dad had trouble communicating, and the more personal they were the more they grew as an unspoken anxiety in his mind. That was why he would often erupt: he just couldn't bring himself to say the simple, basic thing he wanted as soon as he wanted it. For example, when he waited too long to eat and suffered hunger pangs, he was like a bear coming out of hibernation. His patience was incredibly thin, and his anxiety increased exponentially by the minute.

Dad would hint, suggest, ask, and offer, but very seldom would he come right out and say exactly what he wanted. He was strategic in avoiding a direct question. Nothing exemplified this behavior better than feeding time. A customary exchange would go something like this:

DAD: Do you want something to eat? (*kindly offering*)
ME: No, I'm good, thank you. (*being honest, understanding it was a polite offer*)
DAD: You're not hungry?

ME: No, not really—you, Dad? (*offering him the opportunity to express himself*)

DAD: Nope. I just thought you might want something to eat. (*long pause*) When do you want to eat?

ME: Probably not for a while.

DAD: Well, we better start thinking about when the hell we want to eat!

ME: How about 5:30? (*hearing agitation in his voice as my first alarm*)

DAD: What time is it now?

ME: Four. (*hearing him grumble*) Do you want to have a snack?

DAD: No . . . do you? (*hearing the hope in his voice*)

ME: Dad, you sound hungry. Are you hungry?

DAD: I could eat if you eat.

ME: Want me to make you something?

DAD: I'll share whatever you make.

ME: I'm not really hungry, Dad.

DAD: OKAY, FINE. FUCK IT! I'M NOT HUNGRY!

Bam! There it was. Instead of just asking for something to eat because he was hungry, he would get himself all worked up to the point where he got mad and denied himself gratification, just because no one would join him in a snack. He was all right if someone ate with him because then he didn't feel like the only one eating or needing to have food prepared. It was as if it was taboo to be hungry when no one else was—but instead of verbalizing that feeling, he would end up exploding.

I learned pretty quickly to get ready with snacks when it was near feeding time and share whatever nourishment I had readily available. Dad was so easy to please. He loved to sit and share food. He would smile and practically giggle as he enjoyed something tasty with you. It was pure heaven if you were enjoying it with him too.

"This is goood, isn't it? Here, have some more. You're not eating. You gotta eat this. Isn't it grrreeeat!"

One Christmas, not knowing what else to get my dad, I bought a collector's tin of Oreo cookies. It may have been one of the best gifts I ever gave him. He proudly lifted the tin and pointed firmly. "Now, *this* is a great gift. Get the milk!" We sat and probably ate over a dozen cookies each, chatting about how long we needed to let them soak and how important it was that the milk be ice cold. Something so simple turned out to be a memorable moment.

As a family, we all enjoyed privacy. We came to respect Dad's lack of tolerance for annoyance of any kind. The fewer interruptions and irritations there were the better our time together was. He could keep a few requests for autographs on the street in perspective, and even appreciate them. But interruptions during dinner at home, especially dinner with us kids, were almost intolerable. It became Dad's ritual around 6:00 P.M. to rip the phone off the hook to be certain mealtime would not be interrupted. Because God help us all if the phone rang during feeding time.

Such was the case one Christmas break when I was about eight or nine and John-Henry and I were with Dad in Islamorada. Everything was calm that evening as we were waiting for dinner. Dad was watching TV; John-Henry and I were upstairs devising a plan to meet up later with our local friends. Dad seemed disappointed when we wanted to visit our friends rather than hang out with him, so we learned that it couldn't be our idea or at our request. We had to encourage our friends to take the initiative and call to ask permission. Silently, John-Henry crept downstairs to put the phone back on the hook, then raced back upstairs so that he could call his fishing friend Richard. It was a perfect plan. We were out of Dad's earshot and could arrange a secret evening with friends without anyone getting upset.

While my brother was scheming over the details with Richard— whose parents would pick us up, when and how they should arrive, and what we could do—I wandered off to the privacy of Dad's bathroom to use the toilet. After doing my business, I effectively made a catcher's mitt out of toilet paper, wiped thoroughly, and flushed the glove down with a couple of tries. I trotted back to my brother to hear the rendezvous details.

"Here, talk to Jenny, she wants you to come over too," he said. "I have to go to the bathroom." As I talked to Richard's sister, my brother went to Dad's bathroom too.

Suddenly Dad was yelling for us from downstairs.

I hung up and ran down to see my father.

"What are you doing?" Dad asked.

"Nothing. Just watching TV."

"Well, get ready for dinner. We're going to eat soon. Old Teddy Ballgame has a meal for you!"

Off I went upstairs to tell John-Henry. I found him in Dad's bathroom frantically looking for a plunger. Simultaneously we looked with immense fear at the rising tide within the bowl.

Like two complete novices, my brother and I prayed. We tried to will the water to stay below the rim of the toilet. Despite our best efforts, God was not listening and the water continued to rise. It was relentless, bringing with it bodily deposits and pieces of my baseball mitt. Then it overflowed and hit the floor. Oh God! We begged, pleaded, and grabbed towels all at the same time. The water kept coming, and we were soon running out of towels. My brother condemned me to the task of hand-delivering the evidence of my guilt to the other toilet. I made several trips with my hands full of soggy toilet paper to the other upstairs bathroom.

We were two little kids scared to death that we would make our father angry. In the back of our minds we could see the perfect storm coming. Like three runaway trains with a common destination, three situations guaranteed to set him off were coming together in the worst way: an indoor flash flood caused by a plugged toilet; a phone that was put back on the hook against Dad's wishes;

and, at the center of it all, the hungry Beast at feeding time. We were done for.

"John-Henry, Claudia, DINNER!"

We made a plan as we scrubbed our hands. We would amble down the stairs as if nothing had happened and nothing was wrong. Then, after dinner, we would find the plunger and fix the toilet. It was the only way out of this mess.

As we got to the bottom of the stairs, Dad got up from his chair and walked past the phone. As he passed through the hall that ran under his bathroom, *drip, drip,* went the water from above.

"Goddamn it! What in Christ's name! We have a goddamned leak somewhere!"

Ring! Ring! went the telephone on the wall, which seemed to ring louder than it had ever rung before.

"Jesus fucking Christ, I took this goddamned thing off the hook!"

The Beast answered the phone with great intensity. *"HELLO-WHOISIT?"*

"Hi, this is Richard. Can John-Henry come over?"

"NO. HE CANNOT. WE HAVE A LEAK SOMEWHERE. HE'LL HAVE TO CALL YOU BACK. GOOD-BYE!"

Then Dad grabbed the whole apparatus, tore it off the wall, and flung it across the living room. My brother and I just stood there, like two fawns in the lights of the runaway train. As Dad stared at the hole in the wall he had just created, we all realized that there would be no calling the plumber.

Chapter Seven

⌣

WITH MY PARENTS' DIVORCE, I HAD TO GET USED TO THE
idea of my dad spending time with other women, and for
most of my life there was one woman in particular I had to deal
with: Louise Kaufman.

After the divorce, Louise became Dad's live-in girlfriend. I
learned to live by the philosophy "keep your friends close but your
enemies closer" when it came to Louise. It's no secret that she was
my enemy. She didn't like me, and I certainly didn't like her. But my
dad liked her, so I had to respect her regardless of how difficult it
was. Louise had taken my mother's spot in Dad's life, and she was
capable of filling a role my mother was unable and unwilling to take
on: take the battering of every storm Dad sent her way.

Once, interviewing my dad, sports reporter Roy Firestone asked
him about his feelings toward Louise.

"Oh, she was a honey."

"And when you gave her hell," Firestone asked, "she gave you
hell right back?"

"She'd make me so damn mad," Dad replied. "I'd say, 'Goddamn you.'" He would grind his teeth and pretend he was getting in her face, only to hear her say:

"Yeah, you go ahead and hit me, I'll *kill* you."

"A little fiery Scotsman. Terrific gal. Love of my life."

I would describe Louise as the epitome of a groupie. She was in Dad's life for a very long time. They'd met in Islamorada before Dad was divorced from Doris, his first wife, around 1954. The one thing Bobby-Jo and I agreed on was that this woman had come between our mothers and our dad. Through the years Dad continually rejected her every time he chose to marry someone else, yet she was steadfast and religious in her allegiance to a man who was tough on her to say the least. She worshipped the famous ballplayer, but "bitched and whined" about his behavior, never taking a strong stance or defining her boundaries of what she would and would not accept. The end result was that he walked all over her.

Dad did not have much patience or tolerance for women. He saw women as weak when they would cry or complain about something trivial like getting old, putting on pounds, or some other man's wife being more attractive. I forbade myself to exhibit any of these "typical" female idiosyncrasies. I learned to change my ways very quickly. I was not going to be condemned for such behavior. To Dad, women were broads and bitches. They needed to be taken care of, and you "couldn't make them happy if you were Jesus Christ himself." They couldn't handle any guy talk or criticism, or understand that a man has got to do what a man has got to do.

Except Louise. It was impressive how many verbal bashings Louise took from Dad. So many times she just turned the other cheek or simply ignored what was really going on. Every swear word he uttered at her stuck to her, but somehow she kept coming back. She was callused and resilient against every criticism. I'm not saying she was not jealous—she was, and especially of my mother and me. I'm not saying she didn't complain either—she did, and it was always about us kids or our mother. I understand her reasoning. Despite my parents being divorced, Dad loved my mom's cooking, laughed on the phone when she was giving him the latest news about us kids, and loved her challenging ways. I know for a fact that it was easy for Mom to convince him to stay for days in our Vermont home during the summer when he passed through town to pick us up. There was a connection between my parents that could not be broken. I have always said that if the two of them had not been so much alike, they would have been inseparable.

I believe that Louise and Dad could have developed a very loving, mutually respectful relationship if Louise had the courage and self-love to walk away from the disrespect Dad showed her. I think it would have strengthened their relationship, and I certainly would have respected her more. Instead, she scolded him and yelled at him when he would swear and storm around. When she reprimanded him for using the Lord's name in vain, Dad would look to the sky and curse even louder. She was six years older than Dad, and not beautiful like his wives. She was not tall or athletic, and she was not a former model or a great cook. Ironically, she was a devout Episcopalian, but more importantly, she was able to take everything Dad dished out. As long as she lived, my dad was not alone, and Ted Williams loved her for that. She was described by her children as a "lover and a mother" to Ted Williams. That description always made me cringe, but since Dad did not want to be alone, it's certainly true that he needed someone who would put up with his behavior as only a mother can. For whatever reason, she did not leave him, and I will always appreciate her for that.

She did, however, come between my dad and each of his three wives and his children. The year Mom took us to live in Islamorada, Louise would drive by my dad's house, knowing that we were there, drop off her dog Coco, and then call Dad frantically asking if he had seen her poodle. Of course Coco would know Dad's familiar yard and would be whining by the door. Three hours later Dad would return from "dropping off Louise's dog." Sadly, this was why our year in Islamorada didn't work out, even though Mom had thought their marriage might be rekindled.

After Mom and Dad divorced, Louise was finally allowed to move into Dad's life. She was there to stay, and there was nothing I could do about it. From then on, I saw my dad only during the summer, every other Christmas, and on special occasions. The moments I did spend with him were so emotionally overwhelming and action-packed that it was probably a good thing to experience them in limited doses—not to mention the bitter elixir of Louise that I now had to swallow and Dad seemed to need.

More than anyone else, my brother helped me to appreciate Louise and recognize her value to Dad. "You want Dad to be happy, don't you?" he would often ask. "You don't want Dad to be alone, do you?" I did want Dad to be happy, and I couldn't be there all the time. If my mom couldn't be the number-one woman in my dad's life, and if I took precedence only when I was in the immediate vicinity, then Louise would have to do.

As a child, you rely on your feelings. You don't have command over the English language yet, and it's difficult to express yourself appropriately and with conviction, especially in the face of your enemy. I could feel with every hair on my body that this woman did not like me. I got many bruises from her strong, enameled nails digging into my arms as she yanked me to my room or shoved me into a car or pushed me out the door. Something I never understood was the way she wanted me to address my father. She tried to train me to say "Yes sir in the major leagues" every time I responded to my father. She insisted on my saying "Yes ma'am" to her as well, and I tried to remember and respect her request. But the "Yes sir in the major leagues" response didn't make any sense to me. I don't think I even knew what "major leagues" meant at such a young age. It seemed so phony and weird. I didn't like it. Finally, it was my father who figured out what was going on.

"Do you even know what you're saying?" he asked me once as I snuggled next to him in the big recliner.

"Louise says I need to show you respect and say that when you ask me a question."

"Oh boy. . . . You just call me your ol' dad. Try and remember to say 'Yes ma'am' to her—that oughta make her happy."

Another Christmas break, when I was about nine or ten, my brother and I went to Florida to visit our father alone. We were so excited to spend the holiday in warm weather and go fishing with the greatest fisherman in the world. Mom had diligently taught me to braid my long blonde hair so I could keep it out of the way whenever I was around my dad. For some reason, my dad hated long hair. He thought it was "dirty" and would somehow "get into your soup."

One early morning when we were going out on the boat to fish with Dad, I lagged behind as I fumbled with my long hair. Right over left, right over left—I was trying to braid it in record time, and Dad was already yelling for me to get the show on the road. John-Henry popped into the bathroom and urged me to hurry up. I was trying so hard, but couldn't seem to braid my hair that morning.

Louise barged into the bathroom.

"Don't you ever make your father wait!" she yelled as she grabbed —no, yanked—my hair and proceeded to pull it out as she braided it. "Now go!" she said, still yelling, and pushed me out the door.

"But my sunscreen!" I exclaimed. "I haven't put on my sunscreen."

"That's too bad. You've already made your father wait too long."

Florida sun can be awfully cruel. I was so sunburned by the end of that day that I had blisters all over my legs and shoulders, and especially my back. My lips were so chapped that I couldn't talk. My brother stayed up with me that night in the guest room, feeding me ice chips. I cried quietly as John-Henry rubbed Vaseline on my shoulders. I probably had sun poisoning. I remember throwing up and John-Henry sneaking off to the kitchen to get me ginger ale. We didn't dare wake our father. We didn't want him to know I was sick and get angry because I hadn't put on sunscreen. I didn't even leave the room the next day. When I did, I was sure to cover my body as much as possible so that our father wouldn't be upset by the unsightly burn.

When I got home, the evidence of my sunburn was still quite obvious. My mother was furious when I told her the story. She picked up the phone and called collect to Mr. Williams's residence. She was not going to pay for this. It was one of the most vicious verbal wars I had ever heard. After Mom was done tearing Louise to shreds, Dad got on the phone and got the best former Mrs. Ted Williams lashing he had ever received.

A few years later, when I was about thirteen, John-Henry and I were witness to one of Dad's tongue lashings directed at Louise, and even I have to say, I cringed and was not prepared for it. It's hard to justify what Dad said, but it did not come without provocation: it came from Louise's jealousy of the strong bond my father and I had. She loathed it when I would curl up in my dad's lap and watch television, cooing and giggling over something we were sharing. She resented that when Dad was with us there weren't so many outbursts. One time she'd had enough. I had crawled up into my dad's lap in my pajamas. I guess at thirteen I didn't know how to "sit like a lady."

"You shouldn't sit on your father's lap like that!" Louise snapped as she walked by us in the big comfy chair.

"What the hell's the matter with the way she's sitting on my lap?" barked Dad.

"She should know better than to sit like that with her legs straddling yours," Louise hissed. "Her mother should teach her how to be a lady."

"Jesus Christ," Dad exploded.

"Well, she looks like a hussy sitting on you like that."

"Shut the fuck up, *you dried-up old cunt.*"

I sat right up from my sprawled-out, apparently unlady-like position and looked for my brother. He was looking right at me. We were all silent. How could *that* ever be forgiven? Dad glared straight ahead, watching the television as his jaw jumped and his teeth grinded. Slowly and carefully, I left my comfy spot. My brother and

I escaped outside to play off the heavy words that lingered in our heads.

Surely that was the end. Louise would surely leave on that note, I thought as we ran around the yard. It was just a matter of time now. They were definitely going to break up after that.

But they didn't. At any moment Louise could have walked out on Dad, but she did not. There were times when I thought she should, just to make a point and let him know she wasn't going to be treated like that. She could always have come back. But she never left, and Dad never changed his ways with her. Dad never married her.

NOT SURPRISINGLY, MY MOTHER ALSO STRUGGLED WITH LOUISE and with her own place in Dad's life. I believe one thing that bothered my mother about Louise was the fact that she was able to endure Dad longer than Mom had been able to. On some level, my mother compared herself to Louise, and won on all accounts, except that she could not withstand the intensity of my father's verbal outbursts while also caring for her children.

I think Mom never remarried because she continued to believe that, with age, Dad would become less agitated, realize he'd let a wonderful woman get away, miss his two children, and finally come back to her. My mom continued to love my dad, and no man who came after Ted Williams could compare. Like a lot of people, my mother pined for the relationship to be rekindled. She believed in marriage and married only one man in the hope of being with him for the rest of her life. Dad never remarried either, and whenever he would come through town to pick us up to go to Canada, he stayed with Mom. There was wonderful chemistry between them, but it just wasn't stable enough to survive beyond a week without some turmoil.

Sadly, Mom grew resentful over the years, and then the negativity crept into her being. She started to resent that I could maintain a real relationship with Dad but she could not. On some level, she became envious of my relationship with my father, even though she'd been such a big part of keeping that relationship alive. My relationship with my father was very controlled on my part: I had figured out what I could and could not take by simply observing the other women in my dad's life. I have Louise to thank for that, as well as Bobby-Jo and my own mother. In reality, they showed me what *not* to do in order to have a successful relationship with Ted Williams—especially as a female. My relationship with Dad may not have had the depth of my brother's relationship with him, but it was the best that I could expect, and I embraced it.

Also, it was exactly what I needed to determine the traits I would look for in a husband. There is a saying that daughters marry their fathers and sons marry their mothers. I don't believe that is always the best choice. In fact, sometimes it should be just the opposite. Later I would seek out what I had missed from my father. I learned some very valuable lessons, both good and bad, from my father. He was the one who taught me to take what you need and leave behind what you don't need. He taught me to be who I am and not apologize for it. I am well aware of my own character flaws, but I also know and am proud of my integrity, principles, and genuineness. These standards worked well for Dad and he certainly lived by them. I learned to appreciate and enjoy the parts of Dad that I liked and to compartmentalize the rest, ensuring that his negative traits would not affect me mentally or emotionally. I relished the good and ignored the bad.

This also bothered Louise. She was envious that I could tailor my times with Dad to ensure that we enjoyed only the best moments and that I could forecast the tough moments in time to exit the scene before Dad had an outburst. That I could do this also upset Mom, who was unable to maintain a close relationship with Dad for long periods of time. Both of these women wanted all of Ted Williams, and it burned them up when they could not change his ways. I didn't try to change him. I just wanted him to accept me and love me. All I ever tried to do was bring peace to his life and make him proud and make him laugh.

For this reason, I believe I was able to understand Ted Williams better than any other woman in his life. Did I innately understand him because I shared my father's genetic code? Did it come from the unique relationship between a father and daughter? Was it due to the slight detachment of a second daughter caused by the disappointments of the first one? Whatever the reason, I could appreciate and love my father from a safe distance. I could quickly sense the anger and frustration welling up in Dad. I started to identify the brewing storms before they even arrived. Eventually, I got good enough to forecast them, deflect them, and simply tell Dad to let the demons go. Everything would be all right. Half the time I didn't even know what it was that was bothering him, but when I let him know that I knew it was coming, the outburst seemed only half as bad for both of us. Finally he would inhale deeply, exhale heavily, and then let it all go, his shoulders slumping.

My father's disciplined approach to whatever he decided to accomplish was what made him great in his endeavors. That same disciplined approach, which could also be perceived as stubbornness or indignation, was exactly what allowed us, his children, to encapsulate that facet of him and love everything around it. With our love and acceptance, our father realized that his flaws were not as offensive to us as to most people. We were way beyond the first layer of his personality. We understood his character and simply accepted it. He didn't have to prove anything to us. He didn't have to exhaust himself trying to be someone he wasn't. My brother and I loved our father for exactly who he was. Just because you can't change someone doesn't mean you can't understand him and love him.

I'm not saying there weren't times when my father wounded me—he did hurt me, and some of the things he said still stick with me. Sometimes I had to work hard to remind myself that he was angry at life, or at circumstances, and that his anger did not reflect how he felt about me. If I had allowed every verbal outburst to affect me, I probably would have resorted to alcohol, drugs, or some other self-destructive behavior in order to cope. A person can take only so much verbal aggression before it affects them. I guess that's why Louise will always be somewhat of an enigma to me: no normal person could have endured what she did—but she wasn't normal.

As more and more time went by, my mother would complain about the relatively small amount of money she got for alimony and child support. Often I would have to sign over my own allowance or good-grades checks to my mother because she could not seem to manage her money effectively. She struggled financially, and she would wonder whether she should have been tougher and stuck around with Dad just to avoid the financial strain. She would rationalize that, if she had, at least her children would be around their father and she wouldn't have to worry about when the next check was coming. Some people stay in marriages for the money, some for the children. My mother did not choose either one, but she would come to doubt her decision, expressing regret and saying things such as, "I should have been able to put up with it. Look at Louise—she does, and she gets whatever she wants . . . a new car, health insurance, new clothes, and God knows what else."

I didn't like hearing my mother bemoan her own standards, the standards she had lived by so steadfastly. I learned to admire her fortitude and her determination not to be like Louise and not to take the disrespect that my father showed so many other women. But I also understood that, after years of waiting and hoping, it had finally become clear to her that Dad wasn't coming back.

Chapter Eight

A S TIME WENT ON, I DISCOVERED THAT MY MOST DIRECT line to Dad was through sports, even though I was a girl. Sports was something that he could understand, a language he spoke, and I wanted him to know that I spoke it too. I might not have been the best ballplayer, but I was going to get my dad's attention with my athletic prowess. Instead of using a glove and a bat, I decided to use my legs and run. *Watch me run, Dad! Watch me run and win. I'll make you proud. You are going to be so impressed. Watch me now.*

It happened at an invitational cross-country race. I was in the sixth grade, and according to my coaches, Mr. Murphy and Mrs. Whitehead, I had a very good chance of winning this race. If I did, I would be the first girl to do it. They *knew* I was going to win, and I could sense their certainty, but I wasn't so sure . . . I saw faces I had not raced against. As if that weren't enough, my dad was there as well, and he had never been to any of my races before. It was unusual that Dad was in Vermont in October; he'd come this year for my twelfth birthday. There was an added stress I was feeling that I did not anticipate, and it was weighing heavily on my already shaky legs.

Unbeknownst to me, my father approached Mr. Murphy.

"Coach, I think we have a problem," he said.

"Really? What's wrong?" said Mr. Murphy.

"My daughter thinks she's supposed to win this race."

"She very well could."

"No, I don't think you understand," my father emphasized. "She thinks she is going to win the *whole* race—including beating the boys."

"Yes, she could do it. I think she will."

Apparently Dad did not look convinced. Neither was I.

As I stood at the starting line among my classmates and the runners from other schools, I felt the butterflies fly around in my stomach and my knees were doing the jig all on their own. *Let's get this run started already.* I couldn't feel my hands, and my heart was pounding in my chest. Dad was standing off to the side, just watching me. *I have to win this race. I have to.*

BANG! I jumped and flew, all at the same time. Everything I had learned about not starting too fast went right out the window. It seemed like a fifty-yard dash at this point, and I was in third place. I had one and a half miles to go—oh boy. Surely Dad had just seen this costly mistake. Oh, where were the woods? I wanted to hide among the trails, calm my heart, and find my stride. *Watch me, Dad.*

We entered the woods, and I started picking off each runner as I came alongside them. I was breathing heavier than ever. I could have sworn I tasted blood in the back of my throat. Suddenly, I found myself alone in the woods. This could mean only one thing. I was in the lead. I dropped my shoulders, lengthened my stride, and knew that soon I would emerge from the trail and onto the track. There my dad would see me, and when he did he would be so proud—he wouldn't believe that a girl, his little girl, would win this race. *Watch me, Dad, because here I come.*

I exited the woods and there across a small section of field was the track—only six hundred yards left. But the path was not empty. There were two runners ahead of me. Now another race was about to start, but this time my opponents had a two-hundred-yard lead. It became the race of my life. This was it. I could not be third. If I didn't win, I wasn't sure I'd ever have another chance to impress my father. *This is where you leave everything you have on the track, Claudia. Don't regret this moment. You have to win this race. Dad is watching, and he brought his camera. This will go down in the Williams history book.*

"I think we have a problem," Dad said again, eyeing my coach a bit more seriously. "She's gonna get third."

"Ted, Claudia has a great kick. You haven't seen her kick yet."

"Well hell, third is pretty damned good."

I lowered my head, leaned forward, and started the hardest kick of my life. *Here I come. I'm gonna catch you, kid. Go quietly—maybe he won't hear you coming. Run hard—go hard—now!*

I'm not sure how I did it, but I can still remember the pain. My legs tingled, and I thought I just might die right there on the track trying to catch my competitors. The first boy was easy, he was wheezing and puttering out. As I came up behind the boy now in the lead, the little twerp kicked it up a notch. *Oh my . . . now you've really got to dig deep—only twenty-five yards left.*

Being five-eleven is a gift my parents gave me when they got together, and I intended to use every bit of those blessed genes right now. Shorty didn't stand a chance. *Here I come, Dad, watch me now, catch me now, because I'm running straight to you. . . .*

Mr. Murphy later told me that my father was crying as I came around the last bend of the track. He said tears were just rolling down his face.

Dad felt huge when I buried my face in his chest. I was so tired. He couldn't believe I won. He kept saying, "Jesus, I thought you were going to get third! Second would have been good too, you know! Jesus, I didn't think you could do it. Damn, you really sprinted. Are you sure you don't want to be a sprinter?"

That wonderful moment was worth all the effort, but it was

short-lived. Just as the race was over and his praise was flowing, other parents started coming up to Dad for autographs. I was slowly pushed aside and went off to stretch with my friends. I watched my father from a distance and wished—for me and for him—that he could be just a normal guy, just another dad there to watch his daughter win a race.

WHENEVER POSSIBLE, I LOOKED FOR CONNECTIONS WITH MY father through sports. As it turned out, sports was just the tip of the iceberg.

As a young adult, I started to discover that I was like my dad, and not just because of my height. There were other things, both physical and mental, that made me realize that we were bonded by so much more than proximity.

Of course, that race was not the last time I'd feel the pressure and difficulty of being a girl around my dad. In fact, the older I got the harder I had to work to prove myself to him. I didn't want him to see me as he saw Bobby-Jo; I wanted him to see me as he saw John-Henry.

Even though I was born nearly twenty-five years after Bobby-Jo, I started out with a full count against me. I had only one chance to present myself as a worthy daughter to my father, a small window in which to show him that not all girls were created equal, that *this* daughter would be different. I wanted to show him that a girl can grow up to be a woman who does not take, demand, embarrass, or disappoint. I was going to prove that I would never ask him for anything other than love and respect. I would not embarrass him. I would hold myself to a standard of which he had to be proud. I would try not to shed a tear. I would be strong, and no matter what, I sure wouldn't whine. Whatever my much older half-sister did so wrong, I would do the exact opposite. Instead of her footsteps, I'd follow in John-Henry's.

As Dad's first and only son, John-Henry did not disappoint. It was understood and expected that Dad would have enormous admiration and attention for his only boy. So, with my brother blazing an easy trail three years ahead of me, I tentatively followed, wishing I was a boy too. It was here that once again my mom was the best teacher, preparing me as she did for the challenges I'd face as a girl seeking my father's acceptance. My mom knew the history of Bobby-Jo, and she knew how to mold me into a daughter Dad would acknowledge. My mom showed me where Bobby-Jo had failed as a woman in the eyes of my father. She gave me the tools that, unfortunately, Bobby-Jo didn't have.

I was going to be such a good girl. I was going to get straight As. I was going to be a phenomenal athlete. I was never going to spend a dime, and I'd save all my money. I really didn't need anything, just his approval and acceptance. Every time my dad called and asked how I was doing, I was fine, I was great, I was happy, and how are you?

Obviously, that is a difficult line to toe, and as I became a teenager I hated the superficial relationship I was developing with my father. I felt as if my father was almost afraid of me. He was fearful that he would mess me up too and fail again with another daughter. So, instead of even attempting to right wrongs, he avoided me. There were times, of course, when I wanted to cry to my dad, so that he would make it all better or take the pain away. I wanted to tell Dad all about my struggles and disappointments. Surely he would be able to counsel me and tell me what I needed to do. But my mom had taught me that was futile. It was not an option for me because Ted Williams did not know how to do that. And that meant, if he couldn't do something about a situation, if he couldn't manipulate or control it or do what he saw fit, he hated it. And if he hated something, he cursed it and wanted nothing to do with it. I had a lot of foundation to build first before I could take our relationship to the next level of transparency and reality.

And so for the first fifteen years of my life I did not turn to my father for guidance. I observed him and studied him and listened to what he liked and disliked. There were quite a few items on my list of things "to do" and "not to do" around Dad. Then, after much studying, I discovered something remarkable. I realized more and more, with every interaction with my father, that I was actually a lot like him. I was starting to figure him out.

I wasn't perfect at it. There were always hiccups along the way when I would forget the lessons I'd learned about him or a momentary emotional weakness would take over. When I went away to Northfield Mount Hermon High School, I was almost immediately homesick. One day Dad called on the dormitory pay phone, and a housemate came and got me. I was thrilled to talk to my dad. When I got on the phone, his bellowing voice sounded like music. I wanted to crawl through the phone line and cuddle up right next to him on his fluffy chair.

"How are you doing, kid? Are you keeping up on your grades? Any boys?" he kidded sarcastically.

Immediately tears welled up in my eyes as I envisioned him on the chair half-smirking, half-smiling, and I choked on my words.

"Are you there? Hello? Jesus Christ!" he muttered. "CLAUDIA, ARE YOU THERE?"

"Yes, I'm here."

"Well, what the hell's the matter, damn it?"

"I'm homesick. I don't like it here."

"Well, what the hell do you want me to do about it? Call your mother, damn it!" *Click.*

I sat there in the hall holding the phone, holding it to my ear, feeling the tears roll down my face. I was miserable. The one person I thought might somehow save me had just slammed down the phone. I had just disappointed him. How much ground did I just lose with that one display of weakness?

The truth, I think, is that his reaction was really a way of saying, *I hate that you are sad, I hate that I can't do anything for you right now, and I can't bear to hear you cry.* It took me a while to realize he was not mad at me, he was mad at the situation.

That's how it was for a very large part of my childhood and adolescence. Those were the times when I almost gave up, the times when I wondered how anyone, let alone a woman or a daughter, could like this man—not to mention love him. It was awfully difficult to pretend that I didn't need my father. It was awfully difficult not to yell and scream and stomp my feet at this man to get his attention. But at the same time, it was very scary when he got mad. Although my father spanked me only once, he tested me on numerous occasions with his words. His words could penetrate even the toughest armor, and many times his words stung for days—sometimes months. A few are still with me, like embedded splinters.

And yet, despite difficult moments like the phone call at school, I came to discover that if I could weather those moments, he and I were actually more alike than different. As I grew up, discovering our similarities helped me appreciate him more completely. I could feel what he was feeling and knew what he was thinking because I was coming from the same place. I realized that his blood definitely ran through my veins, and I found him in my life at surprising moments. I have a tough time giving up, and I have no tolerance for losing at anything. I find the will to do things where most people would give up, and I can be very intense in my approach. I'm definitely a perfectionist, and I thrive on enthusiasm. I see nothing wrong with focused obsession.

I am my father's daughter. It's not just the physical resemblance. Most clearly, it's the passion, the senses, and the sensitivities. I innately understood this man, and my family would tell me often that I reminded them so much of Dad. Now, I don't swear like my father did—but I can sure emulate him if I want. I have walked into a dugout only one time in my life, but I know my father's passion and relentless drive to excel. Dad said it very clearly in his induction speech at the National Baseball Hall of Fame: "Ballplayers are not born great. They're not born great hitters or pitchers or managers, and luck isn't the big factor. No one has come up with a substitute for hard work." To be great at something, he'd say, you have to work harder at it than anything else you ever do. Dad believed it, lived it, and did it.

I was not born a great athlete, but I sure am an athlete. I am intense and passionate, with absolutely no patience or tolerance for complaints or trivial inconveniences. My father taught me (or maybe gave me the gene) to do one thing to the exclusion of all others—to stay focused and know what matters in life. I recognize that this is a blessing and a curse. I know that there is a cost to forsaking all else to accomplish one goal. It can strain social and even family relationships. But there is a benefit too. It's the way to achieve at your highest level. For better or worse, my focus and intensity are inherent.

My father also taught me to be brutally honest. He spoke from his heart, his gut, and he shared the kind of thoughts that many people do not dare verbalize. Not many people can handle that type of honesty. He felt that people had an obligation and a responsibility to identify a wrong and attempt to correct it. This obligation applied to people and to God. His delivery was sometimes harsh, but the message was honest and heartfelt. He did not like superficial people or facades. He saw right through them.

It's uncanny how Mother Nature can combine the genes of two individuals and from that union produce an innocent child with attributes of both parents. I learned so much from both my parents, and it is clear that I was loved by both. Through it all, though, I was determined to show Dad I could make it. With my every encounter with this "great American hero," I learned more and more about not only this man but also what I needed to do to reach him. Mom taught John-Henry and me to accept the ones you love, to appreciate Dad regardless of his "flaws." Dad served as an example to always be the person you want to be and always strive to be better. Growing up the daughter of Ted Williams was not easy—it's still not easy. I have to wonder how many children of celebrities must feel the same frustrations that my brother and I felt. No matter what we did, we

were always compared to our father. I suppose my life's experiences
pale in comparison with the lives of the children of today's celebrities. I can only imagine what it is like to be the children of Michael
Jordan, Tom Cruise, Brad and Angelina, Tiger Woods, Madonna, or
President Obama.

While I had a difficult enough time, my brother had an impossible task ahead of him, albeit in a very different way. Unlike me,
he didn't have to fight for our father's acceptance; on the contrary,
our father took a lot of pride in his son. Even though my father had
not been to college, he had repeated ad nauseam that all he wanted
was for both of us to get an education. A couple of years later, when
John-Henry got into Bates College, Dad could barely contain himself. For a Christmas present, John-Henry gave Dad his acceptance
letter. Dad loved it. Eventually John-Henry graduated from the University of Maine and framed his diploma, graduation cap, and graduation program as another gift for his father. Dad loved all of it and
displayed these items prominently in his library.

Though John-Henry didn't have to work to acquire our father's
affection in the same way that I did, he had to contend more with
people outside the family, people who held him to a higher standard
because he was the son of Ted Williams. He didn't stand a chance
in the eyes of critics and naysayers. There was no way he could be
as good as his father. Our society leaves little room for children of
famous people to discover who they truly are as individuals and to
claim their unique identity. And those who do succeed in making
a name for themselves are rarely credited for their own hard work
or volition. I am always impressed by those athletes, such as Ken
Griffey Jr., who can break the mold. It seems like you have to exceed
your parent's performance before being credited independently.

Like me, John-Henry had athletic aspirations. He wanted to
play baseball, but didn't have a lot of opportunity to play while
growing up in Vermont. He could have played in the summer, but
that was also one of the few times when he could be with his father

in Canada, fishing. He grew up to be six-foot-five and comfortable at 210 pounds, strong, with arms of steel and forearms roped with muscle. John-Henry made a few attempts to play ball in high school and then again in college. Despite having a ton of talent and ability, it went unrealized. In the end, he chose spending time with his father over playing. In my opinion, my brother could have been an excellent baseball player if Mom and Dad had allowed him the opportunity. Instead, he became whatever his father needed. His father was always his first priority.

Chapter Nine

Because John-Henry and I saw our father only sporadically growing up, I made studying him a full-time endeavor whenever I was with him; back then, though, that happened only during summers and on winter breaks. The rest of the time Mom's domain was our world.

It was hard living in Vermont on a farm. Being with Dad was like being on vacation at the Taj Mahal. At Dad's house there was television, there were sugary sweets, there were no chores, and somebody cooked for us. We lounged around, watched TV, read books, and played games, and there was always some amusement park to go to or a local mall to entertain us. This was the life—for about three days.

The stark contrast between the two worlds was difficult for us to understand. As children, we struggled to comprehend why our mom would have left this life—until we saw our father explode. On top of that, Louise's constant complaining about us to our dad when we were there would only infuriate him more. At times it seemed as though her mission was to nag him constantly about what my brother and I were doing (or not doing) in order to get him mad at us. After a while, Vermont would start to look like a welcome retreat and a safe place once again, even if it meant a ton of chores and hard work.

My brother and I had to pile wood almost every night to ensure that we had enough supplemental heat for the winter. Our late 1800s home was cold and drafty, and heating it required two wood-burning stoves and two fireplaces. We would go through almost three cords of wood every winter, which meant cutting down lots of trees during the fall and throwing the wood into the cellar. Every night after dinner my brother and I would have to go down to the cellar and pile wood for at least half an hour—or for a full hour if we were being punished for something. I think our father eventually realized the hardships his children were facing, especially during the winter months, and he started to send an extra check for the oil heater so that we would not have to depend solely on wood heat.

The chickens, the geese, a sheep, a horse, two dogs, and a cat all needed feeding and cleaning and caring for. Our chores were never done, and living on a farm with animals and a drafty house costs money. So it's easy to understand that living in Vermont got old, especially in the winter. In the early spring, to make a little extra money, Mom would make maple syrup. That meant we were hanging sap buckets on all the maple trees and collecting it every day. In the summer, we cut the twenty acres of grass to bale hay for the animals and for mulch hay, which we would bank around the house for extra insulation. On weekends we had to weed the garden and build the stone wall. We learned a lot on the farm and certainly knew what hard work was. There was little free time. One Christmas Dad sent us a TV, and Mom promptly threw it out into the snow. So for fun we would play chess or listen to *Prairie Home Companion* on National Public Radio as we colored or did our homework. My brother and I loved animals, respected the food that was on the table, and appreciated the simple things in life. I can promise you this: as children, we did not live lives of fame. You wouldn't believe where and how we grew up, but I wouldn't have changed it for the world. I've met a lot of famous people, and when I meet their children, I am often grateful our mother raised us the way she did.

Growing up on a farm is hard work. We appreciated that it was educational and wholesome; however, at times it was painfully boring and tiring. Our work was never done. Even for Mom, the hard work was sometimes a bitter reminder of what she used to have, and I believe that started to eat at her.

Despite their divorce and the distance between them, Mom was always trying to take care of Dad. She was on a perpetual health kick, constantly educating us on the latest in medical research and the latest alternative treatments for common maladies. She would send Dad healthy recipes she knew he would love, and at Christmastime she would send along with us a gift she thought he would enjoy. On the day we were to see our father at the 1982 Old-Timers' Game, my mom decided to bring a very special gift to him. After all, it had been twenty-two years since Teddy Ballgame had worn a Red Sox uniform at Fenway Park.

We drove into Boston, where we met Dad and all stayed together in a suite for the weekend. John-Henry stayed with Dad and I was with Mom. Dad had recently shared with Mom that his cholesterol levels were up, and so Mom thought she'd introduce him to a new vitamin that was getting a lot of attention at the time because it was a natural alternative to prescription medication for lowering cholesterol. Always the nurturing nurse at heart, Mom had decided to give Dad some niacin. As you might know, niacin is vitamin B3. You can buy it now in an extended-release formula that reduces the flushing, tingling sensation that most users experienced when it first went on the market. When Mom and John-Henry and I first started taking niacin, we were all concerned when we turned blotchy and red like tomatoes. But every morning the three of us would go ahead and experience our twenty minutes of flushing, knowing we were warding off high cholesterol and improving our "good" HDL cholesterol.

I think there is a little bit of trickery in all of the Williams clan. We were always thinking a bit outside the box. Mom, John-Henry, and I knew that when we told Dad of niacin's benefits he'd fall for it, hook, line, and sinker. We just wouldn't mention the temporary side effect.

The next morning for breakfast we ordered room service. Mom passed out our vitamins and then gave Dad his wrapped bottle of niacin.

"What's this?" Dad asked.

"It's a vitamin that is very good for lowering cholesterol. The kids and I have been taking it along with our other morning vitamins. You really should start taking some supplements, Ted."

Dad ripped through the wrapping and opened the bottle.

"Christ, this sounds GREEAAT! How many can I take?"

"Just take one for now, and then you can up it to two."

When Mom wasn't looking, Dad popped two into his mouth as he winked and smiled sneakily at John-Henry and me. We stared at him and smiled back obediently, chewing our breakfast. We squirmed in our seats, anticipating our father's first experience with the vitamin.

About fifteen minutes after Dad had drunk his morning coffee, he started turning pink. He scratched his arms a little and started looking around. His eyes landed on his bright pink children, who were expectantly grinning at him.

"Dolores!" he yelled. "You better get in here! What the hell did you give us? The kids and I are all red. Something is going on! We're having a damned allergic reaction or something. DOLORES!"

Mom was in the other room fixing her hair and getting ready for our Fenway Park appearance. She calmly walked into the adjoining suite. As soon as Dad saw her he exclaimed, "Jesus Christ! You got it too! We better call the damned doctor!"

We couldn't contain ourselves any longer. We burst out laughing and giggling.

"It's okay, Ted," Mom smiled through a stifled laugh. "It's a common side effect of the vitamin. You'll be fine."

"Are you sure? What the hell kind of vitamin is this?"

My brother and I were rolling at this point. Dad was just sitting on the edge of the bed, puzzled by the tingling sensation he felt.

"All right," he barked. "How long does this last? I'm supposed to be on the field in thirty minutes."

"Don't worry, it'll be all gone by then," Mom soothed.

"It sure as hell better be. Jesus! I took two, Dolores!"

"Well," Mom said, calmly containing her smile, "you might be red a little longer than us."

We watched our father for his response. He looked at us and then back at Mom. We must have been pretty funny-looking, wide-eyed and red, smiling at our dad.

"Ha ha. Real funny, you two."

"We just want your *cholesterol* to get better, Dad," I smiled.

"Yeah, Dad, we want you to be healthy."

My mom just stood there looking beautiful in a leather jacket outfit, with her black curly hair framing her bright pink face; she was smiling at her ex-husband. We knew she still loved our dad, otherwise she wouldn't have cared about his health. Dad looked up at her and said, "You got any more surprises for me?"

We all burst out laughing again, and Dad just shook his head.

"Oh boy," he said sarcastically, making his Kermit face at us. "Are you two all right?"

For years after that he would always joke with us at the breakfast table, asking if our mother had any other *great* vitamins for us. He was always trying to trick the next person by telling them how great this natural cholesterol-lowering vitamin was, and then the whole experience was relived and we would laugh and reminisce all over again.

While my mother was waiting and hoping for Dad to return, she grew bolder and more daring. She started showing up in Canada when she knew we were all there, including Louise. I remember one summer in Canada when Mom showed up to celebrate John-Henry's and Dad's birthdays—they were just four days apart—with a triple-layer chocolate cake, a bottle of champagne, and presents for the birthday boys. She also went to Florida a couple of times on the pretext of taking care of Dad; she was, after all, a nurse. She would be wearing her best dress and bring Dad's favorite dish or dessert. Dad loved every minute of it, and Louise didn't dare say a word, for if she had, she would have been the one who was scolded. In Dad's eyes, Mom did nothing wrong—and she was a lot better cook than Louise.

It's an eight-hour drive from Vermont to Blackville, New Brunswick. So, of course, Dad would insist that Mom spend the night in the guest cabin. Mom was in no hurry to leave. As one can imagine, Louise would be beside herself. I can honestly say it didn't bother my brother or me very much, because we loved seeing our parents together. They would talk about the fishing and the neighbors as if it was just yesterday when they were hanging out together. Mom was just as enthusiastic about the outdoors as Dad, and she knew just what to talk about to get Dad animated. Roy Curtis, the fishing guide, and his wife, Edna, the Canadian cook, loved Mom. They both had helped her with her children and admired her country girl genuineness. She was funny, and she loved fishing and Canada. On top of it all, she was beautiful. I actually think Dad got a kick out of Mom's ballsy surprise visits and may have even enjoyed seeing Louise squirm.

John-Henry and I knew what Mom was up to. Mom wanted back into Dad's life and wanted to prove to him that she could take whatever he would dish out. Mom was tired of waiting. She was trying to show Dad that she could do it, she could fill the role he wanted from the woman in his life. She would be sweet and not take it personally or complain when Dad was stormy about something.

But both my parents were incredibly stubborn, and neither knew how to bend. If you wanted to spend any time with them and cultivate a relationship, you had to conform to their ways. They would both give you the shirts off their backs, but they could not change their ways. It was surprising how much the two of them were alike. At times I would wonder whether one of them was trying to be like the other, or whether they had actually adopted each other's idiosyncrasies.

Chapter Ten

GROWING UP IN THE SECLUDED WOODS OF VERMONT, ON A farm, with a thousand chores and few neighborhood friends, you can get to know a brother very well. John-Henry was my best friend, and my big brother who protected me. I looked up to him. He was so smart, seemingly without even trying. We had only each other to rely on and trust. We worked together, played together, and got in trouble together. We were in this unique family situation together, and we discovered together how unpredictable our lives would be. We never knew what to expect of either of our parents. Very little in our lives was ever "average" or "normal."

My first memories of my brother are of following him around trying to be just like him. That meant playing in the woods, fetching the balls he would hit into the horse field, and touching frogs and snakes. Our only playmates were our cousins when they came over. The next nearest house with children was about two miles down the road, but those children were older. Besides, we had too many chores to do and Mom was not going to drive us, so we usually just played with each other.

Given our rural upbringing, animals became a very important part of our lives. We learned so much about ourselves and about life just by the experiences we had with our pets, the farm animals, and the wildlife. Our animals became our friends. We were always taking care of them, bringing home strays, providing shelter, nursing abandoned babies back to life, grooming, feeding, training. You learn discipline, responsibility, kindness, respect, and loyalty on a farm. We witnessed the ways of Mother Nature and the cruelties of humankind. Sometimes we would lose a chicken to the neighbor's dog or a wild fox. The deer we fed would be shot, and it broke our hearts to see one strapped to a vehicle. Aside from fishing, my brother never hunted a day in his life.

John-Henry loved frogs. He loved catching the bullfrogs in our muddy pond and insisted that I kiss each one. When it rained and the frogs decorated our driveway, John-Henry ran ahead of the car to be sure none of them would be run over. At one point he had about a dozen fish tanks in his room with fish, frogs, and snakes all living in a happy habitat of glass houses. He was always finding animals that needed saving, and we would doctor them all. We found a wild mallard duckling that had been abandoned, and my brother raised it. He fed Puddles worms every day and taught him to dig in the dirt with his bill to find his own. That duckling would squawk and try to fly after John-Henry if he got too far away. At night John-Henry put Puddles to bed in a paper grocery bag with torn newspaper for his nest. Puddles took showers with John-Henry and slept at his feet.

Then there was Bangor the cat. John-Henry and Mom were coming back from Nova Scotia, where Mom had a cabin on an island. They stopped in Bangor, Maine, for a rest. Mom was low on money, so they slept in sleeping bags in the bed of the truck at a rest stop. That was when my brother heard a kitten crying and set out to find it. It was near a Dumpster, lost, shivering, flea-ridden, and dirty, but John-Henry still tucked it into his sleeping bag. She never left him after that.

One of my brother's best friends had a family dog that needed medical attention they couldn't afford. They thought they'd have to put it down, but John-Henry couldn't stand the idea. He sent them a box of pictures autographed by Dad with a note attached that simply read, "Get the dog fixed."

He gave a lot of himself to his animals, protected them, and always provided them with the best. Guinevere was a female Doberman pinscher we rescued from the pound. She was starving so badly that you could see every bone in her emaciated body. That night for dinner, instead of eating the meatloaf Mom was preparing, my brother convinced her (with my help) that we should give the seasoned ground beef to our new friend. The dog ate over a pound of ground beef, herbs, and eggs, while we ate salad.

Guinevere was one of our best dogs and our favorite pet. She was splendid and sleek with striking eyes. When she was hit by a car, we were devastated and rushed her to the vet. The vet wasn't confident that she would survive and explained that the required surgery was risky at best, and expensive. Mom was ready to put her to sleep. My brother and I both wailed, but it was John-Henry who insisted that the vet attempt the surgery. He announced that he would pay for the operation. I remember thinking, *I want to be just like my brother. He makes things happen.*

He loved animals, and he wanted, *needed,* their love back. There were a couple of times during my childhood, though, when I found my brother's behavior with animals puzzling. The more the animals wanted freedom and independence the more John-Henry wanted to hold on to them. He bought a small dog harness with a long leash for Bangor and tied her to his bedpost so that she wouldn't leave him. He took great care of her, fed her, and provided her with water. She was never hurt at all, but he didn't want her to leave him. He didn't like it when his birds would bite, and sometimes he flicked his finger on their beak to let them know. Again, it wasn't at all that he meant to hurt them. He just didn't like it or seem to understand when his animals didn't show him complete love and devotion. He would stare his birds in the eye and scold them for biting, as if they could or should understand him. He had done everything for them, and all he wanted in return was their allegiance and their love.

While he was at Exeter, John-Henry and a small group of boys—a few of them also sons of celebrities—went on a trip to the Amazon River. Some of the boys found an enormous bullfrog in the jungle and decided they would dissect it with a jackknife just for fun. John-Henry stepped forward to defend the frog, and the knife was turned on him. The boys teased him for being a frog lover and challenged him to try to stop them. When my brother turned to the trip leader for help, the man dismissed it as boys being boys. John-Henry did not dismiss it. He was very unhappy about the cruelty he witnessed as the boys tortured and killed the frog. My brother told Mom and Dad when he got home.

"That's bullshit," Dad said, disgusted. "What the hell is the matter with them . . . that's bush league." Dad used the term "bush league" to label actions that were amateurish, like something that would happen in the minor leagues.

Mom was more proactive. She promptly called the headmaster and gave him hell, then proceeded to take John-Henry out of Exeter.

Dad did not balk at her decision. By this point in our lives he knew about and appreciated his children's love for animals. He got a kick out of John-Henry's aquariums and was pleased by our devotion to our animals. Dad was a big proponent of the catch-and-release program that was started in Canada to preserve the salmon populations, and his hunting days ended when he realized how much we cared for animals.

Around 1984 we found a small black kitten by the side of the road. She was very sick, and our mother tried to convince us to not even pick her up. She was drooling at the mouth, her eyes were caked closed, and she was trembling. She couldn't walk without falling down, and she was severely undernourished. We begged our mother to take the kitten to the vet. It was already late, so she called the vet rather than go there. After hearing the symptoms, the vet voiced concern that the cat was probably very sick and wouldn't survive the night. He warned us to keep the kitten away from our other animals. My brother and I tried our best to nurse the kitten back to health. We fed her warm milk, gave her a bath, cleaned her eyes and mite-infested ears, and combed hundreds of fleas from her fur. We made a bed out of old clothes in a cardboard box and put her by the fireplace to keep her warm. We stayed up most of the night trying to calm her crying, but she didn't survive. The next morning our mother called the vet back and asked him how we should dispose of the kitten. The vet strongly suggested that we burn the carcass. He was very concerned that if we just buried the cat, our other animals, especially our dogs, might dig it up and also become sick.

Grumpa had an old fifty-five-gallon drum by the shed out behind his house in which he burned some of his trash. My brother and I carefully wrapped the dead kitten in an old T-shirt. We thought we were being wise to use lighter fluid instead of gasoline to cremate her, which proved to be a bad mistake. John-Henry doused the T-shirt and placed the bundle at the bottom of the drum among some twigs. When he lit the match and bent over to drop it into the drum, the fumes ignited and there was a flash flame that burned his hands and caught his shirt on fire. John-Henry started running toward our grandparents' house. I screamed, "Roll!" He dove to the ground, screaming in pain. It was a terribly scary moment.

At first glance his burns did not seem too bad. He kept telling Mom that he was in severe pain, though, and needed to go to the hospital. Mom didn't seem very concerned and was angry at us for not being more careful. We thought we were being *very* careful. She told him to put some aloe on his burns and take an aspirin. John-Henry continued to insist on going to the hospital. He had no blisters or obviously burned skin, but he was very red. When he started throwing up and crying, Mom finally took him to the Brattleboro

Memorial Hospital, where they determined that he had second-degree burns. Unfortunately, the hospital was not accustomed to treating burns, and when John-Henry's hands and chest swelled and formed blisters, they did not know how to treat him appropriately. It didn't take them long to realize that they had a case they couldn't handle, and they recommended that he be transferred to Shriners Hospital for Children in Boston.

Dad was furious with our mother when he heard the news. He told her that she should have never let us burn the cat. It was an ugly time as John-Henry lay in the hospital, hurting badly, and the tension between Dad and Mom peaked. My brother and I both saw how cutting our dad could be, and our mother was hurt.

Burns are very painful, but John-Henry was brave throughout his recovery. Unfortunately, the burns worsened to the point that he required skin grafts on his hands and chest, and he would be scarred for life. He was treated like royalty at the Boston hospital, and Dad checked in on him every day. My brother felt guilty that he was being treated so attentively when there were children there who were far worse off than he was. He realized how lucky he had been.

We were all there when he was discharged, including Dad. John-Henry insisted that Dad meet some of the other children who were on his floor and sign some autographs for the nurses and doctors who'd taken care of him. Dad gladly agreed.

He and John-Henry went straight to Florida on a fishing trip afterward, and I returned home with Mom. Dad hated to see his son scarred and would frequently ask him over the years how his hands and chest were doing. I have seen some pictures from that trip, and it appears that Dad took some photos of the scars, almost secretly, as John-Henry was putting on his shirt. As part of his ongoing treatment, he had to wear compression gloves for the grafts on his hands and a tight chest bandage to keep the scars from rising. Dad would wince and curse every time he saw his son without his shirt. For quite a while after the incident, my brother was afraid of fire. Even when someone just pulled out a lighter to light a cigarette he would take a step back. My father made contributions to Shriners for years after his son was treated there and always spoke highly of the quality of care and treatment they provided.

EARLY ONE SUMMER MORNING MOM, JOHN-HENRY, AND I WERE out in the back field picking wild blueberries. Dad loved Mom's blueberry pies, and since he was coming to pick us up any day now, she was trying to have one ready for him.

"Christ, this is the best damn blueberry pie I ever ate."

We were eating more than we were gathering, but it was fun and light work compared to our other chores. Our mother tapped us on the shoulders and motioned for us to turn around. There, standing about ten feet away from us, was a young fawn. It started walking right up to us. It was the most beautiful thing I had ever seen. Its wet and shiny black nose reached toward us, its nostrils flaring, trying to smell us. We just stood there captivated, considering ourselves lucky to witness such innocence. Then its ears twitched in the direction of a sound we barely heard, and with a flick of its tail it turned, leapt into the air, and disappeared into the tall grass.

Weeks later our mother went into the forest to cut some wood and came across a dead deer. It had been poorly shot, then ripped up by dogs in the hindquarters, and it had probably suffered as it died. She was sure it was the mother of the fawn that visited us, and she was furious. We went into town that very day, and Mom bought at least twenty-five NO HUNTING and NO TRESPASSING signs. For the rest of the day we ran around and hammered these signs into the trees that bordered our property. We also decided that we should start leaving grain by the blueberry patch and feed our newly orphaned friend.

By that fall we had an average of twelve deer in our back field. We would camp out by our window in the back of the house, watching as they emerged from the forest. We were sure that we knew which one was Innocence. By the first snowfall there was a whole family and their distant relatives in our field, eating the hay and grain and wild apples that we had picked for them.

One afternoon in the early fall we were working in our yard when a stranger drove up our driveway. He stepped out of his truck, which had guns hanging on a rack attached to his back window. In a bright orange hunting jacket, he approached us and addressed our mother.

"I noticed you have a lot of signs on your property."

Mom responded suspiciously. "How do you know I have a lot of signs on my property? Were you hunting on my land?"

"There does seem to be a lot of deer activity. I'd sure like to hunt your property."

"Absolutely not. No, you may not. This is private property. If I catch you trespassing, I'll call the police. You understand?"

"Listen, lady, it's hunting season, and I have a right to shoot a deer if I want. You don't own them. If I shoot a deer and it comes on your property, I have the right to go get it."

"Oh no you don't. You get the hell off my property, you son of a bitch." Mom stuck her long neck out as if to challenge this big, burly, scary man. She wasn't afraid. She stood her ground and did not flinch.

"You don't have to be a bitch about it." He spat out brown tobacco spit as he turned to leave. He jumped in his truck and tore out of the driveway, shooting gravel at us as his wheels spun out.

"Go to hell, you bastard!" Mom yelled after him.

We stood there watching the mean-eyed man drive away. Then Mom turned and looked at us as if to say, *What do you think of your mother now?* "Way to go, Mom. You showed him!" John-Henry and I cheered.

It's the first time I remember my mother being really angry and swearing. Mom has been unfairly described as a woman who had a sailor's mouth. My mother says she *never* swore until she met Ted Williams. It was only after their divorce that she started using powerful curse words to emphasize what she was feeling. She had learned from the best and witnessed firsthand how effectively those words could be used to make a point.

Little did we know at the time that this was the beginning of a long series of neighborhood battles. After a long fight we would lose the war and be left with many tragedies and heartbreak. Every evening we would look for Innocence and her friends and make sure they were all accounted for. Late one night I was awakened by Mom hurrying through the house. My brother was up and digging around in our huge black pilgrim chest. I stood in the dark of my bedroom doorway watching my mother and brother. I felt the sense of urgency and was frightened.

"What's wrong?"

"Someone is driving in our back field," Mom explained. "We're going out there to see who it is. Stay here."

My brother found what he was looking for and pulled out a double-barreled shotgun. Wide-eyed, he handed it to Mom, and out of the house they hurried.

I watched from my window as they drove toward the back field in our red Jeep Wagoneer. It was a story of headlights and motors. As Mom's Jeep approached, the other vehicle's lights turned to face her. The engine revved, and the lights turned down the direction of the driveway. Mom's lights followed close behind. I raced up to the attic and peered out the window to follow the light parade. The first vehicle, which I now saw was a truck, was speeding down our driveway, and Mom was right behind it. At the end of the driveway, the enemy truck turned onto the dirt Pine Banks Road and raced away. Mom's Jeep came to a stop there and idled for a while. Then she turned around and drove back up the driveway. She stopped again in the back field, and the headlights rested in one direction for a while. It seemed like an eternity as I stood watching the lights, wondering what was going on.

Finally, John-Henry and Mom came into the house. I was waiting for them in the middle of the kitchen.

"They shot a deer. We found blood. But we got their license number. It was the same truck," they explained together.

"Oh nooooo," I moaned, thinking only of Innocence. "Did you use that gun?"

"We don't have any bullets," John-Henry grumbled.

"I'll call the police tomorrow," Mom said, looking determined and focused.

The next day at school I couldn't concentrate on anything except what had happened the night before and what was going to happen next. When I got off the bus, I went straight up the hill. There was a police car in our driveway. I walked into the house quietly and listened as John-Henry and Mom gave a detailed account of what had happened the night before. I heard every word the officer was saying. There was going to be an investigation. He was going to file a report and question the owner of the vehicle. It was hunting season, though, and he explained that it might be difficult to prove anything.

The shots in the night had awakened Mom, and then she'd seen the truck's headlights. They were "deer-jacking." When you shine a car's lights into the eyes of deer, they stand perfectly still, gazing into the brightness—the famous "deer in the headlights" pose. They're easy targets for "hunters."

Mom started sleeping in the attic. The very first part of our driveway off the main road is steep, and as a car first pulls in its headlights shine through the attic window. She bought shells for the shotgun and an endless-loop cassette tape to record the gunshots at night to prove to the police that our neighbors were illegally poaching deer on our property.

Dolores Williams was becoming a game warden. She was going to protect her land, her deer, and her rights. John-Henry was first deputy, and I was second. John-Henry and Mom started learning to shoot so they could get accustomed to the kickback of the shotgun. Mom also pulled out Dad's hunting rifle from the chest to use herself. The two of them were armed for the next encounter.

Mom took recordings she made of gunshots in the night to the police and presented her evidence. Unfortunately, this still was not enough proof, according to the police, so Mom asked for Dad's help.

"Tell 'em you'll give them a couple of autographs if they come to the house to see if they hear the damn shots. Let them do their job, for Christ's sake."

With that, Mom returned to the police with memorabilia in hand for barter. For a couple of nights we had a sheriff staked out in our attic. He in fact heard some shots, but realized the sound was coming from someone driving up Pine Banks Road and just shooting guns out their windows. It was going to be very difficult to catch the poachers in the act, and the harassment continued. Our mailbox was shot out, we found bullet holes in the side of our barn, and someone eventually plowed into our gate, leaving it bent.

This went on for years. On weekends we'd have stake outs, waiting for the deer-jackers. My brother and I climbed our favorite pine tree and waited, watching for any suspicious activity. Late one night in the early fall of 1986, when I was fourteen and my brother was seventeen, we sat perched high in our tree. A truck slowly pulled into our driveway with its headlights off and only the cab dimly illuminated. We were about to alert our mother with our walkie-talkies, but then the truck did something unexpected. Instead of traveling past us to the back field, it turned right into our overgrown lower field. The driver pointed the truck toward the top of the hill and turned on the high beams. There, caught in the glare, was a small herd of deer.

"Do something," I implored John-Henry.

Any moment now they would shoot one of the deer.

"Cover your ears."

My brother didn't hesitate. He aimed high above the deer and fired the shotgun in the cover of darkness and from the safety of our secluded perch. It was just enough to break the stare of the deer and scare the hell out of the deer-jackers. The deer flicked their white tails and jumped away. We stared into the darkness. I feared the deer-jackers might guess where the shot came from. John-Henry kept still and quiet. He was brave, and I pretended to follow suit.

Mom's voice came crackling through the walkie-talkie.

"Don't move. Stay in that tree!"

Instead of using our long meandering driveway, Mom got in the Jeep and cut straight down the hill, the same hill that she had moved the house up. She parked horizontally across the driveway, blocking the exit. In the dim moonlight we saw our mom jogging toward us with Dad's African safari rifle in her hands. There was no exit off our property. There was going to be a standoff.

We must have really scared the shit out of those deer-jackers. They had no idea where that shot had come from, and it went right over their truck. It was loud, and it was clear that someone with a gun knew they were breaking the law.

"The police are coming," Mom said in a loud whisper. She looked up into the dark of our tree. We could barely see her. She stood behind the huge pine, watching with us to see what would happen next.

The driver shut off the headlights, and the truck crept slowly back toward us. I was so afraid they were going to see Mom standing behind the tree. I wanted her to climb up the huge pine with us. John-Henry raised his gun and sat focused on the vehicle. When they saw the car blocking the driveway, they knew they were caught red-handed. The driver switched the lights on, and the truck burned a doughnut forty feet from us. He gunned the motor and headed back toward the field. From our vantage point, we could see blue lights coming up Pine Banks Road. Any minute now the police would be here.

"They're going to try to ram their truck through our hemlocks," Mom said. We watched as the truck tried to shove itself through the trees bordering our property. It got stuck. We could hear the wheels spinning and the engine screaming.

Suddenly, John-Henry started climbing down the tree.

"Mom, come on! We have to flag the police before they come up our driveway!"

The row of hemlocks was just a few feet from the freedom of the main road. The criminals might escape from their truck, but they couldn't free it from the hemlocks before the police got there.

I started climbing down too.

"Stay right where you are!" Mom yelled sharply at me.

John-Henry and Mom ran down the driveway, jumped into the Jeep, and drove down the main road to where the truck was stuck. The police were pulling up. I was still back in the tree peering out through the branches, observing the light show once again, but this time I heard the voices yelling.

There was no deer carcass, so the deer-jackers couldn't be fined for poaching. But they were cited for trespassing and for destruction of property and had to pay to get their truck towed from where it was hung up in our trees. They were pissed. Mom had just kicked a hornets' nest.

Dad couldn't believe our story.

"I hope to hell I don't wake up one morning and read about you guys in the paper! Get some floodlights and put them all around the house—will you please?"

After that rattling experience, Mom bought another dog, a German shepherd we named Jazz. Shadow, our Doberman pinscher, and Jazz became added security for us and our wildlife. We trained them not to chase the farm animals or the deer. Untrained dogs will pick up the scent of a deer and chase it for miles in the woods. They give off distinct, yipping barks when chasing an animal and are easily trained to find deer. Hunters who have shot a deer often use a dog to help them track the wounded animal. Domestic dogs are also notorious for chasing cats, as well as birds and especially chickens. But not ours. Shadow even adopted a baby chick that was left to die in an abandoned nest. She would carry it in her mouth and place it by her belly, keeping it safe. Jazz was a very good dog. She was obedient and not interested in any of the animals.

Our father became more and more interested in the saga of the deer-jackers and their illegal poaching. He suggested to Mom that we buy Guinea hens from Africa. While he was on safari there, he had learned that Guinea hens were excellent at alerting other animals of danger.

"Just get a dozen of those fowl, and you'll hear them a mile away if something is bothering them."

Mom found an exotic bird keeper and ordered a dozen African Guinea hens. Dad wanted to be involved and ended up paying for our gray-spotted birds. Every few days he would call to find out the latest. With their harsh, cackling calls, the Guinea hens made great partners for our watchdogs. They would alert Jazz that something was up. They were all good animals, and we considered them part of the family.

As if all that weren't enough, Mom also bought a small derringer that she holstered to her brassiere. The former Miss Vermont USA and ex-Mrs. Ted Williams was now a pistol-packing badass momma.

For a while all seemed calm. We had sent a very strong message, and now, with a padlocked iron gate across the driveway entry, we felt it was safe for us and our animals. Every night before bed one of us would walk down the hill and lock the gate.

For my thirteenth birthday, Mom and Dad gave me a horse. I was so excited, I couldn't believe it. Chestnut brown with a shiny black mane and long tail, Bella Nina was strong and regal, not to mention huge, standing at almost seventeen hands tall. She was a retired standard-bred but had failed as a brood mare; to save her from being put down, Mom and Dad gave her to me as a pet. I loved her instantly, and she instantly became my best friend. I would lie on her back, bathe her, brush her, ride her, and take her swimming. Sometimes I even slept with her in the loft of the barn. "Bella niña" means beautiful little girl. She was more than just pretty, though. She became a protector. Bella Nina befriended the deer and would graze with them. We'd see her even during the day, among the deer, eating the grass or licking the salt block on her fencepost. The deer-jackers wouldn't dare shoot at night for fear of hitting the horse. There was no excuse for a horse being shot on your own property, no matter what time of day or night it was.

Dad had a bumper sticker on the back of one of his vehicles. It read: IF GUNS ARE OUTLAWED, ONLY OUTLAWS WILL HAVE GUNS. Dad was a supporter of the National Rifle Association, but these outlaws were making him question his support.

When he called from Florida to check in on us, he always wanted to know the latest about the deer-jackers. "Are you sure you know what the hell you're doing? Call the goddamned game warden and tell them to take care of this problem."

The local authorities were quick to help out—everyone knew where Ted Williams used to live. Eventually, though, they realized that it was Ted's ex-wife who had an issue with the deer-jackers and that Ted himself wasn't that involved.

The deer-jackers were outlaws with guns. There was no stopping them. They attacked our farm life and ravaged our family of animals. They set their dogs loose on our property, where they'd chase our birds, killing and carting off our chickens and goslings. All of our animals were precious to us, and their lives mattered. The Guinea hens would alert us that a predator was around, but it was often difficult to catch them in time. It seemed there was nothing we could do. It was tormenting to see our animals get hurt, suffer, and die. They were our friends, they were part of our family, and they were getting killed one by one. We had a family goose named Peeper. She followed us around everywhere until we got her a mate. When she too was killed by the neighbor's dog, John-Henry was determined to use that gun for the first time.

The next time the Guinea hens alerted us, we let the dogs out. John-Henry was close behind with the rifle. The neighbor's dog was chasing Ballerina, the chicken that Shadow had adopted and raised. John-Henry raised the gun to fire, but Shadow beat him to the enemy just as the bad dog clamped its jaws on our black chicken. Jazz joined the fight with the orange mutt, and a terrible battle ensued, with bites and rips of fur and coats. We raced to the side of our pet chicken, and my brother picked her up. Shadow and Jazz dominated the fight, and finally, with a tucked tail, the dog turned to run. But that was not punishment enough for killing our birds. My brother stood in the driveway holding our last chicken in one arm and the rifle in the other. He braced the gun against his body and shot from the hip. It was the first and only animal I know of that my brother shot and killed. He shot it in the chest. The dog dropped right where it stood, without even a yelp.

We turned our attention to Ballerina. She was fatally wounded. Shadow already knew what was happening and kept trying to lick her friend, whining as Ballerina died. John-Henry was crying, but I think it was from the impact of actually killing an animal.

We buried two animals that day. It was sad for many reasons. We decided as a family that we wouldn't buy any more chickens. Guinea hens were fast and could easily fly into the trees. The geese were big and made a lot of noise, and they fought with strong wings.

The hardest decision we made, though, was to stop feeding the deer. We didn't want them to think they were safe on our property or to begin trusting people or even our scent. Every night for a very long time, many deer would still come around looking for food, especially during the cold winter. It was difficult to watch. They'd nuzzle in the snow, hoping to find something to eat.

One winter I begged my mother to please leave some food out for them. The coming months were supposed to be especially brutal, with freezing temperatures, heavy snowfalls, and lots of ice storms. She agreed. John-Henry had now gone off to boarding school, and it was just me, Mom, the dogs, and Bella Nina. We decided to change where we would put the food out for them. We put out carrots and apples and grain right by the barn where my horse slept. We thought it was a very safe place for the deer, because the barn was right up against the back woods that led to many uninhabited acres of the

Vermont hills, but feeding them there proved to be a deadly mistake.

Early one morning the dogs were whining by the door. When Mom opened it to let them out, they took off toward the barn. I was just getting up. It was the weekend, so I didn't go to school that morning, but by habit I usually woke up around 6:00 A.M. I was in my bedroom when I heard two gunshots. I froze and listened. Fear struck me, and I flew toward the kitchen. My mother heard the shots too and ran behind me. I raced up the horse path. When I reached the barn, I looked around everywhere, yelling, "Shadow! Jazz! Come!"

Bella Nina was spooked. Her tail was raised, and she was snorting in the direction of the back woods. We heard rustling and tromping in the distance. I started marching in the direction of the noise, but Mom grabbed my arm and shook her head.

"Shadow! Jazz! Come!" I screamed.

They never came, and they never returned home. They ran off into the secluded woods where the deer would hide and so would the deer-jackers. Years later, when Mom allowed a forester to cut down some trees for lumber money, she would find two rotted collars among a pile of bones.

In 1986, on my fifteenth birthday, my mother met me on the driveway when I got home from school. I knew instantly that something was terribly wrong. The tears in her eyes told me everything. She didn't need to say a word. I knew.

"I have some sad news, honey. Bella Nina is very sick. The vet is pretty sure she's been poisoned."

"No, Mom. Don't say that," I pleaded. I dropped my book bag and ran straight up the hill, my mother following me, carrying my books. On the top of the hill, in the wooded area by our house, right next to the stone wall, my horse lay breathing heavily. The vet was by her side and pulling a tube out of her. He had attempted to pump her stomach, but when he found the distinctive blue pellets of rat poison in her grain bucket, he had realized there was nothing he could do. I dropped down by my horse's side.

"Oh, Bella, please don't die."

Rat poison kills by causing internal bleeding. There was blood coming out of my horse's soft, velvety snout. She was struggling to breathe and trying to stand up.

"I'm sorry, Claudia, but Bella Nina is suffering. We have to put her down."

The veterinarian looked up at Mom and asked if he should shoot her or put her to sleep. The first method was far cheaper.

"Please put her to sleep. I'll pay for it," I said, stroking my incredibly strong, regal friend.

Instead of opening presents that day, I watched our friendly farmer from down the road open up a huge hole in the ground and push Bella Nina into it.

I didn't see my father that December for the holidays. My mom, my brother, and I spent it together. Our father must have started to realize how extremely significant animals were in the lives of his children and former wife. That Christmas Dad sent us James Herriot's *All Creatures Great and Small* and *All Things Bright and Beautiful*. Inside he inscribed to both of us, "To my children, who love all animals. I love you both. Love Dad."

Chapter Eleven

I TOLD MY FATHER ONE TIME THAT I HATED HIM. I WAS FIFTEEN years old, looked straight up at him, stared right into his eyes, and told him, "I hate you!"

It was the summer of 1987, in Canada. I was sitting on the porch watching the river flow by, enjoying the quiet and the wilderness all around. I had not gone fishing that morning. It was a bit too early, so I had slept in, and now I was waiting on Roy Curtis, John-Henry, and Dad to return. Edna, Roy's wife, and I sipped tea and ate her homemade doughnuts. As I heard the truck roll down the gravel hill toward the cabin, a mother Merganser duck and at least fifteen baby ducklings came floating down the river. Knowing my brother's appreciation and love for animals, I ran out to meet the truck to tell him. As I was exclaiming about the cute little babies soon to be right in front of the cabin, Dad jumped out of the truck. John-Henry knew what was about to happen, but I had no clue. As we walked around the cabin to see the ducks, out burst my father from the front door, carrying a shotgun.

I froze.

"What are you doing?" I implored. Dad raised his gun and shot right into the cluster of babies and their mother. I screamed. Without thinking, I raced down the hill toward the babies. My dad shot again, killing the mother. By the time I got to the bank of the river only little fuzz balls and feathers were floating by. I couldn't believe what had just happened. Then, in the midst of this massacre, I heard one little duckling peeping. It was just swimming around in circles right at my feet. I picked it up and held it to my face, crying. When I lowered my hands to take a look at it, I saw that the buckshot had gone through one of its eyes. It was struggling to hold its head up and peeping the whole time.

I couldn't believe what had just happened. I could hear my father in the background yelling something about guns and listening to your father—blah, blah, blah. I didn't care. I was fuming. I crouched down by the river, holding the little duckling, suffering right along with it. I was so sorry for the little baby. I was so sorry for what I was about to do. My mom had taught me that on the farm one way to kill the young spring chickens was to snap their necks. This little Merganser was suffering, and I didn't know what else to do. I held him in my hands, and as quickly and as strongly as I could I snapped its neck.

I stood and looked up at the cabin where my father was still standing, holding his weapon. I put my hands on my hips, stuck my neck out as far as I could, and screamed at the top of my lungs, "I HATE YOU!" I started to say it again, but it only came out as a high-pitched scream. I turned my back to him and sat down by the edge of the river and wept.

I continued to sit by the river, crying, waiting for my father to come down and say he was sorry. I kept waiting and crying. I started throwing rocks into the water as hard as I could, waiting for an apology. About an hour later my feet were wet, my butt was wet from sitting on the river rocks, and I was cold. I picked up the duckling and dug a hole where I laid it to rest. I found the biggest rock I could and put it over the miniature grave. Then, taking a sharp rock, I scratched the word "Baby" on it.

I jumped when I heard my father yelling from the top of the hill. I was so angry at him. He was a cruel monster and I hated him. "Dinner!" he kept yelling. I never wanted to see his face again. "Come up here for dinner right now." I rebelled and stayed right where I was, staring at the rock. B-A-B-Y . . .

After a while I walked up the hill, marched right through the front door, and headed toward my room. My dad was saying something about preserving the salmon and how much damage the Mergansers caused . . . blah, blah, blah. I didn't even pause. I stomped into my room and slammed the door. Then I opened it so that I could slam it again.

I didn't leave my room for three days. I allowed only my brother to come in. He brought me food and tried to explain why Dad did what he did.

Dad believed that killing Merganser ducks would help with salmon conservation. Of all the fish Dad caught in all the waters of the world—black marlin off the coast of Peru, sharks off the coast of New Zealand, tiger fish on the Zambezi River, sailfish, bluefin, yellowtail, tuna, trout, muskie, snook—his "big three" were the bonefish he angled for in Florida, the tarpon off the Florida Keys and Costa Rica, and the Atlantic salmon in Canada.

He loved and admired the Atlantic salmon the most. He first fished for them on the Miramichi River in New Brunswick in 1955, at the invitation of Canada's tourism board. Every summer Atlantic salmon fight their way up the river to spawn in freshwater. Dad loved the beautiful natural setting and the fact that few of the locals cared or even knew that he was an American baseball star. By the early 1960s he'd bought some land and built a camp in a secluded spot with the river just out the back door. It is now known as Ted Williams White Birch Lodge. It would be his summer getaway for three decades. He formed a long, warm friendship with Roy Curtis, his river guide, and

Roy's wife Edna, who cooked for the cabin and later kept an eye on John-Henry and me when we came up in the summers.

I knew how important the salmon were to Dad, but I was unmoved by my brother's words. A sister can tell when her brother is lying. I could tell John-Henry was just the messenger. Dad was trying to apologize vicariously. I wasn't buying it, and I wasn't bending or budging.

I was not going to take being disrespected anymore. I had clearly outlined my boundaries and wasn't afraid anymore to face the possible consequence of being dismissed by Dad, as other women had been. The moment I stopped trying to be liked and stopped caring about what he thought of me as a female, he started worrying that he had driven me away forever. I had gone well beyond meeting him halfway, waiting for him to recognize me. Now it was up to him to meet me the rest of the way. I "left" him for three days. It was as though he could only admire and respect a female who had the courage to stand up to him and do what was right for herself. He knew I didn't need him but only wanted his recognition and affection.

It was a turning point in our relationship. I think he tested women and pushed them to see if they would abandon him, just like his mother had. Ted Williams was not going to change for anyone he did not find admirable. Roy said to me years later that after that day my father never picked up that shotgun again.

From that pivotal moment, our relationship started to change. Dad couldn't ignore me anymore. Wherever Dad went now, I was invited. That summer of 1987 permanently changed my relationship with my father—not just in terms of how he saw me, but in how I saw him.

One of the first places Dad, John-Henry, and I went as a trio that summer was to Cooperstown, New York, to attend the National Baseball Hall of Fame induction of Catfish Hunter, Billy Williams, and Ray Dandridge. For the three of us, it was our first adventure together. It was a trip with Dad, but more than that it was a trip with a friend who couldn't wait to introduce us to his other friends from his past. The Kid wanted us to see his statue that stood next to Babe Ruth's in the entrance. He wanted us to see his accomplishments and give us a grand private tour of the museum.

I met some wonderful old-timers. The best part was seeing how Dad's fellow players received him and hearing their conversations. It was clear that these gentlemen *loved* baseball and had immense respect for one another. It was fun to hear them talking shop. It was as if I could travel back in time and feel what it was like to play then, while also catching a glimpse of who my dad was. A new man appeared to me.

This was when I started to learn who Ted Williams the baseball player was. He wanted his two kids to appreciate where he'd spent twenty-two years of his life. He couldn't wait to introduce us to the great Mays, Musial, Mantle, DiMaggio, and Doerr. For baseball fans, these introductions would have been a dream come true. I learned more about these old-timers than I knew about the current players. However, as I sat with my dad on the porch of the Otesaga Hotel, I didn't realize that he was talking to the man with whom he'd had an epic duel in 1941.

"Kids, this is the greatest player I ever saw."

Our dad introduced us and continued: "I enjoy being with him every chance I get, and I've admired him so much as a player. I KNOW how great this guy is."

Joe DiMaggio was quiet. He smiled at my brother and me and shook our hands. He was tall and thin and seemed a bit distant. I looked at my dad sitting next to him and I thought to myself, *You're pretty good too, Dad.*

The two men seemed like buddies as they talked baseball. I was struck by how much admiration my dad expressed and how friendly he was with this gentleman. He was humble and respectful to the Yankee. DiMaggio's fifty-six-game hitting streak versus Dad's .406 batting average had been all anyone could talk about in 1941. Dad would win his first of six American League batting titles that year. DiMaggio won the MVP.

I never heard my father say one negative thing about a fellow baseball player. In 1949 Dad narrowly missed winning his third Triple Crown, losing out to George Kell of the Detroit Tigers. In the last game of the season, Kell stood on deck with one out when word arrived that he had won the batting title if he did not bat again. He threw his hat in the air in relief. Kell won the batting title .34291 to .34276, a difference of .00015 points. Dad never complained about losing the title that way and respected Kell's decision.

And he always spoke with the highest respect about Joe. "I'm pretty near embarrassed when they compare me to DiMaggio," he said.

I couldn't help but wonder why Dad didn't sound more confident in his own abilities and accomplishments. I was impressed even with the little I knew of my father's career and statistics. Surely he was comparable to this man?

I began to appreciate that if only my dad's whole life could have been as simple as life on the diamond, things would have been a lot different. Inside the stadium, life is very direct, very cut and dry. You either get a hit or you strike out, you're either on or not, you either win or lose. The great accomplishments on the field are the simple stuff. Step outside the stadium and life instantly gets a whole helluva lot harder.

I was amazed when John-Henry told me that the ballplayer Dad was talking to had once been married to Marilyn Monroe. And I was really impressed when John-Henry told me that he also talked to DiMaggio and, according to my brother (who was having "girl troubles" at the time), got some advice from the Yankee Clipper:

"If you love someone, don't ever let them go."

OUR TRIP TO COOPERSTOWN WAS JUST THE START. ON JULY 31 OF that same summer, Dad and I went fly-fishing together for the first time. Thankfully, though, it wasn't really my first time; during those summers when I wasn't able to go Canada with John-Henry and Dad, Mom spent time teaching me how to fly-cast in our backyard in Vermont. Since patience was not one of my dad's strong suits, she knew that if I was to stand a chance in the presence of the "greatest fisherman in the world," despite being his little girl, I better know what the hell I was doing. My dad could be intense in learning situations, using colorful, sometimes harsh, and not exactly encouraging words, but that was Dad. My mom knew this, and I practiced hard to earn the right to fish alongside my father. So I had fished on my own before, with my mom and my brother—just never with Dad.

We were on the Miramichi River at the Moore House Pool, one of Dad's favorite fishing holes. We got up at the break of dawn and piled into the front seat of Roy's green truck. Dad was drinking some coffee and eating a doughnut that Edna had baked the day before. I nibbled on mine, sitting between my dad and Roy. I was still tired, trying to wake up for the quest that awaited me.

When we reached the banks of the river, my dad opened up the silver metal box that held all his handmade flies. I was allowed to select my fly. I wondered which one would catch my fish as I scanned the miniature pieces of art. Finally, I selected the Cossaboom. The truth is, I chose the fly because it was the prettiest. It was gold and orange and yellow, with a big black head.

"The Cossaboom, huh? You sure you want that?" asked my dad.

"Yes please, I would like that one."

Dad tied the fly to my line and explained the knot as he tightened it around the eye of the hook. He tested its strength by jerking on the line, then tossed the Cossaboom into the water.

"All right, kid, let's see what you got."

I tentatively waded into the river, slipping on the moss- and slime-covered river rocks under my felt-covered boots. I felt very unsteady and wondered if I might fall. *This is it,* I thought to myself. *Here's my chance to prove myself. Let's hope Mom knew what she was teaching me. I've probably got one shot at this.* Not many people survived fishing with Ted Williams—and if they did, the day ended with them thinking they were lousy at it and should go back to school just to learn the basics. Dad was highly critical of anyone who fished alongside him, and he made sure they knew what the hell they were doing. If they didn't, God help them.

My mom was a wise one. She knew what I was going to face, and she'd prepared her little girl. Her teaching paid off. I found myself standing in the Miramichi River in waders that were about three sizes too big and came crowding up under my armpits. I stood there in the deep, cold, nearly four-foot water that rushed against me, forming ripples and hugging the waders tight around my legs. My dad watched from the riverbank for a while and finally said, "I can see your mother taught you! At least she learned something from your ol' dad."

I smiled to myself. That was exactly what Mom said he would say. Satisfied by my casting ability, Dad walked farther up the shore and waded into the river about a hundred feet behind me. I could feel him watching me. In a normal voice, he coached me, tweaking my technique here and there.

"You keep casting like that you'll likely catch something," he said confidently.

The river carries your voice, so you can hear very well on the water. I was happy to be fishing the pool first; I figured that meant I would be done first and probably wouldn't catch anything anyway. I was new at this fishing business and just lucky to be in on the escapade.

After a long twenty minutes of nothing, I decided I would try praying to God and ask nicely for a fish to come along and somehow be interested in my fly. And then, for good measure, I prayed to not mess up. "Come on, fishy fishy . . . please bite my fly."

Over an hour into casting, with my arm so sore I thought it was going to fall off, I began to wish I had never come along. I was miserable. My dad had taken a break on the riverbank and was watching me, giving me further instructions on how to rectify my mother's teaching mistakes. This was turning out to be torture. I hadn't even gotten a nibble. I started to pray again to this God I really didn't know—*please let it rain, create a hailstorm, make lunch hurry up and get here, or maybe even an alien could show up*—anything to get me out of this slippery dangerous river and out of this stupid sport that my dad seemed to think was the greatest thing ever. What was so great about this? To make matters even worse, my impatient father was finding more and more errors with my technique and I'd never catch a fish if I didn't straighten out!

"Keep your rod UP! Keep your EYE on the fly! FEEL the weight of the line on the back cast. LOOK where you are casting . . . Jesus Christ . . . PAY ATTENTION!"

Why did you want to do this again? I asked myself. *Fishing is the dumbest thing ever. This is what Dad and John-Henry spend all morning doing? What am I missing?*

Just as I had given in to this mindless, boring sport and started staring at birds and planes, something truly amazing happen. My fly got hit by what felt like a great white shark that just happened to live in the Miramichi River. A lightning bolt of energy flew up my rod and into my hands. I thought I was surely going to be pulled away by this mammoth or slip on the slimy river rocks and be drowned by the largest salmon in the world who had just taken off with my fly. Suddenly, everything I had been taught I forgot. My first instinct was to just hold on to my rod for dear life as it jerked and pulled, trying to free itself from my hands. I went right back to praying to the same God and chanted, *Please don't let me lose this fish, please don't let this fish get away, pleeaasssse. . . .*

Sure enough, from the shore came my dad's booming, screaming, demanding voice. "Get the goddamn rod UP! Pump the rod and start reeling in your line, damn it! Pump and reel, pump and reel!"

Oh God, how am I ever going to survive this day if I can't land this fish? Stay on that hook, fish, please let me reel you in, please let me show Dad I can do this. Stay with me. . . .

It took me at least twenty minutes of fighting to get this king of fish into shore. It was so graceful, but it also jumped and whipped itself so powerfully. I never dreamed that a fish could put up such a fight. I was sure I had lost it a couple of times, but Dad knew better. My fish would take off, and over my right shoulder Dad would point out that it was jumping upriver, trying to escape the line stuck to its mouth by the barb of a very sharp hook. As soon as there was any slack, I reeled as fast as I could, shortening the distance between me and the fish, bringing it closer and closer to the green nylon net that Roy had placed in the water to scoop it up.

When *she*, a queen, finally came to rest, her beautiful shiny body lay exhausted in the net. She was gasping in the waterless air. Her gills were bright as blood, and her slime coat glistened. She was so perfect. As I reached down and touched her, tears filled my eyes and I was overwhelmed by emotion. I did it. I had caught my first fish with my dad. I stood there looking down at the wild Atlantic salmon speckled with black beauty marks and a thin black line down the middle of her silvery side. The morning light caught the shimmering array of colors on her body, and her belly was as white as snow.

Suddenly, I felt sad and terribly sorry but grateful, all at the same time, for my fish. She was the biggest fish I had ever seen alive, and I had caught her only to bring her to her death. I didn't want to see her clubbed over the head. She had fought so hard and struggled so long to try to regain her freedom, and I had struggled and prayed in hopes of capturing her so that my father would be proud of me. I wanted to thank her, thank her for allowing me to have this very special moment in my life with my father. But more than that, I wanted to set her free and save her life. I was so grateful that I was able to prove to my dad that I could catch a fish, and now she deserved to be set free. I looked up at him, scared to ask if I could *please* let her go.

"You did a great job, damn it. Good job. It's a hen, you know. . . .

She's probably about five years old, and she is one of the very few that made it back here, to her birth spot, to spawn. She will lay over ten thousand eggs, and we'll be lucky if one percent survive. She will die soon. Roy, get the camera."

My heart broke and tears started filling my eyes.

"We'll have to let her go," my dad said looking straight into my eyes and smiling.

We'll let her go? I could not have heard sweeter words. I smiled and quickly blinked away my tears.

"She is very special. For conservation purposes, hens are the most important."

She *was* very special. She would play a very important role in my life, because from that day forward I was a fishing buddy. I could cast, I could fish, and I had caught a twelve-pound Atlantic salmon. It was going to be a great ending to an exhausting, wonderful day. My fish would be set free and would be able to go home and lay her eggs. She would live another day and complete her tremendous journey as nature had intended, and we could go home with a great story.

On that day my prayers were actually answered. Somehow I managed to catch the only fish for the day—but even more importantly, I gained a little bit more respect and pride from my father. It was like a rite of passage. I would be allowed to go on future fishing trips. I had proven myself to be worthy of fishing with the great Ted Williams.

"You did a helluva job, sweetie. I'm proud of you. You couldn't have played the fish better."

When Roy returned from the truck, the world almost came to an end. My dad had forgotten the camera. But although this special moment wasn't captured in the Williams scrapbook, it remains one of my favorite stories. When I feel lonely and want to find Dad, I go fishing.

So that summer, the summer of 1987, as Dad was nearing seventy, his relationship with both me and John-Henry really started to change. I think he began seeing us as young adults and started relating to us on many levels—not just as adolescents but as people who would understand him, accept him, and carry on his legacy. And that's exactly what he found. My brother and I started noticing fewer and fewer eruptions—at least when he was with us. There was no reason to get mad. We were all of a similar mind-set. I was about to be sixteen, and John-Henry was nineteen. Dad didn't know how to be a father, but he knew how to be a kid. And that's exactly what we became—three kids hanging out.

Chapter Twelve

After I won that cross-country race in the fifth grade and got my father's attention, I began to crave more of that kind of recognition. I started running all the time. After practice at school, I would come home and run some more.

My mom would follow me in the car, usually at night after I'd done my chores and homework, up the dirt Pine Banks Road. She put ankle weights on my legs, trying to build up my strength. I believed at that time that my only connection with my father had to be through sports. At the same time, I needed an outlet to channel my frustrations and the fear that I would never amount to anything in my parents' eyes. I needed to feel free, and exhaust my inner turmoil. Running was not the sport best suited for my body type, but it was the only reprieve I knew at the time. Running became therapy, an escape both literally and figuratively.

Neither of my parents took my dedication to athletics seriously. They were amused by my efforts but didn't realize how much I needed and wanted to excel as an athlete. My mother wouldn't buy me running shoes because she thought my interest would be short-lived and paying $60 for shoes was ridiculous. I ran in Keds sneakers for probably three years. Finally, when my coach explained to me that I was very flat-footed and needed more arch support, I took some of my saved money and bought a pair of Kangaroo sneakers. My mother meant well by adding the ankle weights, but I ended up injuring my knee with the added weight and couldn't train as much after my sophomore year.

Unfortunately, when I lost running, I lost my release. My teen years came on with all their fiery rebellion, from which I now had no positive coping skills. Making matters worse, my brother had left for boarding school at Vermont Academy, so I was home alone with Mom. It felt like the last man in our family had abandoned us. My grandfather had passed away, and Mom and I leaned heavily on John-Henry. He was a direct line to Dad. He seemed to be able to make things happen and resolve conflicts. But he grew tired of the endless mundane chores and our overly protective and controlling mother; he wanted some freedom.

With my brother gone, my mom kept the reins tight on me. It seemed like Mom didn't allow me to do anything. We started fighting, and our fights quickly escalated. I would rush out the kitchen door, frustrated, and force myself to run, even through the pain. I was fifteen, John-Henry was eighteen, and the age gap felt like it kept us worlds apart. John-Henry had a car and could drive away to his freedom. I had my legs and a bike. When I injured my knee, I discovered I loved biking too. I would tear up and down our gravel driveway until my legs trembled with fatigue. I loved pushing myself to the point of exhaustion, and then I'd push a little more.

One of my last arguments with my mother ended with her saying, "I swear, you are just like your damn father!"

I knew from that moment on we would have our struggles. I needed a change. We had no other parent figure, and Mom had taught us everything she could. My brother and I needed to be set free to explore our lives. I always said my mother did an excellent job of raising us until about the age of thirteen. I'm glad she was as tough as she was. My brother and I never got involved with bad crowds, drugs, alcohol, or anything illegal. She was very strict but very loving, teaching us the importance of respect and appreciation. She was overprotective, though, and discouraged us from even trying something if she thought we wouldn't be any good at it. She was trying to cultivate in us what *she* thought we would be good at.

One activity she tried to push me into was singing. At a very young age, maybe five or six years old, I had started to sing. I loved singing, and at that age I had no fear and would ask anyone who would listen if they would like to hear a song. In the first grade we had a music teacher I absolutely adored—he reminded me of my grandfather and Santa Claus. I couldn't wait to go to music class and sit as close as possible to him so that he would hear me singing. He ended up telling Mom that I should be given singing lessons because he believed I had talent. Mom dismissed the suggestion, believing I was far too young. A couple of years later, now in third grade and another school, I had a music teacher who was a young guitar player named Jesse. He also recognized my singing talent and encouraged Mom to get me music lessons. Finally Mom agreed and took me, at the age of ten, to audition for the Brattleboro music school. They warned my mother before we even came that they were unlikely to take someone so young. My voice was probably not mature enough, and voice lessons were expensive.

We traveled with Jesse to Brattleboro, and he played his guitar as I sang a few songs. After I auditioned, Ms. Messier went and got the music director, Ms. Nall, then asked if I would sing another song. I happily agreed. Less than a year later, I was given the lead role in *Amahl and the Night Visitors*.

"Opera?" Dad boomed on the phone. "How 'bout you sing some nice jazzy songs? You could sing for your ol' dad anytime."

Mom explained that she would need more money if I was to

pursue voice lessons, and Dad paid up. That Christmas Dad came to Vermont to watch my brother and me perform in the opera. He couldn't believe it—and the small town of Brattleboro couldn't believe that Ted Williams was in the audience.

"Now who do you think you got those genes from?" asked my father after the performance.

It had to be my father. The timbre in his voice and his musical inclination hinted at a hidden talent. Although my mom wanted to claim the bragging rights, she had to agree that even when he just hummed "The Battle Hymn of the Republic," you could hear a good voice in the Splendid Splinter.

Although I loved singing, I could not see myself committing to it as a career. So when I told Mom that I wanted to do something athletic, she replied, "What do you want to do that for? You should just do that to stay slim. Why don't you keep singing?"

When I tested my aspiration out on my father, he replied, "You can't make any money doing that. You should be a teacher, an English teacher. You'd be a great teacher."

I wasn't fitting into any mold, and everyone was frustrated with me. I was lost, and looking for my own way.

When Yvonne, a friend of my mom's from her modeling days, offered me an opportunity to continue my education in France, I jumped at it. It would serve so many purposes. I would be free to discover who I was. I would learn another language and pursue a well-respected education in the International Baccalaureate program. I begged to go. I never dreamed my mother would let me leave, but to my great surprise she did. I found out a year later why.

GOING TO PARIS TO FINISH HIGH SCHOOL TURNED OUT TO BE A learning experience in more ways than one. At sixteen, I was able to show my father that I was courageous. I could face adversity and survive. Dad was concerned about me going to Paris without my mother, but reasoned that, so long as I was with a close friend of hers, it was tolerable. Being without my parents in the city of Paris challenged me on many levels. But in the seclusion of the big city, I was free to discover who I was. I could succeed, fail, grow, and somehow persevere independently, without being judged, criticized, or mislabeled because of who my father was, what my half-sister had done before me, or how I compared to my brother.

There were difficult times in Paris. I couldn't speak a word of French, and I failed a lot until I learned the language. I carefully chose what to share with my father; as far as he was concerned, I was studying hard and learning to speak another language. He was very proud of that and bragged about it. I shared with him the places I had gone and the things I had done. He loved that I could hop on a train and be in Switzerland in just a couple of hours. I think he liked hearing of my sense of adventure and how brave I was.

His phone calls were always funny. There wasn't much about making phone calls, receiving phone calls, hearing the ring of a phone, or operating an answering machine that didn't annoy the hell out of Dad.

"Ah Christ," he would say when he heard the first ring. "I'm not here!" He'd grind his teeth and clench his jaw, saying, "I don't care if it's Jesus Christ himself, I'm not here!" When forced to leave a message, here are some of the things he would say.

"This is Theodore Samuel Williams, your father. Dinner is at 5:30."

Another common message was, "It's only your father."

But our favorite that made John-Henry and me laugh every time was simply, "How're your bowels?"

Dad never spoke on the phone, he YELLED. Even when he was just answering it, he'd yell, "HELLO!" There was one public phone in the youth hostel where I lived. As I walked toward it, I could hear a voice yelling over and over, "CLAUDIA WILLIAMS! CLAUDIA WILLIAMS!" Usually someone with a heavy accent answered, and all Dad would say was my name. It made me chuckle. I explained to him that most of the exchange students could speak English, but he would reply, "Never mind, I want to be sure they know I'm looking for YOU!"

I was proving to myself and my parents that I wasn't a helpless girl. I was a survivor, and I was independent and could make good choices. I didn't share my struggles with them because it served no purpose. They were the common problems that most teenagers have to deal with. I faced them all and dealt with them on my own. I made some mistakes, but every teenager does—it's more important how you recover and deal with future choices and consequences than what you've done wrong at that moment. Considering I was sixteen, alone in Paris, and without my parents, I did pretty well.

I'm guessing that most daughters would tell their father about their struggles, but I did not. I had learned from my experience in boarding school that I could not. I wanted to—I wanted to tell him how I had survived some scary moments and some tough, lonely times—but I knew I just couldn't. If I'd made any mention of mistakes or danger or poor choices, my dad would have been furious—at me. He would have told me that I should have known better and that I must have done something wrong. He would have told me to get my ass home—now. I did not want my father to be disappointed in me or think for a second that I had poor judgment.

So I told my brother. He was impressed and proud of me, living without my parents in the big city. He came to visit me after about a year, and I gave him the grand tour of my new home. We roamed the streets of Paris, I took him sightseeing, and we ate pizza every night at a new pizzeria. His little sister was growing up.

I corrected the mistakes I made using my own morals, strong values, and determination to show my family that I was not weak and didn't need rescuing. I wasn't going to disappoint myself, my family, or my friends. I was admired and loved by new people, and my athletic abilities were once again noticed and encouraged. I started cycling, and a respected French national trainer told me that I had a lot of talent. I met his cycling team and wanted to stay and train with them. I thought I was going to be the next Jeannie Longo. I loved being recognized for my athletic ability. I so needed that validation.

The best part was that my life in Paris was all based on who I was and had nothing to do with my father. The French didn't follow baseball, let alone know who Ted Williams was. I felt accepted and wanted. I didn't want to come home. I wanted to stay and develop my cycling ability.

Chapter Thirteen

THE ONLY REASON MOM ALLOWED ME TO GO TO PARIS WAS because she had been diagnosed with cancer and did not want her children to know or to watch her go through her treatment. It was 1988. I was in Paris, finishing high school, and John-Henry was at Bates College. We were unaware that anything was wrong. The only person Mom told of her diagnosis was Dad, because, with no medical insurance, she needed his help. She didn't want us to worry about her, and she made Dad promise he wouldn't tell us either.

She flew to Kansas City to be treated by a doctor she had met while in nursing school whom she trusted and respected a great deal. I remember that when I called she never answered the phone—she wasn't home. Finally she called me. When I asked her where she'd been, she said she was in Kansas visiting friends and didn't bother telling me because she figured I wouldn't care. I could hear in her voice that something was off.

"What's the matter, Mom?"

"Oh, honey . . . " Her voice trailed off. "Nothing . . . I'm fine. I love you."

Now I really knew something was off. As loving as she could be, she very seldom said those words. I remember asking her as a child, "Mom, do you love me?" I was a girl whose love language was words of affirmation. Mom communicated love more through acts of service and through gifts.

"Mom, are you all right?"

There was an echo on the phone line as we talked across the Atlantic Ocean. I heard my mother clear her throat.

"I've been sick, but I'm gonna be okay, and I just wanted to talk to you and hear how you're doing."

"What do you mean sick? What's wrong?"

"Well, I had a bit of cancer in my breasts, but I'm going to be okay."

"Oh my God, Mom! I'm coming home!"

"No, no, no. I won't be there. I have to stay out here a little longer. I've met a nice lady, and I'm taking singing lessons."

I was very upset, but she kept telling me she was fine and not to worry. Unfortunately, she was far from fine. She had been diagnosed with infiltrating ductal carcinoma in the left breast. There was only a small mass in her right breast, for which Mom selected to have only a lumpectomy. The disease was considerably worse in her left breast, and the doctors wanted to do a complete mastectomy with the removal of all lymph nodes. Mom refused to have a mastectomy. She insisted that they just remove the mass and leave the breast itself. She would undergo radiation but not chemotherapy. The doctors strongly advised against this, but Mom insisted. She directed her own treatment, forcing the hands of the doctors to experiment on her with a form of treatment that would not be protocol for another twenty years. She told them to just go in behind the breast and take out all the cancerous tissue.

They ended up doing just that, but her radiation treatment was aggressive. As my mother would describe it, after they removed the tumors in her left breast, the biopsy showed cancerous cells present at the margins, so they removed more breast tissue and some lymph nodes. She still refused the mastectomy. They implanted five tubes through the skin of her left breast so that they could pass the radiation implants through them. She was also treated with external beam radiotherapy to the entire breast area.

My mother had large, voluptuous double-D breasts in her modeling days. After her cancer treatment, they were barely a B.

In the aftermath of surviving breast cancer and radiation, my mother seemed to unleash all her inhibitions. She became very bold with her desires and self-expression. I'm not sure whether it was due to feeling mortal or feeling invincible, but she lost all social filters. She began to thrive on her shock value. In her mind, she had lost almost all those identifiable and desirable attributes that had made her popular in front of the camera, but she hadn't lost her knowledge or her spirit.

In addition to the loosening of her inhibitions, my mother's behavior began to change in other ways—most notably in how she interacted with Dad. When she first met him, Mom had been on the brink of stardom with the potential for a great modeling and acting career right in front of her. Had things gone differently, she would have become financially independent and able to survive without the help of anyone, especially a man. With these thoughts in her mind, she started to resent the fact that she'd married the man she fell in love with, because it reaffirmed that now she was completely alone; she'd survived the cancer, but still he hadn't come back. She began to miss the career and the recognition that she so deserved. Instead of being a retired model, she'd become a cancer survivor stuck at home on a farm in Vermont. Raising two children had not been as rewarding as she had expected or hoped. Motherhood was not nearly as glamorous as the modeling and acting world she had left behind. She would often say, "I should have never gotten married." And when she was really mad and frustrated, especially with John-Henry and me, she would say, "I should have never had children."

As her resentment grew into anger, her manner of self-expression changed dramatically. She started swearing more, almost as if to emulate Ted Williams; in fact, she'd often write down his expressions to use them on others. She started wearing more provocative clothes than her country duds and became flirtatious with younger men because she knew she could be and she enjoyed the power she still possessed over them. It was something that made her feel attractive and believe she was worthy.

She'd always been comfortable standing out, and as her daughter I had been embarrassed by some of the things she did. She had come to one of my cross-country races, for instance, wearing a Swiss cowbell around her neck. When she saw me on the wooded course, she rang the bell. I finished the race with one of my best times—I was so embarrassed I raced as fast as possible to get off the course.

Now her behavior became more outrageous. One Halloween she decided she was going to a party that would be having a costume contest. She decided she was going as a witch. Not very original, one might think, but with her makeup knowledge, she transformed herself into a very dramatic creature. Everything—from the witch's hat to the nails, from the knee-high fashion boots to the asymmetrical dress—was stunning. So was her exposed right breast, the one that had survived cancer, now painted as a pumpkin, with vines curling around her exposed back. It was beautiful, but that didn't mean I wanted her to go out in public looking like that. In fact, I begged her to stay home. She refused, seeing nothing wrong with her appearance. She thought it was captivating and exciting, to say the least.

Unfortunately, the small towns of Vermont did not understand her flair for the dramatic, and my mother shocked and offended many people that night. She still won first place, but she also won the cruel gossip of small-town people who couldn't understand her nerve or unique personality. They gossiped about her behind her back and labeled her "the Pumpkin Witch on the Hill." For a few years in a row she returned to the same costume party to shock some more people. Each year she would expose a different body part.

She was more than brazen—she reveled in it. She decided she would rise with pride to her new moniker and started growing giant pumpkins to enter at the local fair. She won there too, with a pumpkin weighing over three hundred pounds. They invited her to participate the following year. Mom agreed—but only if she could set up a kissing booth. The townspeople didn't know what to expect of her next.

Now I was afraid to return home and see people I knew, especially when I went into town. I just knew people were laughing and poking fun at "the former Mrs. Ted Williams." She couldn't go anywhere without someone pointing her out. She shared all of her latest endeavors with her family and friends by creating cards out of the photographs taken of her and her giant pumpkins and photos of her in her costumes that seemed to come right out of the pages of *Vogue*. She knew every trick of the modeling trade and understood how to re-create any look she'd seen in a fashion magazine. Despite how unrealistic it may have seemed to the average person to actually wear haute couture on the small-town streets of Vermont, Mom would still choose the latest in fashion and wear it at any event possible.

She used hairpieces and fake eyelashes to accentuate her beautiful features and distract attention away from her wrinkles. Not many people understood her or found her style appropriate, but Mom would always say that one has to dare to be a little crazy in order to be great and as long as they're hissing and spitting, you know you're on top.

I didn't always understand my mother's philosophy or her antics, but I did admire her courage and nerve. I was just too embarrassed to be around when she was up to something. I was afraid for her and disturbed by the reactions I might see from other people as they turned to talk about her. I was more like my father, who, in spite of his loud voice and bombastic ways, valued privacy and discretion.

Like him, I don't like being embarrassed. One of my greatest fears is of being unfairly judged by others. I am casual and relaxed and do not go out of my way to get attention. I always said my brother was just like his mother. He looked like Dad but acted like Mom. He too was fearless.

In the end, I would discover that it did bother both my mother and my brother to learn what people thought of them; it hurt their feelings, but they would never let it show. They both sacrificed their lives for others' joy, comfort, freedom, and love. Despite the belittling, the cruel jokes behind their backs, the many jealous lies people would tell about them, they persevered in what they thought was right, because both my brother and my mother lived for the day. They were bold and courageous—knowing life is too short to be afraid.

Chapter Fourteen

By my senior year in France, I was seriously contemplating not going home to go to college, but staying in Europe to become a professional cyclist. My mother came to visit me and assured me that if I did that my father would disown me. When she failed to change my mind, she sent John-Henry over. My brother was able to convince me. He knew me and knew that staying in France was not worth becoming estranged from our father, so I followed him back to the States.

I hadn't even thought about where I might go to college. John-Henry took me to Springfield College in Massachusetts. We toured the campus, I filled out the registration papers, and a week later I was moving into a dorm. I went to college not having a clue what I wanted to do.

When I got there, I decided to take all my money out of savings and buy myself a car. When Dad heard I was car shopping, he called me up.

"Don't buy a damn car. It's the biggest waste of money. The moment you drive off the lot it will be worth half what you paid. I'll tell ya what I'm gonna do. I'm sending you Louise's car, and you can drive that."

I was excited to get a car, even if it had belonged to Louise. I didn't care. I got my license at nineteen and took the test in my gray Ford Tempo. I was touched by my father's gift and called him up to thank him for my wheels and also for allowing me to save my money. I told him I had an idea. I asked him if I could ask his advice on something. There was complete silence on the other end of the line. Then I told him that I would like to take my savings and invest in a stock. My bat hit dead center on the ball and it soared. I had just hit a home run.

"You want to buy a stock?"

I heard more pride than surprise, but most of all I had impressed him. He was floored that I had called him to ask for his advice and guidance.

"You wanna buy a stock . . . All right . . . lemme tell ya what you have to do. How much money you got?"

The excitement in his voice was the best feeling I had ever had on the phone with Dad. He was so excited and enthused he almost sounded angry and impatient. I couldn't even answer his questions. He just kept talking.

"It doesn't matter. Whatever you got, I'm gonna double it for ya! You wanna buy a blue-chip stock. A goddamned solid blue-chip stock. You know what that is, right?"

He was talking so loudly at this point that my Japanese roommate looked up, concerned.

"I was thinking of General Electric or IBM."

Another home run deep to center.

"You bet your ass! Those are great choices. Great choices!"

He started yelling in the background for Louise to hurry up and get him the damned morning paper. When she wasn't quick enough, I heard him dragging the phone, grumbling and rustling through papers impatiently.

"All right! Hold on, I'm looking right now. Louise! Get me my magnifying glass."

I was smiling, almost laughing. I was ecstatic.

"All right, kid, let's buy IBM. It's at 90 right now. That's a little high, but what the hell, it's a damned good stock and it will probably split soon."

Now he started talking jargon. I didn't know what to say, so I asked, "When can I sell it and make some good money off of it?"

Swing and a miss. Strike one.

"Never!"

"How will I ever make money from it?"

His excitement quickly turned to frustration. Strike two.

"Never mind. Just save it forever. Don't even look at it."

"Okay, I'll forget all about it." I shrugged my shoulders and smiled.

"Thatagirl. It will drive you crazy watching the son-of-a bitch. Just don't ever sell it."

"Okeydokey," I said triumphantly. "I got it!"

The older I got the more I realized that the thing that exhausted and frustrated Dad the most was the constant drain other people put on him, even his own family. Everyone was always asking for something, especially money. Dad was taking care of everyone. His heart was large, and his compassion for others less fortunate was unending. He financially supported anyone who had the nerve to ask. He paid for the cars, college educations, and insurance. He was sending money to everyone, and it was consuming him. He did not have the fortitude to say no. Instead, he did what he believed real men should do. He would grind his teeth and pay, regardless of what it cost him. Taking note of this, I strengthened my resolve to win his admiration and affection.

I decided I would start working on campus. I worked in the campus post office, I was a hall monitor, and I worked with campus security. I would share every paycheck amount with my father. One day out of the blue in 1997 my father called me to tell me something very important. You would have thought we'd won the lottery. He was beside himself.

"I got some great news, kid. Great news for us! Guess what I saw in the paper this morning?"

I hadn't looked at it in years, because I was following his instructions not to, but I knew.

"Did it split?"

"Can you lend your ol' dad some money?"

Just as quickly, I responded, "How much you need?"

Grand slam.

THERE ARE FEW TIMES IN LIFE WHEN YOU HAVE THE OPPORTU-nity to establish yourself as a genuine and honest person. These character-building moments came aplenty with Dad, as he was always testing my brother and me on our integrity and our principles.

One of the things I loved about Dad was his ability to be purely genuine and brutally honest. He would reveal himself completely and expected the same of others. For most people, considering how fake we can be, it was a bit unnerving. We polish our fronts to hide behind them and avoid the reality of the simple truth.

During my teen years, my dad would routinely ask the silly, sarcastic (and probing) question, "Are there any boys?" In my mind, I believe he was inquiring just to see if he could still make me blush over the phone. When he asked in 1990, when I was nineteen and at Springfield, there was in fact a boy. And I really wanted Dad to meet him.

"Would it be all right if I brought my friend down over Christmas break?"

"Your friend?"

"Yes, he is a friend . . . a boyfriend."

"Oh yeah?" he asked sarcastically. "What does *he* do?"

"He is a graduate student."

"Well, I'm not buying him a ticket down here."

"No, no, you don't have to do that. We were planning on driving."

"Oh Jesus! Can he drive?"

"Yes, he can. We'll be there in a couple of days. Is that all right?"

"All right. But . . . DRIVE CAREFULLY."

This was the first man I had ever brought home to meet my father. The whole ride down to Florida I had time to think of what *could* happen . . . what was about to happen. I prepped my boyfriend on the trials we would surely be put through. This was a crash course on how to take my dad and understand the sarcasm that was going to be laden throughout our stay, the peppering of questions that were definitely coming.

I was on pins and needles. Suddenly I saw my beau a lot more critically than I ever had before. *We should probably stop on the way down and get him a haircut,* I thought as I sneaked a peek at him out of the corner of my eye.

Something that I think made my father a great dad was his courage to be nosy with his daughter. There were no boundaries, no waters left uncharted. I believe a lot of fathers shy away from confronting their daughters. They don't take a strong stance with them, challenging them on their choices and their actions. They leave it up to the mother, and in my opinion that is a terrible mistake. At some point in a young woman's life she will model her choices in men based on her experiences with her father. She will seek the qualities she likes, and avoid the ones she does not. I now realized my male companion was about to represent a lot more than just a boyfriend. In my mind, this seemingly simple visit had grown out of proportion and become an event that would expose my father's influence on me when it came to choosing a male mate.

The drive to Florida could not be long enough; the fifteen hundred miles flew by. There was no escaping the hot Florida trial and cross-examination we were both going to go through. What was I thinking?

We arrived right before dinnertime, which I knew would be like walking into a field of land mines. The Beast loved to eat, and he was always lurking around dinnertime.

I led the way into the grand house through the back door. There was no one in the kitchen. I had my male suitor wait for me as I went to seek out my father.

I found Dad in the bedroom watching television. I rushed over to him. He drew me in with his long arms and smothered me in a huge hug while I buried my face in his shoulder.

"How's my little girl? How was the drive? Where is this guy? Who the hell is he? Are you hungry? We're going to eat soon."

"He's in the kitchen."

It was the only question I heard.

The roll of the drum started as I scurried ahead of my dad to warn the hunted that the hunter was coming.

I stood next to my defenseless intimate pal.

"I hope you guys are hungry!" yelled my dad as he tromped through the living room before catching a glimpse of the guilty party. I felt naked standing there, and my friend was just as exposed. It was as if it was written all over us that we had done "it." We weren't just friends. I've prayed a few times in my life. This was one of them as Dad rounded the kitchen door and put his sights on the two of us.

Just as we had discussed in our on-the-road training, my guy lurched forward and stuck out his hand to shake my father's. "It's very nice to meet you, Mr. Williams."

There was a moment of silence before the first shot was fired.

"So you're the guy my daughter wants to bring down here and share her time with her ol' dad?"

"Thank you for allowing me to come down," my buddy said on cue.

"Well, Christ, sit down. We're going to eat. I hope you're hungry."

Like synchronized swimmers, we slithered into the kitchen chairs. Of course, my dad sat at the head of the table and just watched me in silence. The interrogation light was on and focused right at me. I felt the heat on my cheeks, as though every secret lustful moment or thought I'd shared with my friend was tattooed right across my forehead. I prayed for the cook to serve the food. *Please bring food to put in mouths—so words can't come out.*

I don't remember what was served for dinner. As Dad took the first bite I thought there might be a chance for escape, but I was harshly denied. With his mouth full of food, Dad focused in on me and shot again:

"So this is the guy you're sleeping with?"

It pierced like an arrow right through my solar plexus. My head tilted up and back, and I took a hard swallow. I looked at my father and realized this was one of those moments. This was the moment when I would either choose to stand tall, take ownership of the relationship, and start revealing my character or downplay it and try to pass off my companion as just a friend.

My guilty lover kept his head low, very low, as he tried to hide behind the plate. I continued to stare at my father, who stared right back at me in silence.

"Yes, Dad, we sleep together."

If I had been standing, I would have fallen. I might have even died.

Then, through the kitchen door, came my savior.

"Hey, Sis," smiled my protector. John-Henry was going to put an end to this painful moment. He knew exactly what was going on, and being three years older, he'd already gone through this interrogation (albeit from a completely different angle, being a boy). As he took his place at the dinner table John-Henry's smile could not have been a more welcome retreat. My brother knew just the role to take on at this moment of truth.

"So what do you think of him, Dad?"

My brother was smiling and enjoying the sight of both of us squirming.

"Well, the jury is still out on *this* guy. We'll have to see. Yeah, I'm talking to you."

There was a hint of playfulness. My father squinted at his victim. He was definitely curious about my choice of a male, but he also was thoroughly amused that his daughter brought her first boyfriend home to meet her dad. It is a difficult milestone in any father-daughter relationship, but I had told the truth and passed the test.

Clockwise from top left, Dad with baby
John-Henry; beautiful Mom holding
John-Henry in the Keys; unlike any
other wife (Peru, copyright Norman
Parkinson Limited/courtesy Norman
Parkinson Archive); Mom modeling in
Australia, the day before she meets Dad
[Helmut Newton, *Vogue Australia,* 1964 —
copyright Helmut Newton Estate)

Clockwise from top, Mom and Dad
relaxing in Vermont after working
in the garden; Baby Claudia/Vanilla
Ted/Butterball; tender moment
between Dad and his son

Above, Vermont home on its new location; *left,* Ethel Wettach (Mom's mother, my beloved grandmother)

Life on the farm

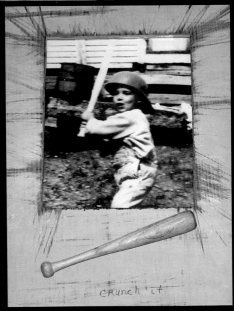

Clockwise from top, the family on the
day Mom surprised Dad moving the
house; Christmas in Vermont; "Crunch
it": young John-Henry swinging a bat
in a frame made by Dad

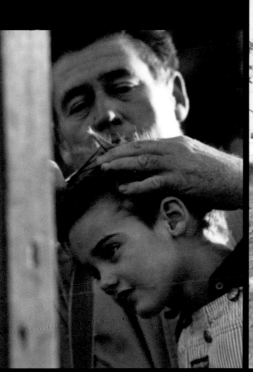

Clockwise from top left, Dad the barber; springtime in the Keys with Dad; bringing Dad a flower

Clockwise from top left, happy fishing with John-Henry off Dad's dock in Islamorada; young John-Henry fishing on a boat with Dad; Mom's first bonefish; safe with my brother, coming up the hills of Vermont

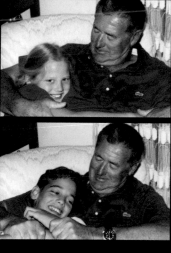

Clockwise from top, brother and sister in Canada (ca. 1978); getting comfy with Dad; little sluggers in Vermont waiting for Dad to pick us up on the way to Canada

Clockwise from top, choosing our flies on the bank of the Miramichi River; the greatest fisherman in the world; Dad and his buddy, Guide Roy Curtis in Canada; a mellow man tying flies in his basement at his fishing camp in Canada

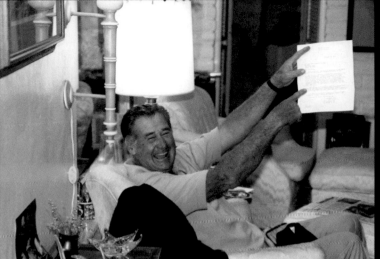

Christmas morning, when Dad opened John Henry's acceptance letter to college

Left, father and son at spring training (ca. 1990); *right*, John-Henry about to go to college

Dad batting at Old-Timers' Game (1982)

John-Henry as batboy at Old-Timers' Game

John-Henry and Dad signing photos

Clockwise from above, Dad often surprised John-Henry with personalized notes in the stacks of photographs he was signing. This one is inscribed: "To John-Henry. Too bad you don't hit like your old dad, but you have a ton of other abilities I didn't have. I love you. No. 9. P.S. Keep going"; Red Sox photograph inscribed: "To my wonderful son John-Henry & do I love you. Always take pride in what you do & say. Your old Dad, No. 9"; Dad and Babe photo inscribed: "To John-Henry. One of the potential greats but didn't have a chance to play. From your old dad, Ted Williams"; Minneapolis Millers swinging photo inscribed: "To my wonderful son who's getting on the ball more and more and I'm proud of you. Your loving father"

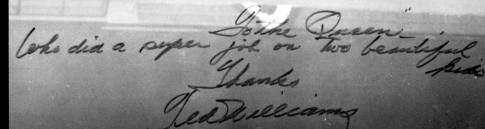

Clockwise from top, Dad personalized a photograph to Mom for Christmas 2000: "To the Queen—who did a super job on two beautiful kids. Thanks, Ted Williams"; a special Vermont Christmas photographed by Dad; together again in Citrus Hills, Florida (1994)

Clockwise from top, first trip to Cooperstown, the "three musketeers"; John-Henry and I surprise Dad by throwing out the ceremonial first pitches on Ted Williams Day, 1991; second trip to Cooperstown

The special day when Dad received the Presidential Medal of Freedom from President George H. W. Bush

Left, always proud to be a Marine, Dad and fellow Marine, Maj. General Larry Taylor, USMC (ret); *above,* Dad and Senator John Glenn talking about flying prior to Glenn's space shuttle launch; *below left,* Aerosmith's Steven Tyler and his lady visit with Dad just before the shuttle launch

Above, Dad and me on the California coast during my graduation trip (1993); *left,* Dad and John-Henry loading the boat to Alcatraz

John-Henry and me on the California coast during my graduation trip (1993)

Clockwise from top left, the start of a baseball memorabilia company; Dad, John-Henry, and me at Dad's home in Citrus Hills, Florida; me and my dad; the "three musketeers" fishing off the Florida coast

Chapter Fifteen

One early spring day John-Henry called me at college to let me know that I needed to come to Boston.

On May 12, 1991, the fiftieth anniversary of Ted Williams hitting .406, the Red Sox were going to celebrate Ted Williams Day. Dad was seventy-three, and the Red Sox had asked if John-Henry and I would surprise our father and throw out the first pitch.

"Throw out the first pitch? You mean like go out onto the mound like the pitchers and throw the ball?"

"Yeah, you can do it. I'll see you this weekend."

Sure, easy, no problem, I can do it. Panic set in. I take everything very seriously. I don't think my father had ever seen me throw a ball before. And now I was going to throw in front of my dad, and a baseball crowd, at Fenway Park.

I stood in my dorm room staring at the phone. *I can't embarrass my dad. I have to throw well. I can't throw like a girl.*

I had made sure that none of my classmates at Springfield knew who my father was. I was very quiet and kept my family life private. But this called for drastic measures. I decided I would seek out Chris and Mark, my two buddies who were in my biology class and on the baseball team. I found them in the cafeteria and sat down next to them.

"Hey, what's up, Williams?"

"Will you please teach me to throw a pitch?"

They both laughed, but then saw how sincere I was.

"Why?" They chimed in unison.

I paused for a moment and then said, "Well . . . my dad is the Red Sox baseball player Ted Williams, and this weekend is the anniversary of his hitting .406, and they're planning a surprise by having my brother and me throw out the first pitch, and I don't want to look stupid or throw like a girl."

Both young men stared at me with their mouths open.

"No way. You lie."

I smiled and shrugged.

"Are you freakin' serious?"

"Please teach me to throw. I have to throw the ball very well."

"Holy shit." They looked at each other in disbelief.

"If you help me, I would like to invite you to come along with me, and we'll stay after and watch the game."

"There is no way you are serious."

"I'm very serious. Please help me, but please don't tell anyone else—okay?"

They didn't even respond. They were stunned.

My first lesson was that afternoon. I had no clue what I was doing. I definitely threw like a girl, and they let me know it. They coached me and explained everything they could, right down to how I needed to hold the ball if I wanted to throw a curve.

"I just want to get it over the plate."

I practiced every day for the next week. My arm was so sore I couldn't even lift it. The boys told me I had better ice my shoulder and take a lot of Advil. They were on a mission to get me to throw sixty feet, six inches, the distance from the mound to the plate. They were very excited, and word spread very quickly throughout the campus. I had been identified.

I drove my gray Ford Tempo into Boston with Chris and Mark on Sunday. I was meeting my dad and brother, and then we would be escorted to the edge of the field. Doing public events with Dad was always last-minute planning. There was no lingering or standing around in one place too long. It was right this way, hurry up, and then "let's get the show on the road."

I was shuffled down to the edge of the field, where John-Henry and Dad were waiting. My pitching coaches were close behind me. I wanted to warm up, but that would have ruined the surprise. We got to the edge of the field, and I introduced my friends to my dad. They were ready to get their autographs already, but the pregame ceremony was about to start, so I left them to find their seats while I joined my brother by the dugout. I was wearing a long, black-and-white, polka-dotted dress, and black, bowed shoes. Quite the baseball uniform.

I gave my Dad a big hug.

Standing next to my brother was Chris Isaak, who would sing the National Anthem. John-Henry introduced me, and the next thing I knew we were walking out to the field. In the background I heard the announcer say, "And throwing out the first pitch are two of the most important people in Ted's life, his children John-Henry and Claudia."

I felt like I was in a bubble. I didn't look up. I didn't want to see the crowd.

"You want to go first?" my brother asked.

"No, you go first."

John-Henry stepped out onto the mound and looked like he knew what he was doing. He did the whole windup and threw the ball wicked hard. It was a wild throw. Tony Pena scrambled to catch it before it hit the backstop. I heard the crowd go, "Oooo."

Now it was my turn. I hiked my shoulder-padded sleeves up and did my windup just like I was taught. I may not have had the velocity that my brother had, but my pitch lofted through the air and landed softly in Tony Pena's glove. Thank God.

The catcher trotted toward me and gave me a kiss and a hug. Everything happened so fast that I didn't even have time to think. John-Henry was smiling at me.

"Nice job, Sis."

We walked off the field side by side. Dad was laughing, and I thought I saw a tear in his eyes.

"Oh boy! You guys did great! Where did you learn to throw like that?"

I thought he was asking me, but he was looking at John-Henry. He was needling my brother, smiling at the same time. He grabbed my brother's strong biceps and slapped him on the shoulder. "At least you looked good." He was clearly so happy. Then he turned to me and drew me into his strong arms. He squeezed me and patted my back.

"Christ . . . YOU should have been a ballplayer."

The few people around us couldn't help but feel the pride and giddiness. Dad was surprised and laughing, shaking his head.

It felt like he might be on the verge of tears. I like to think that it was because we had surprised him that he decided to give his own surprise. When he was finally announced and welcomed onto the field, he did something he hadn't done in over fifty years. When he got up to speak, he thanked everyone for being there and for the wonderful ceremony. Then he turned his attention to the stands and addressed the fans. He was shaking a little, and my brother and I realized our steely father was nervous. He had hidden in his pocket a Red Sox cap.

"I'm especially happy, though, to have a chance . . . so they can *never* write ever again that I was hardheaded, can *never* write again that I never tipped my hat to the crowd. . . ."

The crowd went wild as he pulled the cap out of his pocket and put it on his head.

"Because today I tip my hat to *all* the people in New England, without question the greatest sports fans on earth."

It was obvious that this moment meant something special to him. There were very few times that Ted Williams showed he was vulnerable, but I thought he seemed very fragile as he spoke those words. He was admitting that it had bothered him to be criticized for not tipping his hat. He wanted to thank his true fans who'd stood by him. The begrudged, tumultuous relationship between Dad, the sportswriters, and the fans was coming to an end, and he wanted to thank his faithful supporters for helping him never to be broken by the press. He wanted to thank them for their love and their loyalty, and most of all for the cheers and standing ovations that had helped him during every at-bat and won him over forever.

TED WILLIAMS DAY WAS THE FIRST OF MANY EVENTS THAT MY brother and I began to attend with our father. He was often invited to different kinds of celebratory functions and honorary ceremonies, and he often turned to us to be by his side at these gatherings. My father appreciated how my brother and I had matured, and he saw us as important traveling companions to have with him. We were beginning to form something of a traveling trio, which was how I ended up visiting the White House later that year.

Dad and George H. W. Bush first met at the Chapel Hill Naval Air Station in 1942, where they both trained to be pilots. Dad was twenty-four, Bush eighteen. Bush had played baseball at Yale and, as a Red Sox fan, had been thrilled to witness Dad's amazing season in 1941. He also loved fishing.

At the start of 1988, my father and George Bush reconnected in a way that changed history. Bush had been Ronald Reagan's vice president for two terms and was now seeking the Republican presidential nomination. Early that February, he had finished a disappointing third in the Iowa caucus behind Senator Bob Dole and the televangelist Pat Robertson. His advisers believed that to win the crucial

New Hampshire primary later that month, he needed to be seen less as a Washington insider and more as a man with whom the average New Englander could identify. Who better to help with that than the greatest hitter the Boston Red Sox ever had?

Ted Williams, who distrusted most politicians and had certainly never campaigned for one, rushed to New Hampshire to help his old friend. It's said that he showed up early for his first Bush rally and was waiting backstage when Bush arrived in a bad mood.

My father's voice boomed out, "Any problems, Mr. Vice President?"

Bush smiled and relaxed. "Not now," he said. "Everything's going to be fine now."

Teddy Ballgame strode onto the stage with no introduction. None was needed. The crowd burst into wild cheers and leapt to their feet. When they finally quieted down, my dad introduced Mr. Bush, who now got a very warm reception. They toured the state side by side for the next several days. Mr. Bush readily admitted that the giant, cheering crowds that showed up everywhere had come to see Ted Williams, not him. He was just basking in the Splendid Splinter's reflected glory. But it worked. He won the New Hampshire primary handily and, of course, went on to become the president of the United States.

On November 18, 1991, thirty-one years after Ted Williams hit his last home run, President George H. W. Bush bestowed on my father the Presidential Medal of Freedom, recognizing his accomplishments on the baseball field and his service to his country as a Marine, not once but twice.

My brother and I were there for this wonderful occasion, and so was Louise. John-Henry and I were so proud of our father. We were going to the White House to see the president of the United States give our dad the highest civilian award possible. I had never been to the White House before, but John-Henry and Dad had spent a night in the Lincoln Bedroom the previous July, when President Bush held a ceremony in the Rose Garden honoring Dad and Joe DiMaggio on the fiftieth anniversary of their great 1941 season. "I didn't think I'd get to meet royalty so soon after the queen's visit," Mr. Bush said during the ceremony, referring to Queen Elizabeth's visit the previous May. "But nevertheless, here they are." After the ceremony, DiMaggio, Dad, John-Henry, and various dignitaries flew on Air Force One to Toronto for the All-Star Game.

I believe that was when Dad and John-Henry spent the night in the Lincoln Bedroom. As Dad would later tell Dave Kindred of *The Sporting News,* President Bush came to him in the middle of the night and took him to another room, where he pulled open a dresser drawer. Dad said he was startled to see hundreds of old fishing flies there, real classics, some maybe two hundred years old or more. Another drawer held an assortment of reels. Dad was thrilled to know the president was as avid a fisherman as he was.

I studied and prepared for a week on how to address the president, what to do, what not to do, and what to wear at this very special event. I don't have any children of my own, but I think I know how it must feel when a child is recognized and honored for their accomplishments. In this case, it was as if the roles were reversed in our relationship with our father. The Kid was cared for by his kids, and we felt like proud parents.

As we approached the White House in a limousine, I figured there would be a multitude of security questions, background checks, requests for photo IDs, and so on. But at the security gate the guard walked up to the limousine, our driver announced the guest, the guard looked at our passports, and then he waved us through. I am almost certain the guard saluted Dad.

We pulled up in front of the White House. You could tell Dad was excited from the fact that he was quiet and on his best behavior. As we walked through the front doors a man approached us who looked a lot like the president, but shorter. As soon as he saw my dad, he lit up. It *was* the president. He headed straight for us and gave Dad a huge bear hug.

Dad started to address him as "Mr. President" and attempted to introduce me, but the president of the United States interrupted him and said, "George."

"Mr. President," Dad said anyway, "I would like you to meet my daughter, Claudia."

I couldn't even recite my rehearsed line of "It's an honor to meet you, Mr. President."

President Bush put his arm around me and said, "Claudia, I've heard so much about you."

All I could do was smile. I was stunned. I managed to stutter, "Thank you, Mr. President. It is very nice to meet you."

I don't think he even heard me—he was too thrilled to see my dad. He patted John-Henry on the back, and then, from his pocket, the president of the United States pulled out *a baseball*. I smiled and looked at my brother in disbelief. I wanted to ask the president for *his* autograph.

As other guests arrived the president was obliged to greet them. We lingered in the entrance hall. I saw President Ford and former First Lady Betty Ford. Then, as so many times before, people started gathering around my dad in the entrance hall of the White House. It was surreal. President Ford shook his hand and shared some laughs. Former Speaker of the House Thomas P. "Tip" O'Neill wandered over to Dad. He seemed like such a jolly ol' fellow. They also had a friendly exchange. Dad was signing programs and whatever else people could get their hands on.

I decided I would start my own autograph collection right then and there. John-Henry was by Dad's side, and Louise and I slowly got pushed to the back of the pack. We worked our way toward the East Room of the State Floor, where the recipients would be presented with their awards. I honestly believe the ceremony was started a bit late because of the autographs that were being signed. I had yet to get one.

As the honored guests and their families and friends found their seats, I grew curious about what the president of the United States would say about my dad. I looked around the beautiful room with its chandeliers, gold drapes, American flags on stands, and the presidential seal on the front of the lectern. I sat there thinking about what an honor this was. *My father* was one of ten people that day who were being recognized for their life accomplishments.

My mind drifting, I began to wonder what I could ever do in my life to truly impress my father. What could I do that would even remotely compare to what he had done? I sat there wishing I was smarter, wishing I had the credentials to get into medical school or law school, wishing I could do something really impressive, just like my dad. As inspired as my father made me feel, I'd also never felt so lost, so insignificant. I didn't even know what I was capable of, or where to start. How could I make a positive impression on a man as great as my father? It was one thing for him to bring Fenway Park to its feet, but now, seeing him in a room filled with the most powerful people in the world, the people who led America, I was learning about how profoundly he'd shaped our country. For the first time I began to see him not through my own eyes but from the perspective of these great individuals who all seemed reduced to boyishness around him.

I'd grown up without fully comprehending who my father was, and suddenly I was face to face with the full breadth of his legacy. I felt tiny. I wanted to start all over again knowing what I knew right then. Greatness comes in many forms, but unless you can clearly focus on what you want to achieve, the way my dad did, it's easy to get lost. I was twenty years old and had no clue what I wanted to do. And my parents didn't approve of the one thing I felt most passionate about—being an athlete.

We were asked to stand as the president of the United States and the first lady entered the room. The president seemed so friendly in that setting. All at once my self-criticism was swept aside and my feelings of pride in my father came flooding back. From behind,

I watched Dad bow his head as he listened to the president. I followed along with the program to honor author William F. Buckley, clergyman and civil rights leader Reverend Leon Sullivan, conservationist Russell Train, baseball great Ted Williams, former first lady Betty Ford, former speaker of the House Tip O'Neill, former Puerto Rico governor Luis A. Ferré, historian and humanist Hanna Gray, Ambassador Vernon Walters, and Professor Friedrich Hayek. As the president said a few words about each of these extraordinary individuals, I gazed at my father's name on the beautifully embossed presidential paper. *That's my dad,* I thought to myself. *My dad. . . .*

Here are the exact words that the president of the United States said about my father.

> Baseball great Ted Williams, whom I don't see sitting here—oops, there he is over on the—don't say anything—[*laughter*]—is an American legend, a remarkable figure in American sports and a twice-tested war hero. At the height of his athletic career, he answered the call of patriotism, serving his country in both World War II and the Korean War—a true champion in the eyes of many Americans. An author wrote of his retirement from baseball, "And now Boston knows how England felt when it lost India." [*laughter*] Ted, congratulations.

As the president read those words and smiled at Dad, my father sat quietly and only once nodded his head as he maintained eye contact with his presidential friend. At the conclusion of the ceremony, President Bush said that the United States was *indebted* to each of the recipients.

> You have touched us. You have enriched us. You have
> shaped our nation's destiny. And you've also shown us

the strength and joy of a simple but powerful idea: the idea of freedom.

The idea of freedom.

The first lady and the president hung the medal on each of the honorees. I was surprised to see tears in John-Henry's eyes. I put my hand on his shoulder, but he shook me off. As Dad stood up to accept his medal, the crowd started applauding and everybody stood. Goose bumps rippled over my skin as my father walked toward the president and the first lady to receive the special recognition. He was beaming as he stooped to allow Barbara Bush to reach his neck. It was as if time had slowed down.

At the conclusion of the ceremony, the guests and their families adjourned to the State Dining Room for lunch. To my delight, I was seated next to Tip O'Neill. I am ashamed to admit that I don't remember who else was at my table. I remember seeing my dad two tables away, sitting with President Bush. The two of them looked like school buddies. Dad caught my eye, and both of them waved to me. I half-laughed and smiled back. Surreal.

Mr. O'Neill wondered if I was the granddaughter of Mr. Williams when he saw my name. I politely responded that I was actually his daughter, and the conversation took off from there. Coming from Massachusetts, he explained, he was a lifelong Red Sox fan and had watched my father play growing up. He went on for a while, rattling off stats and stories about Dad. Every once in a while he would ask me questions about my dad's career, but I didn't know the answers. I was clueless and felt lost in history. I should have studied up on Dad, not on how to address the president of the United States. I was born eleven years after Dad hit his last home run, and still knew little about what went on in the 1940s and 1950s.

Finally I smiled and said, "Mr. Speaker, I believe you know more about my father than I do."

He laughed and then proceeded to ask *me* questions. I wished at that moment that I had just let him go on about Dad and asked *him* questions. I was afraid I was not going to sound very impressive being the daughter of Ted Williams. I didn't go to Harvard or Yale. I didn't even know what I wanted to study. I didn't play softball or any other team sport. I felt stupid answering questions about myself until finally we found common ground. When I shared that I had finished high school in France and completed the International Baccalaureate, he slipped right into speaking French. The speaker of the House and I started chitchatting in informal French. I tried to use only the formal form, but he kept using the informal. We worked our way through lunch, talking about the great city of Paris and where I'd lived and what I had done and seen. I turned to check on Dad, and both he and the president were smiling at me.

When the day came to a close and we piled back into our limousine, the first question my father asked was, "What were you and Tip speaking about? You two were lost in conversation. Every time I looked over at you, there you two were laughing and talking with your hands and so on."

"It was something else, Dad. We were speaking French together. He was telling me all about you and your baseball career. I told him he knew more about you than I did. Congratulations, Dad. I'm proud of you."

To which he replied, "Thanks, honey. That was a very nice thing for the president to do."

A man never stands so tall as when he stoops to help a child.
—TED WILLIAMS

AS TIME WENT ON IT BECAME CLEAR THAT OUR JOURNEYS WITH Dad were not always going to be opulent or star-studded, but that didn't make them any less important—especially when it involved kids in need. Although Dad may not have been described as a level-headed, emotionally stable, even-keeled, warm and fuzzy, or patient father, he always became a different person when he was around children in trouble. They never failed to bring out a side of him that few people ever saw firsthand, a tender side that he rarely displayed and never broadcast.

Such was the case when John-Henry and I went to Dana-Farber with him in 1991. Throughout his retirement, he'd continued his involvement with Dana-Farber and the Jimmy Fund, often attending fund-raisers and helping to raise money. He never took any false pride from this. "It's something you should do without having people rave over you," he writes in *My Turn at Bat*. "I love kids, that's all, it's no virtue, and I don't see any reason to cash in on it." It was one of these kids, the son of a sports photographer, who gave our father another of his nicknames, Teddy Ballgame.

Dad and the painter LeRoy Neiman, in conjunction with the Jimmy Fund, created and sold a lithograph of Neiman's painting *Williams at Bat* to raise money. Neiman had painted a beautiful depiction of Dad in a swing stance, and he and Dad signed a limited number of the lithographs. My brother and I spent most of the morning at the Cancer Institute watching the photo and press session of our father and Neiman signing the pieces and answering questions.

As the session was coming to a close, and after the press had left, a few children were brought in to meet Ted Williams and LeRoy Neiman. I think it was the first time I had ever seen my father interact with a child. He pushed himself back from the table and leaned toward the children. He had the most welcoming smile on his face, and his eyes were so kind. The children were not timid or shy, but it was Dad who stole the show and the attention of our visitors, becoming as lovable as Santa Claus, asking the children silly questions like, "How was the food? Did you get anything good to eat in this place? Are there any rules?" He asked whether they played baseball (even the girls) and quizzed them about current players. He had them demonstrate their swings and tweaked their little hips with his huge hands, physically showing them how they needed to lead with their hips in order to generate a powerful swing. Just touching them and wiggling their bodies made most of them laugh, and Dad laughed right along with them. He announced to the children that he had a very serious question. Silence. Everyone thought he was going to ask about their health or treatment. Instead, he asked, "Do you guys get any ice cream in this joint?" A flood of responses came his way. He'd then ask something else in complete seriousness, only to elicit another silly response.

As my brother and I watched, we were in awe at how easy it was for Dad to connect with these little kids. Eventually, we were all accompanied to the hospital floor, the children leading the tour to show us their play room, therapy room, and individual rooms. The children had now captured our father's undivided attention. When Dad had a question, without hesitation the children described in detail what was going on in their treatment, what the different tubes were for, what kind of cancer they had, what their hair used to look like. I remember one child describing in detail a picture he had drawn in art therapy. He had depicted the cancer cells being fought by his army of strong cells; in the background, atop his castle, he was winning the war. Dad listened patiently and watched attentively through the lengthy description.

"That's one good-looking castle—fit for one strong king."

Only when we were parting ways with the children did Dad turn his attention to the adult giving the tour.

"Now, let me ask you a question." He stood a little taller, and shoved his hands in his jacket pockets. "Are those little guys gonna be okay?"

In the question was a hint of fear and a touch of anger. I heard it, and I know my brother did too. There could only be one response. I hoped it would be the one Dad needed to hear in that moment. He asked again, this time more demanding.

"The little guy who showed me his picture—is he going to be all right?"

I suppose we met these particular children because they were healthy enough, at least at the time. The response was one of cautious optimism. It was made clear to us that these children's lives were forever changed by their disease and the battle they would have to fight.

When the day was over and we were waiting for our ride in front of the hospital, our father turned his full attention now to the skies. His jaw clenched and his lips pursed like vise-grips. He exuded tension and anger from his entire body as he started to curse. His frustration could not be restrained.

"And they say there is a God. . . ."

Everyone knew what Ted Williams was mad about. There was no excuse for children to be sick with cancer. Surely someone who could turn water to wine, walk on water, and raise the dead could prevent the cruel disease of cancer from affecting innocent children. It challenged his faith and his willingness to believe in God.

Chapter Sixteen

WHEN I WASN'T TRAVELING WITH MY BROTHER AND MY father, I was at school working on my degree. In spite of my reluctance to go to college, I took my education seriously and ended up graduating cum laude. I never took a break. I stayed at college working on campus and taking classes over the summer. I graduated in three years, with a BS degree in psychology and just two credits shy of a BA in art therapy and art.

Truthfully, though, I thought much of it was a waste of time and money because I had no focus or direction. I thought I might go on to get my master's in psychology, but the pull of Europe and my athletic dreams was far stronger. I had fulfilled my father's wish that I get a college education, and now it was time to get back to Europe. I couldn't wait.

Before that, though, I wanted to enjoy the *best* graduation present.

Throughout my senior year, my dad would ask me what I wanted as a graduation present. My answer was always the same.

"I want to go on a trip with only you and John-Henry to California and see where you grew up." Time alone with Dad became more and more valuable as my brother and I matured. Both of us longed for opportunities just to be with our dad, alone, and enjoy the moments. We valued our limited time with him. When it was just the three of us, there were no outbursts, there was just easy, fun, creative games and stories. Dad was as interested in us as we were interested in him. We would share dreams, experiences, regrets, and wishes. We were united and supportive of each other, and it was a great sense of family.

"What about a car? You want a car? How about some money? Do you wear any jewelry?"

"Just me, you, and John-Henry on a road trip. That's what I want."

We were to depart for California right after my graduation. Louise was not invited, and she did *not* like this. I would discover just how much she didn't like it on my graduation day. It went without saying that Louise was not invited to my graduation either. My mother and father, my brother, my best friend, and my boyfriend were the only ones I wanted there.

Having the last name Williams put me near the end of the line. I couldn't wait to walk into the building and find my dad sitting in the stands like every other dad, being proud of me.

As we marched out in unison toward the stage, I searched the bleachers. I spotted him immediately. He was beaming. I was so excited. Everyone was waving and smiling at their families, showing off their caps and gowns. A gold rope around my neck represented graduating with honors. John-Henry was taking pictures, and Dad was just smiling like I had never seen. I broke formation. I ran toward my father, right across the middle of the large room, and scampered up into the stands.

"I'm so damn proud of you." He hugged me tightly, and I held on.

"Now go get back in line—you're messing up the whole production."

I turned and looked back. There was a gaping hole where I should have been walking with my classmates. Worse, I had started a trend. A bunch of other kids had decided to follow my lead and go find their families too. I looked at my group and thought I better get back. Just as I turned to go I caught a look on my father's face that took me aback. What was *that*? I had *never* seen that look before. Something was wrong. Something was terribly wrong. From that moment on, I could not get that look out of my mind. I obsessed over what it might mean.

After I walked across the stage, my father and brother hurried out of the building to avoid the crowd of Massachusetts fans coming his way. We were to meet back at my brother's place for a celebration. I would have to wait at least another two hours before I could confront this ominous mystery. I grew frightened of what I was about to discover.

My boyfriend drove me to John-Henry's house and dropped me off. It was a good thing he couldn't stay, because what I was about to find out was shocking. As I took the elevator to the top floor of John-Henry's apartment building I racked my brain for any and every possibility it could be. John-Henry met me at the door. He was on his way out to pick up some stuff at the grocery store.

"Is something wrong with Dad?"

"No. Why?"

"I don't know . . . I thought he seemed a little off."

"I don't know of anything. I'll be back in a bit."

I walked into the apartment and tentatively looked for Dad. I found him in my brother's room propped up on the bed watching television.

"Hey, Dad," I said with bated breath.

When Dad saw me, he started gripping the comforter and crushing it in his hands. He wouldn't look at me. I thought he was going to rip the covers off the bed and spontaneously combust.

"There is something I have to ask you," he seethed through clenched teeth.

"What is it, Dad? What's the matter?" I was scared at this point.

He couldn't even speak. He was shaking his head, fighting what he was about to say and just gripping the covers over and over.

I took a step toward him and he said, "No."

I pleaded, "What's wrong?"

"Did you ever tell John and Mary that you sleep with me?" he asked while grinding his teeth.

I knew the words, but I also knew what was implied. I could not believe my ears. John and Mary were very good friends of Dad's. I couldn't fathom why in the world they would say such a thing. I stood there stunned.

"No . . ." I stammered. "But . . . when we were kids we slept with you. . . ." I didn't know what to say or how to say it, but even that sounded wrong, and Dad recoiled and cringed at my words. "They knew what I meant!" I yelled.

I stood at the edge of the room, leaning up against the door jamb, feeling weak. *How the hell did this get misconstrued?* What an awful thing to imply. Then I heard my answer. "*LOUISE* told me you told John and Mary that we sleep together."

Louise. She hadn't said the word "sleep" either. I could tell in the way Dad said the word. He might as well have said the other word, but he couldn't even bring himself to say it—just like I couldn't even bring myself to comprehend *why* she would say such a destructive thing.

Louise Kaufman died three months later. I never saw her again after she had planted that horrible seed. I'm glad I didn't see her ever again, because all the strength, restraint, and self-discipline I had always used to behave appropriately when I was around her would not have been enough for the confrontation from me.

She had inflicted her last wound. She hated my relationship with my father so much that she had to put an evil twist on something innocent—just like when I was a kid sitting on his lap. She had tried to break our bond by demeaning what was normal behavior in a child, insinuating that it was something inappropriate.

I represented everything she hated. I had lived my life by a standard she could not fault. Every time she tried to turn my dad against me there was no truth to substantiate any of her accusations. She was always trying to split up my father and me. It had probably put her over the edge that I had not invited her to my graduation and my beautiful mother was there instead. It probably twisted her gut even more to know that she was denied the graduation trip that followed. Another woman, just like the three wives before her, had come between her and Ted Williams, *my dad*. She was rejected once again, and the only way she could think of to taint my relationship with my father was to suggest something inappropriate and terribly humiliating. She had stooped so low to try to get at me.

"Dad . . . I never, *ever* would even think of saying anything like that."

"I know. I couldn't fuckin' believe it."

And with that he sat up and picked up the phone.

I thought, *Good, give HER hell. PLEASE.* But instead, he called John and Mary and set the record straight. He hated that he even had to explain it. I stood and watched him defend me and explain that Louise didn't know what the hell she was talking about, but that surely she didn't mean to imply anything wrong. He gripped the phone like he wanted to choke it every time he mentioned her name. The conversation didn't last long.

After he hung up, he picked up the phone again. *Now he's going to dial the hag*, I thought. *Now she's gonna get it.* Instead, he slammed the phone down and went back to bed. He was exhausted. I never heard what happened when Dad next spoke to Louise, but I know he didn't mention her name once or even call her during our entire trip.

But the damage was done. I could never snuggle with my father again. Bedrooms became a dirty place, and when Dad was lying down he was unapproachable. I wasn't a little girl anymore, and I never again felt the same affectionate comfort around my dad as I once had.

It was years later that my brother and I discovered perhaps why Louise had gone to such lengths to destroy the bond between father and daughter. According to a source close to the family, a female acquaintance had once called Dad to confide that her children had been sexually molested. When Dad found out, he was furious. She wanted money, she needed help, she told Dad. Dad sent money—a lot of money—and tried to help her and the children. But then she backtracked, waffled on the story, and said she wasn't even sure if it was true. Knowing this woman's history of lying, it's possible she was making the whole thing up, especially since nothing more ever came of it. Regardless, when Dad found out about this, he never wanted to see this woman or hear about her troubles again. He'd lost all respect for her and even the possibility of sexual abuse was enough for him to sever all ties with her.

When Louise couldn't break the bond between my father and me, she decided to poison our relationship by suggesting something lewd and inappropriate. She had seen how effectively it destroyed the connection between Dad and this other woman. Now, she had a way to destroy another female who stood between her and Ted Williams . . . me.

That night I was furious. I was so mad, I couldn't stop crying. I buried my head in the pillow in my room and just bawled. Then I screamed and pounded my fist. I hated her. I hated what she had done on such a special day.

When John-Henry came home, he found me in my room.

"What's wrong? What the hell happened?"

I just started wailing again.

"Claudia!" He grabbed me by the shoulders and shook me. "What's the matter?"

I couldn't even talk. I just stood there crying.

"Claudia . . ."

"Louise told Daddy that I told John and Mary that we sleep together," I blurted and choked.

"What? Oh, Jesus. She's a bitch," John-Henry grumbled.

"I hate her!" I said blubbering.

John-Henry sat down on the edge of the bed, and I told him the whole story. He just sat there and shook his head in disbelief. He ended up staying with me in my room, trying to make me feel better, trying to make me smile, trying to make me laugh at the situation. There was no graduation celebration, and the food and drink just sat in the refrigerator. We were leaving for my graduation trip the next day, and John-Henry was trying to make the best of the upcoming family voyage.

My graduation trip started the following day. As it turned out, asking my father for that trip was one of the best decisions of my life. Time was what I really wanted—more than anything I wanted time together to see if we could all get along. I wanted to feel part of their team. I wanted it to just be the three of us. Just us. It was more important to me than money, a car, a piece of jewelry, anything—just time together. For the first time it seemed, we were all adults, and it was fantastic because we were able to be ourselves and bond as friends. Even today I visit those memories often and smile at the good time we had. Looking back on it, it feels like we laughed the whole time.

The route was a simple one: fly to San Diego to see where Dad grew up, fly to San Francisco from there, and then drive north to Oregon to visit Bobby Doerr at his cabin on the Rogue River. He was a great friend of Dad's from when they both joined the San Diego Padres in 1936 and then on through their many years together with the Red Sox.

We flew into San Diego and were greeted by Bob Breitbard, a friend of Dad's since they were classmates at Hoover High. Mr. Breitbard took us straight to his museum, the San Diego Hall of Champions, where Dad was featured with personal memorabilia loaned by our family.

That was all very interesting, but I was more anxious to see where my father grew up. I wanted to see the ballpark where my dad played as a teenager. I wanted to see the path he took from high school to his house and to the field. I wanted to see the little house where he lived.

Dad was the tour guide. He explained how he loved the weather in San Diego, how every day he walked about two miles from his high school to the park, and how he would always meet a couple of kids there and play ball. I was surprised to see how run-down the area was, but Dad assured me that at the time it was much nicer. The park was just like any other park, simple, with a faded sign reading: TED WILLIAMS FIELD. The park was a quick drive-by, because we had to go to dinner with Mr. Breitbard and some of his friends.

When we got to San Francisco, our first stop was Pier 39, where we took a ferry to Alcatraz Island. For the first time I saw my dad put on headphones. He used the rental Sony Walkman, which gave an audio tour of the facility, so that as we walked we could listen to the history of the prison and its infamous criminals. Though Dad loved history, he was a seventy-five-year-old trying to use modern technology, and the tour ended up being inadvertently memorable and hilarious. Dad kept being frustrated by the challenge of rewinding the Walkman to replay the story just told. It didn't matter that he just heard it, he wanted to hear it again. He was such a kid at heart, with all the enthusiasm in the world, and wanted to share all his thoughts with us as the tour was happening, but John-Henry and I had our own headphones. Dad would yell above his headphone volume to get our attention, then beg for some assistance to make the "goddamned thing replay" to a section that he'd just heard. People were staring and laughing at the three of us. We were all laughing at the comedy of errors too. We repeated one section of the tour at least three times, and every time Dad's reaction was the same. He couldn't believe what he was hearing.

We ended up so far off the intended pace of the tour that we missed seeing the Mess Hall because Dad wanted to play and replay everything on the tape about Al Capone. If we had followed the pace of the tapes, we'd have been at station 16. If we'd followed Dad's pace, we'd still have been at station 4. As it was, we found ourselves stuck at station 12, listening about station 16, and hearing Dad still talking about station 4. About this time, everyone else was reboarding the ferry. Still, it was so funny to see Dad enjoy something so much.

When we got back to shore, we looked for a place to eat. As we walked along the pier, I spotted a young gypsy-looking fortuneteller. He would read your palm for $5. John-Henry and I decided that Dad should have his palm read. Dad agreed, but insisted that we not let on at all about his identity. I have no idea whether or not this young man knew whose palm he was reading, but in less than five minutes he had described Dad to a tee (mentioning his stubbornness, his success, his long life, and the loss of a sibling at a young age) and stated that one day something he had discovered would be patented. Although I know of nothing that my father patented, we explained that part of the reading as pertaining to his work and study of the science of hitting, which, in effect, he patented.

From there, we went to lunch at Fisherman's Wharf. John-Henry and Dad ordered crab legs, and I had the shrimp. While we were waiting for our food, John-Henry leaned in and said dramatically, "I want to ask you both a very serious question." He had both our attentions. "If you had one wish, what would you wish for?"

I was quick to answer with, "I would wish for world peace."

John-Henry and Dad both laughed. Dad said, "That's very sweet, honey, but that's naive. War can be good for the economy."

John-Henry added, "Yeah, that's just what the beauty pageant girls all say."

"Well, what would you wish for?" I asked John-Henry.

"Hold on. I want to hear what Dad would wish for first," he said.

Dad said, "Eh, I don't know." We pounced, insisting that he answer the question too. Finally Dad said, "I would wish for a steel vault room, twelve by twelve by twelve, stacked from floor to ceiling with $100 bills."

John-Henry and I looked at each other, puzzled by the unique response.

"Why not just wish for a billion dollars?" John-Henry asked.

Dad replied seriously, "I'd have to pay taxes on that."

I responded, "You can't buy world peace."

We all laughed. Then I asked John-Henry, "Well, how about you?"

John-Henry took a sip of water, prolonging the dramatic pause and increasing our anticipation, and then, smiling at both of us, he said, "I would wish for three more wishes."

Dad laughed. "That's pretty damned good."

"I wish I had thought of that," I said.

THE NEXT MORNING WE HAD ROOM SERVICE BREAKFAST AND then took off in our rental vehicle toward Highway 101. John-Henry had the foresight to record many of our conversations as we drove north along California's Highway 1 to Highway 101. We all had our cameras. There's one picture in our scrapbook in which I am taking a picture of Dad, who is taking a picture of John-Henry. The most memorable thing about this trip was the simple good time my brother and I had being alone with our father, all the conversations and laughing.

One of our conversations as we drove along the highway was about baseball. John-Henry was always quizzing Dad on something about hitting. Sitting in the backseat, I wondered if Dad was ever challenged. Finally, I chimed in and asked, "Dad, did you ever strike out every time you came to the plate in one game?"

John-Henry looked at me as if I was a silly girl. Of course that never happened to Dad.

"I sure did," he replied. "It was this little guy, Jim Bunning. He had a quirky little loopy slider that I could not figure out."

"*What?*" John-Henry cried. "I never heard about this." He smiled at me and put the recorder a little closer to Dad.

Dad remembered what year it was, what game it was, what the weather was like, how he was feeling, and what the score was. He was unbelievable.

"Did you ever face him again?" I asked.

"I sure did. I couldn't wait to face him again. I ended up hitting more home runs off of him than any other pitcher!"

"So you figured him out?" I asked.

"You bet your ass I figured him out."

John-Henry added a side comment on the tape, "Research Jim Bunning."

As it turned out, Dad was so incredibly mad at himself the day Bunning struck him out three times—May 16, 1957—that he popped all the buttons of his uniform ripping it off after the game. When he next faced Bunning in July, he hit two home runs off him. Their epic duel would continue over six seasons. Dad did in fact hit more home runs off Bunning than any other pitcher—but Bunning also struck Dad out more often than any other pitcher did.

We made a couple of stops along the way, but never without a struggle. It seemed like we had to get to our destination no matter what. John-Henry and I joked that Dad had to make it to Oregon in world-record time. He seemed to be on a mission. We discovered that The Kid did not like to drive after 5:00 P.M.

"You never want to be on the road after 5:00 P.M. There is nothing but traffic and people going to get drunk. It's a pain in the ass— get the hell off road and get to bed so that you can get up at 4:00 A.M. and start driving when no one is on the road. It's a helluva lot safer too!"

We whizzed by the largest redwood tree known to exist. You can evidently drive a car through it, but *nope, we can't stop*, because we had to get to Oregon to see Bobby Doerr. Dad described the "Avenue of the Giants" to us as we flew past it, but *we don't have time to stop*. I wanted to see the redwood tree house, but *nope, we've got to keep going*. The truth is, we were not on a schedule at all, but it sure felt like we were, and we were late. We all laughed until our sides hurt. Dad kept asking what was so funny when he knew good and well. We all knew this was set to be an enjoyable family trip, but patience is not a Williams trait. These were the best moments, the ones shared by us as a family in the car.

"Hey, let's stop and look at the Paul Bunyan statue and the blue ox!" I exclaimed as I saw some signs for it. Same thing for the "Trees of Mystery" in Klamath, California. *Nope, we have to keep going.* It ended up being so funny. All these tourist attractions and we didn't stop. I took drive-by photos that all came out blurry. It became a running joke as we just kept driving.

We didn't stop until we got to Oregon. Dad must have realized we were way ahead of the "schedule" and decided we could take a quick break. I saw signs for a sea lion cave and insisted we stop there. It was absolutely beautiful. We had to walk down near the rocky shore to see the cave. Dad struggled to keep up. When my brother looked back on that moment, he wished that he'd seen that Dad was beginning to show signs of heart failure. If he'd realized sooner that something was wrong, Dad would have had a better chance of recovering from heart surgery, since he'd have been seventy-five instead of eighty-two.

As we worked our way down the steep path we teased Dad about keeping up.

"Jeeaasuus Christ," he said jokingly and now ironically, "this isn't a race. Let's take it easy . . . rest a little and try and enjoy our family trip."

"You're out of shape, Dad," my brother teased. "As soon as we get back you're starting an exercise program."

"Oh jeez . . ." Dad smiled.

We smelled the cave before we even saw a sea lion. It set you back how much it smelled—a combination of a dead fish smell and the pungent ammonia of sea lion scat. As we approached the mouth of the cave our breathless father sarcastically said, "Yeah, *this was reeeaalllly worth stopping for.* All right, let's turn around and head back."

"Dad, we haven't even *seen* a sea lion yet."

When we walked into the cave, there were dozens and dozens of sea lions sprawled out on the rocks. My brother and I walked right up to the opening. Our father kept saying, "Jesus Christ, don't get too close! Allll rriiigghht! That's enough! Let's go."

My brother and I loved animals, and this was up close and personal. There was one sea lion about twenty feet away from us, and we clicked away on our camera. Our father refused to enter the cave.

"Jeez, it stinks. Can't you smell that?" Dad asked, amused that we were still in the cave. "What's the matter with you guys?"

Finally, we turned around and trotted out of the cave. There was hardly anyone there because, of course, we were up at the break of dawn to make it to our destination. By the time we worked our way back up to the top of the cliff, Dad was exhausted. We stopped at one midway point, and he said, "Let's take a break, get some fresh air, and talk about where we want to get some ice cream."

When we were back in the car, John-Henry took over the driving for a while. We laughed for miles at how Dad didn't like the stench. He was sure there was something wrong with our sense of smell.

We drove up the coast to the mouth of the Rogue River in Oregon, then took a boat tour upriver deep into the Rogue River Siskiyou National Forest, where Bobby Doerr had a fishing camp in the tiny, remote community of Illahe. Like Dad, Bobby had started out a city boy, growing up in Los Angeles. He first visited Illahe as a young second baseman for the Padres in the mid-1930s. He'd been an avid fly fisherman and lover of nature ever since. A very nice man. He and Dad had been very good friends a long time, and it showed. They were quite different from each other. Bobby was quiet, soft-spoken, and calm; he rarely swore, and then only with an occasional "damn" or "Christ"—nothing like Dad's blue streaks. He was also quite a memorabilia collector and had a lot of items associated with Dad, some of which he gave to John-Henry as gifts.

This trip was a milestone in our relationship with our father. We had been together for a week, and for the first time he hadn't blown up. It was clear now that we finally knew how to navigate around him. We could sense the onset of an outburst before he erupted and head it off with a joke or a distraction. I think the key is that we were finally all around the same emotional age.

It's no wonder that Ted Williams was called The Kid—the lasting nickname he earned in 1938, at the age of nineteen. Dad always said it was his favorite, and it certainly suited him. Even at seventy-five, my father was a big kid. They say the day an addict picks up his first substance is the day his emotional maturity stops. When I look back on that trip, I can't help but wonder whether we all got along so well because emotionally we were now all about the same age. Dad broke into the major leagues at eighteen. He was very cocky and confident in his ability because, frankly, he was that good. The drug of the crowd's affection and admiration was all it took to hook Dad—he was addicted to the emotional response he felt and needed. However, the team saw his immaturity as something that needed to be curbed and sent him back down to the minors to try and humble him a bit. I don't think it worked, because to this day I would describe my dad as a big kid, with lots of enthusiasm and bad temper tantrums. He always loved hanging out with a younger crowd, cracking jokes and being a bit of a goofball.

John-Henry and I were in our early twenties, and Dad was still nineteen. We had reached a state of equilibrium. Never once on that trip did he act like a father. We were buddies. It was the start of our Three Musketeers phase.

AFTER THAT TRIP I FLEW RIGHT BACK TO EUROPE, TO SWITZER-land, where I had arranged an apprenticeship with a master ceramist to get the final two credits for my BA. I was in La Chaux-de-Fonds, in the French-speaking section of Switzerland. I fell in love with the place and ended up staying about a year. I also traveled all over Switzerland, running a food concession booth for a circus. It was a small circus, just a little of everything that you would imagine in a circus. The circus people were Gypsies, very poorly educated, with poor hygiene, bad teeth, and plenty of drugs and alcohol, but they were very nice people. They were kind to the few animals they had and made most of their money selling their crafts. I cooked hamburgers and hot dogs, which the Europeans found humorous when they heard my American accent.

I don't think Dad worried about me a bit. I had survived in France without any problems. He liked that I was doing my own thing and getting an education. While I was in Europe, John-Henry and Dad remained two peas in a pod, doing everything together they wanted to do—going to Belize, going to Mexico, fishing, flying in fighter jets and on Air Force One, and, of course, going to ball games.

Mom thought it was fabulous that I was living again in Europe. She and I had already come to a crossroads. We knew we needed time apart, so her attitude was "okay, go do your thing."

While I was in Switzerland, I decided I wanted to go to Germany and learn German. I went to an au-pair agency and said I wanted to find a family I could live with while learning German. A week or two later I went to Bavaria, moved in with a family, and was their nanny for a year. The young mother next door and I became good friends. She loved the way I was with kids, so she hired me for the next year. All told, I was in Switzerland for one year and Germany for three.

Every Sunday, though, I spoke to my father. It was a routine we developed, and in between I wrote him letters.

"How you liking the Fatherland?" he would tease when he called. "Have you met any Krauts?"

My father was always curious about my dating status. I got a kick out of it. I think he was worried that it was going to be difficult for me to finally feel secure enough in a relationship and not be so determined to be independent. He saw how I tried to impress him by being like this, but he also knew he'd played a big part in my being so headstrong. I also think he wanted to feel like I was still his little girl, even though he hadn't been the best daddy.

Chapter Seventeen

I MET MY HALF-SISTER ONLY FOUR TIMES. SHE WAS TWENTY-three years older than me. She died of end-stage liver disease on July 28, 2010, in a small town in Tennessee. By chance, someone saw the news of her death online and told me. Otherwise, I don't think I would have ever known.

The first time I met Bobby-Jo was at Louise's funeral in August 1993; at that point, my father had not spoken to her in over a year. She had written him a letter in May 1993 that was manipulative. She played on his emotions, which was the worst way to address Dad, as it frustrated him and escalated his anger. She wrote that she needed more money because her car was old and in disrepair. She was tired of picking up her daughter from work or school "in the middle of the night," and it was dangerous driving in the rain. She added that she was having some financial difficulties as well as marital problems. She insisted that he take money from her trust, saying she had the right to help her kids. She had already told him that her daughter wanted to go to pharmacy school, but they could not afford it. Dad was sending monthly checks to pay for books and tuition. It would turn out to be a lie—the money was being used for other purposes. When Dad eventually found out she had lied to him, the whole thing angered him so much that he wouldn't even take her phone call.

I came back from Europe for Louise's funeral to be there for my father. John-Henry called me in Switzerland and told me I had better come home quickly. Louise had died of a complicated bowel obstruction. She needed emergency surgery, but the bowel was infected and she died of sepsis. Dad was hurting and my brother was worried about him.

"Claudia, you better come home. Dad needs *you.*"

I was on the next plane.

I saw Bobby-Jo before I actually met her. I knew it was Bobby-Jo by the way she and I both reacted, simultaneously, when we heard our father's loud voice in the other room. In a room filled with people, two reacted the same way. Even from across the room, there was enough resemblance to make me certain it was her. I walked right up to her.

"You must be Bobby-Jo."

She looked at me and said, "Claudia?"

"You look just like Dad," I said, smiling.

She quickly responded that she actually looked more like her mother. She was tall and thin with very short hair. Dad hated long hair. You could tell by her voice, her complexion, and those certain wrinkles that she smoked. Dad hated smoking. On the front door to his house is bolted, not a knocker, but a solid brass sign that says NO SMOKING. Bobby-Jo held a drink of some sort, maybe wine, but I knew it was alcohol by the smell of her breath. I was soaking her in. I was comparing myself to her from head to toe. Finally, I had met the infamous daughter who seemed to drive Dad mad every time her name was mentioned.

"It's so *wonderful* to meet you."

She was baring her teeth in a peculiar smile.

From that moment on, I could feel the rivalry, but I wasn't

going to let that dissuade me from my ultimate goal. I wanted to understand this woman. I wanted to get to know her and observe her every behavior. How could my father produce something he so despised? What had she done so wrong that could not be rectified? Why couldn't they get along?

As Dad walked toward us I could feel the tension rising. Her back stiffened, and she swallowed hard. I wondered if he'd known she was going to be there or if she just showed up. Either way, Dad barely looked at her.

"Hi, Daddy," said the forty-five-year-old in a child's voice.

"Christ, are you still smoking?"

"I'm down to only one pack a day."

"Jesus . . ."

Dad did not have the patience to continue the conversation and kept walking. He was working his way through the crowd of people to view Louise in her coffin. I walked closely alongside him as we headed toward the casket. It was the second time in my life that I had seen a dead body. I was fourteen when I found my grandfather. He was lying in his bed with his hands interlaced across his chest. I knew the moment I saw him that he was dead, but I remember looking at him and wishing he was maybe just sleeping. He looked so peaceful, and I wasn't ready to lose my grandfather.

"She looks great, doesn't she?" He reached out to hold her stiff pale hand.

She looked awful, but I didn't have the heart to tell him.

"She looks good."

We stood there for a while in silence. For the first time in my life I was alone with my father in a room full of people. No one swarmed around the great Ted Williams as he stood by his dead longtime companion. I was afraid to look at him. I was afraid to see him hurt. I didn't want to see the Beast weak. I wanted to hold his hand, but I had never done that before, so I just stood there looking at Louise. There were some of Dad's fishing flies on her dress that she had made into pins, and I thought it was a touching gesture that she was going to be buried with Dad's flies. I had never seen her fish with my father, but evidently she had in the past. Fishing, Canada, being in the basement tying flies, and listening to the ball game on the radio brought out the best in this man.

I heard my father take a deep, staggered breath, and when he exhaled, I gently leaned against him and tilted my head up on his shoulder.

"I love you, Dad."

"You are the most important woman in my life now. I need you."

"I'm right here, Dad."

With that, he turned and walked away, leaving me standing in front of the woman who had done so many manipulative, mean, and conniving things to me. I stood there looking at her, wondering how my dad could have loved such a cruel woman. More than that, though, I worried for my father. He was sad, and I hated that his life would no longer include the familiarity of a longtime companion. His pain was real, and I mourned my father's loss and whatever Louise had given to him.

Then a voice whispered in my ear.

"She hated you, you know."

Bobby-Jo was standing next to me, looking right at me.

"She never had a nice thing to say about you."

I didn't know what to say. I just thought how odd it was that she was telling me this. I had heard horrible things about Bobby-Jo herself, but that didn't feel like the right moment to share them.

"We definitely had our differences," I said. "I feel badly for Dad, though. She served a purpose for him, for sure. She stuck around longer than either of *our* moms did." Louise might have treated me terribly, but I could not ignore what she had meant to my father.

"Oh *please.* She drove him to drink. She was always pushing the drinks on Daddy so he'd be nice and not yell at her."

She was right. My mother didn't drink, and she described Dad as very seldom having a drink other than maybe a beer after a long day out fishing. Louise was always bringing him Southern Comfort with ice. And it was true that Dad was a lot more affectionate and subdued with a drink or two. He usually got very tired, though, and the moment did not last long. He would fall asleep in front of the television, and when Louise shut it off, he would get up and quietly, almost obediently, go to bed.

"You and your brother drove her crazy."

"I thought *you guys* didn't get along," I said, a bit defensively.

"Oh, we were close. She was always around and helped raise me."

"Oh . . . I didn't know that."

Somebody was lying. Louise hated Bobby-Jo. She had nothing nice to say about her, and neither did Dad. This was going to be an interesting weekend, and I hadn't even met her husband or my nieces yet.

There is something about funerals that brings out the worst and best in people. I think it's the reality of death slapping us in the face. We are all going to die. Dad hated funerals. He arranged for only a simple graveside service in Santa Barbara, California, for his mother, and I never heard him speak of his dad's death or mention whether he even knew when he died. He was very uncomfortable around grief. He used to say, "When I die, just play some good jazz music and be done with it."

At Louise's funeral, after the viewing, there was a service. These were tough moments in and of themselves for Dad. However, John-Henry and I were more concerned about the burial. We knew the lowering of the casket containing his longtime companion was going to be the most difficult part for our father, and it was. For the first time my brother and I witnessed our father weeping in grief. He grieved harder than I had ever seen. I grieved too. I grieved for my father's impending loneliness; I grieved for the loss of my father's longtime companion. We would have done anything to take away his pain, and it was difficult to see him so sad. We decided we would stand on each side of him and not leave him alone. That was the plan.

It was a hot South Carolina day, and the cemetery looked huge. Our plan didn't go as we had hoped. Louise's daughter, Barbara Kovacs, sat next to Dad, leaving only one other seat. Luckily, John-Henry got to it in time. Dad struggled to contain his grief and cried into his handkerchief, blowing his nose loudly. We worried for him.

After the burial, we all piled back into vehicles to go to Barbara's house to eat. Dad, John-Henry, Barbara, and I all got into the car. Right as we were going to close the door, here came Bobby-Jo, putting out a cigarette.

"Ah Christ . . ." Dad muttered, mostly under his breath.

She squeezed in as well, her last exhale lingering in the air.

Dad was annoyed and his jaw was clenched.

"How are you doing, Daddy?" she asked, as if speaking to a child.

I was sitting across from my father and brother. John-Henry and I looked at each other. *Oh my God,* I thought as I looked at my brother. *Really? That's how you talk to Dad? Eeek.*

Dad didn't say anything, and the hot August day in a packed car just got hotter. I was sweating everywhere. The air conditioner was not up to par for the conditions in this backseat.

Barbara was sitting on the other side of Dad. She put her hand on his knee and said, "Lootie is going to be missed, isn't she?"

Dad looked very uncomfortable.

"She is in a better place now. God will take care of her," cooed Barbara.

Dad's jaw muscles were dancing. If anything, Dad was angry that the supreme being had taken Louise. My brother and I were just waiting for the time bomb to go off.

In a very stern voice, Dad said, "Well, we're gonna have to leave early tomorrow morning."

Dad was now getting irritated.

"Oh no . . . you just have to stay a while at the house," Barbara said, patting his knee. "We're all going to go have something to eat, and I'm sure a lot of people want to give their condolences."

Dad cut her off. "Well, that's real nice of you, but we've got to go back home."

I caught my brother stifling a smile as he looked out the window. We were leaving this joint as soon as possible.

Finally, we got to the house and climbed out of the car. Bobby-Jo lit a cigarette right up, and Dad walked away from the car and the house. Hordes of people were pulling up in their vehicles and piling out. My brother and I caught up to Dad and stood by his side.

"I feel like a goddamned milk shake—chocolate."

"That would be freakin' awesome," said my brother.

"Me too," I chimed in.

"I wish I could get the hell out of here," Dad said, looking at the two of us.

John-Henry, slightly taller than Dad, put his hand on Dad's shoulder and said, "Just say the word, Dad, and we are outta here."

"Ah Christ, I better go in and say good-bye to everyone."

"Whatever we've got to do, Dad. Let's get it done."

We were a team. I was proud of my brother. He could make just about anything seem manageable.

No sooner had we walked into the house than Barbara brought Dad a drink of something.

Oh *great.* . . .

Then, people I didn't even know started coming out of the woodwork to give their condolences—with stuff in their hands for Dad to sign. I could *not* believe my eyes. I could see Dad trying to ignore that this was happening, but it was impossible.

John-Henry stepped in and cloaked his father.

"Let's go sit out back, Dad, and get something to eat."

Dad followed his son out to the backyard and found a chair. As they were uncovering the food, I gathered a plate for my father and brought it back to him. I had to work my way through a roomful of strangers, at a funeral reception, who were lining up asking my father for an autograph. It was as if they knew this was the last time they were ever going to get to ride the coattails of a relationship to get an autograph from Ted Williams.

John-Henry was trying to deflect as many people as he could, trying to give them the eye, as if to say, *Come on . . . leave the poor guy alone.* It was futile, though.

"Ted, I'm a huge fan, so sorry about your loss, would you mind signing this for my kid?"

Dad was done, and John-Henry was overrun. Just as Barbara was coming back, I slithered into her seat next to my father.

"Hey, sweetie, are you getting something to eat?" asked my father.

"Yup," I lied. The macaroni salad was lousy, and the hot weather had made everything lukewarm, with flies visiting left and right.

"You ready to leave soon?" he asked.

"I'm ready."

"Here, Teddy Ballgame, have another drink." Someone was handing him another beverage. I wanted to jump up and knock it out of their hands.

Like a pack of wolves, people kept moving in. Then a pretty blonde walked up to my brother, and a sly smile crept across his face. Clearly something had gone down between these two. It was Barbara's daughter, Elizabeth. She was laughing and talking with my brother about something that seemed to be incredibly interesting and funny. John-Henry's attention was diverted while I was in the middle of a feeding frenzy. Like father like son. Women were John-Henry's kryptonite. Women dripped over him. He was so handsome, and as women did with Dad, they would embarrass themselves around him. Elizabeth had gotten his attention, and she wasn't giving it up anytime soon.

Meanwhile, I kept looking for the exit. I glared at my brother and gave him a dirty look.

"*Come ON,*" I mouthed to him in frustration. *Dad needs to get the hell out of here.*

John-Henry got the message and came to the rescue. My charming brother sidled away from his female interest and said as he approached, "We're going to leave for now and we'll see you tomorrow."

Finally. "Dad, let's go."

Dad was up and ready, walking toward the back door.

"Ted!" Barbara yelled after him. "We want to say a prayer for Lou-Lou before you leave."

Compliant and respectful, Dad turned, dropped his chin to his chest, and stood still as Barbara asked everyone to join hands.

As the amen found our lips, Bobby-Jo and her two daughters found me. Another detour.

"So," I said jokingly, "I have two nieces! You know I'm your aunt—right?"

Dawn and Sherri were both pretty women. Sherri said she wanted to study pharmacology, and I thought, *Wow, looks and brains. That's so good.* Dawn was the older daughter and seemed friendly and down to earth. *My dad is a grandfather, and his grandchildren are older than I am.*

Just as I was about to turn and go, an older, balding man walked up to us and put his hand on the small of Sherri's back. "This is our stepdad Mark," Dawn said flatly. I didn't feel the love . . . at all. It was Bobby-Jo's husband. Another detour.

Finally, after more autographs to strangers, and further light, superficial talk, we left.

"Let's go to a hamburger joint and get a juicy cheeseburger and a milk shake," Dad said as we climbed into our getaway vehicle. And that's exactly what we did. We ate burgers and shakes on the way back to our hotel, and it was great. We camped out in Dad's room for the rest of the evening, sucking on our extremely thick chocolate milk shakes, watching TV, and finding stuff to laugh about. My brother and I did our very best to keep our dad distracted until he was tired enough to fall asleep.

Our father kept saying how happy he was to have us there. We were both glad to be there for him. We would have done anything to keep our dad happy.

BOBBY-JO AND I MUST HAVE EXCHANGED NUMBERS, BECAUSE I started getting calls from her. At first I welcomed them, because I remained curious about this woman and wanted to hear from her and find out what she thought of our father. Our conversations consisted of comparing notes on Dad and discussing how and why he was the way he was. Our theories were actually very similar. She and I agreed that his deep resentment toward women had to stem from his mother having dedicated so much of her time to the Salvation Army and not to her two boys.

Between the lines I heard a lot of deep-seated resentment and defensiveness from Bobby-Jo, but I also heard a lot of pain. I felt badly for her, and I could relate. She blamed Louise for a lot of her problems with our father and said Louise was always trying to get Dad to believe the worst of her. At times I found myself very guarded speaking to her, but when she talked about Louise there was a lot on which I concurred.

As our comfort level increased, she started calling more frequently and later at night. Each time her speech was more slurred than the last. A clearer picture started to emerge, and I tried just to listen. She was very jealous of John-Henry and envious of his relationship with Dad. She put herself and me in the same boat, and I felt an attempt to split the bond I had developed with my brother and father. To justify her life and her actions, she cast herself as a victim of circumstance who grew up during an even harder time than I did because it was when *her daddy* was at the height of his career.

I actually had sympathy for her. It must have been a lot more difficult growing up with a forty-five-year-old Ted Williams than a seventy-year-old Ted Williams. Bobby-Jo grew up during that part of Dad's career when he was feeling the pressures of getting older and his skills were waning. So he was even less patient and tolerant than the dad I knew. Also, he was away all the time playing baseball, fishing, or serving in Korea. Meanwhile, her mom was struggling with addiction. Unfortunately, without the proper guidance Bobby-Jo seemed not to have passed the test; she never forced her father to treat her with respect and dignity.

As I listened to her she sounded like a scared little girl, unable to evolve into a woman. There is no doubt she had it rough, and surely there were things out of her control. I think the big difference between me and Bobby-Jo is our moms. Dolores Williams put her children first, unlike Dad's mom and unlike Bobby-Jo's mom. My mom made sure I worked through my emotional issues with healthy coping mechanisms and sound rational thinking. I was always reminded to strive to be the person I wanted to be. If I couldn't do anything about something, then it was up to me either to leave it or adapt to it.

Bobby-Jo had no one to turn to except Louise when her parents divorced. But she believed that Louise wanted Ted Williams all to herself and was only trying to sabotage Bobby-Jo's relationship with her father. I'm certain Bobby-Jo believed everything she said and was able to rationalize everything she *presumed* I knew about her. She defended things about herself I'd had no idea about. I just listened.

After I received a call from her at three in the morning, I decided I needed to terminate these conversations. I was getting frustrated listening to her as she complained but never came up with alternatives to make anything better. She was a grown woman, forty-five years old. I didn't feel there was anything I could do to help her. She had made her bed a very long time ago, albeit in difficult circumstances. However, she did not conquer the adversities of her relationship with her father. She never spoke about how she was going to right her ship or try to reconnect with her father. She only blamed and complained. I tried to encourage her to continue trying, but it seemed to me she didn't even want to try.

I can only imagine what my father would have said to her if he'd known she called me in the dead of night. When I told him that I was talking to her occasionally, he was surprised and seemed a little pleased.

"Oh yeah? Is that right? What do you guys talk about?"

"You." I smiled.

"Oh boy. . . . Well, maybe you can help her out a little. See if you can straighten her out."

I couldn't straighten her out. I knew that and Dad did too. He was exasperated by this point and didn't want to be bothered anymore. Bobby-Jo was a reminder of his past, including mistakes he'd made that he now could do nothing about. He preferred not to revisit that tumultuous time in his life but instead keep moving forward.

"It's been interesting talking to her, but we're very different," I told him as we sat in his kitchen. "I'm glad Mom was strong and strict like she was. I think that made a big difference in my life."

"That's for damn sure! Your mother was tough as nails and didn't let you kids get away with anything. Dolores is a damn good mother. Bobby-Jo's mother was a drunk."

With that, he gripped the edge of the table like he wanted to crush it, then stood up and walked out of the kitchen, growling, "Christ Jesus and the twelve disciples know I fuckin' tried. Damn it!"

Chapter Eighteen

Not surprisingly, Louise's death did not moderate my father's skepticism and ongoing doubts about God. As his own mortality became more apparent, that did little to change his mind either.

In February 1994, John-Henry called to tell me some very upsetting news: Dad had suffered a stroke. It actually was not his first; he'd had a small one in December 1991, a month after the Medal of Freedom ceremony. At the time Louise had failed to inform John-Henry because she didn't want him coming down to Florida and taking care of his father. When he found out after the fact, he was infuriated, but thankfully there had been no damage or lasting effects from that stroke.

However, the stroke in 1994 was a big one. Even though it was eight months after our California trip and Louise's death, John-Henry felt responsible. "I need to take care of Dad. He needs to eat healthier and start getting better care. I should have seen this coming."

While Dad was recovering in the hospital, John-Henry removed every bit of alcohol in the house. He did buy some nonalcoholic beer called O'Doul's because he knew Dad loved to mix lemonade and beer together. It is an old fisherman's drink that he used to enjoy. We never heard Dad complain about there not being any booze in the house. Dad's drinking days were over.

I came straight to Citrus Hills, Florida, where he was living by then, and went right to the rehab center. Dad was brave and confident he would recover. The stroke was on the right side of his brain, so it affected the left side of his body. To bring back the motor skills in his left hand, they had him pulling small pegs from putty. There had been significant loss of sight, leaving him with tunnel vision in both eyes, the left being the worst. They had him doing exercises turning his head to the left to see what was on that side, because what you see tricks your brain into believing that's all there is. From then on, when we put a plate of food in front of him he'd see and eat only what was on the right side. When we turned the plate so he could see the other half of his meal, he'd say, "I didn't ask for more food!"

From then on, he often didn't see when someone reached out to shake his hand. When you stick out your right hand to shake the hand of a person in front of you, your hand crosses that person's left field of vision; with his impaired vision on that side, Dad wouldn't see the extended hand. Unfortunately, some fans who met him after his second stroke complained that he'd become a cranky old man—"He wouldn't even shake my hand!" But the truth was that he just didn't *see* it.

I stayed a week or two, until he went back home and got settled in. When I wrote him from Europe, I always made a line with a purple marker down the left side of the page and told him to look for it every time he got to the end of a line of my writing. Otherwise, he'd only see the right side of what I'd written and it wouldn't make any sense.

When Dad was in therapy after the stroke, he met a young patient named Tricia who had suffered a brain aneurysm that left her physically disabled. They took a liking to each other right away. She had no idea who this older man was. Dad instantly wanted to help her, motivate her, somehow make her better, and every day, on his way back from therapy, he would give God a verbal thrashing. How could God let a young girl like Tricia go through what she would have to endure for the rest of her life? The almighty God had done a piss-poor job in Dad's opinion. He would look up to the sky and curse God vehemently. Once, I remember him cursing God and Jesus so badly that I wished for Dad's sake that God really didn't exist because, if He did, He would surely punish Dad for what he was saying.

"You syphilitic son of a bitch with a clapped-up whore of a mother—go to hell!"

Most people could never say that line and have it come out as heartfelt as Dad delivered it. Every bit of rage and confusion over God came out in each and every word and syllable. He wanted to challenge God to a duel and demand answers to the injustices He allowed in the world. "You're a damn fraud! Strike me down if you can, you son of a bitch!" My father could see no justification for a God who allowed innocents to suffer so unfairly.

Simply put, Dad was angry with God. He was compelled to not believe because of his life's experiences and circumstances. My father was a very logical man, determined to think for himself and accept the consequences of each and every one of his actions. As far as Dad was concerned, science could not prove that God exists. You had to have faith, and you had to choose to believe in order to have faith. Dad was quoted as saying, "I can't believe there is a supreme being. I don't have that much faith."

Dad was not about to take that leap—he was unwilling to trust in something that was not tangible, something he couldn't have a meaningful conversation with or ask the burning questions that haunted him for his entire life. And he wasn't about to be dependent on something that in his mind had let him down numerous times. I believe Dad *wished* there was a God, but throughout his life and many experiences he was shown time and time again that we are mere mortals and we die only to return to earth. I think if he could have gotten some physical proof of the existence of a higher being, his intelligence would have taken over and he would have been able to understand the value of religion. He chose to not believe in a heaven or a hell—instead, he challenged the entity in the sky many times and waited for a response.

It bears mentioning that when Dad was crash-landing his F-9 fighter jet during the Korean War, he looked to the skies searching for God.

"If there is anybody up there, now would be a good time to help out."

A few years later, in 1997, Dad's health took another dip when he fell and broke his hip. Some years earlier Louise's grandchildren had given my father a Dalmatian puppy for Christmas. Dad didn't want a puppy around the house—"The last thing we need is a goddamned fucking dog!"—but by the end of the holidays the puppy had worked his way into Dad's heart and he had named him Slugger. He came to absolutely love the dog, and after Louise died he allowed Slugger to sleep with him in the big king-sized bed. Slugger was a good companion for Dad, but he was always messing in the house (which no one told Dad, to avoid an emotional outburst) and would not come when you called him. When a squirrel grabbed Slugger's attention, instinct won out over obedience every time. Caretakers were always afraid that the dog would run out into the road and get hit. Slugger ended up snapping a tendon in his leg because he ran so fast trying to catch a squirrel. This just served to create more frustration and irritation every time anyone took him outside. Dad was always on edge, worrying that the dog would run too fast and hurt himself again, so finally Slugger was put on a leash.

Unfortunately, the dog was to blame for Dad breaking his hip. Slugger had jumped up on Dad, knocking him just enough off balance that when the dog jumped down and got between Dad's legs, down Dad went and broke his hip. Slugger had to sleep in the garage for the next couple of months while Dad endured a long rehabilitation. It was not a happy time for anyone, and Dad's health never really recovered after that.

SOMETIME IN 1998, WHILE MY BROTHER AND I WERE HAVING DIN-ner with our father, he announced that he wanted to ask us a question. It was not unlike Dad to set the stage in dramatic fashion to gain our complete attention.

"I want to ask you both something very important."

This was all part of the setup, and he took some time before he posed his question. My brother and I played along as we waited. Finally he asked: "If you could have anyone at our dinner table right now, and could ask them any question without prejudice, whom would you choose?"

I can't remember what either John-Henry or I said, because what still burns in my mind is my father's response. When it came time for him to answer, he wanted his kids to guess. And guess we did. I think we guessed the whole weekend and never expected the answer we got. General MacArthur? Thomas Jefferson? Abraham Lincoln? Richard Nixon? Martin Luther King? Babe Ruth? Albert Einstein? Warren Buffett? Bill Gates? George Washington? How about Jesus Christ? Still not the answer he was looking for.

Finally, he told us.

"I would like to have evangelist Billy Graham at my dinner table."

What? Again our father had stunned us.

"Why?" John-Henry looked at me like there was something very off with our father. I immediately thought the worst. I feared he was feeling his mortality and after years of cursing God, it was time to ask for forgiveness.

"I would like to ask him what gives him the strength and the willpower to have so much faith for so long without any proof. I would like to know how he explains and understands the injustices in the world. How does he explain evolution? How is it that people question scientific research but are quick to accept miracles?"

We were stunned and speechless. Our whole lives we had heard nothing but anger and discontent with anything related to religion. Our father had cursed the skies so badly that we feared there was no repenting. My brother eventually let go of the enigmatic response our father had given us and forgot about it. I did not. For the first and only time in my life, I attempted to use my father's name to get an audience with someone—Reverend Billy Graham. I called the central office of his church and announced that I was the daughter of Ted Williams and that my father would really like to meet him. I got their attention, and I believe they tried to help. I even went to the Crusade held at the Tampa Bay Buccaneers stadium in hopes of meeting the reverend after the service. I was turned away, however, with the explanation that the reverend was not feeling well and needed to get his rest. I was disappointed. The following weekend I shared with my father what I had attempted to do for him. My father was surprised and wanted to make sure I hadn't been a nuisance. I assured him that I wasn't and that all I was trying to do was get him an audience so that he could ask any question he liked. Billy Graham might have been able to help Dad let go of some of his deep-seated contempt for religion and maybe even see some of the good it could offer.

Evidently, according to a nurse who cared for my father shortly before he died, my father "accepted Jesus Christ as his savior."

I'm not sure that actually happened, but if it did—wonderful. Maybe my father found peace with that nurse and felt comfortable enough to accept Jesus Christ into his life before he died. That's okay by me. My brother and I both thought it was more a response out of respect for the caretaker, and that he might only have been trying to show respect for the caretaker, who kept trying to educate him on God and bring salvation into his life. Either way, we had appreciation for what we had been told and what might have happened. We wanted to cover all bases; our father's mind, body, and soul deserved to be preserved and saved.

Chapter Nineteen

I BELIEVE THE OLD SAYING "YOU ALWAYS HURT THE ONE YOU love." When we are comfortable and can be ourselves with someone we love, both the good and the bad emerge. With the security of knowing we are loved, we're freer to express ourselves without the fear of being unfairly judged. You can reveal your feelings and still be understood and accepted.

John-Henry came down to Florida after the stroke in 1994 to take care of Dad and manage his life and business affairs, and he never left. In the last book that was written while Dad was still alive, *Ted Williams: My Life in Pictures,* published in 2001, he says just how important his son was to him.

"My son John-Henry was born in 1968. I was so happy when he was born. I gave him the name John-Henry because I thought a name like that conveyed strength. He hasn't disappointed me. He's been my strong right arm the last few years."

From 1994 to 2000, my brother made more money for his father than Ted Williams had made in his whole career as a baseball player. The sports memorabilia market had heated up in the 1980s. Signa-

tures became more fashionable and collectable, such that the 1990s
are labeled the start of the "Sharpie Era." The value of a ball, bat, or
photograph signed by baseball's top living legends—Ted Williams,
Joe DiMaggio, Willie Mays—just kept going up. In the 1980s, sports
memorabilia wholesalers came to Dad with offers of maybe $100 a
signature. They'd then double or triple the price in retail.

As the business boomed in the 1980s, it attracted a lot of con
men, crooks, and frauds. Dad was scammed by one of them: Vincent
Antonucci. One day in 1988 Dad walked into Antonucci's memorabilia shop in nearby Crystal River, Florida. Like any good con artist, Antonucci could be very likable. He gave no sign that he was a
convicted felon who had been arrested more than two dozen times
on charges ranging from grand theft to writing fraudulent checks.
He charmed Dad into investing in the business and signing thousands of items. When Dad didn't see a dime back, he started legal
proceedings in both civil and criminal court. His lawyer warned
him that he could spend a fortune in legal fees and never recoup a
penny. Dad didn't care. He had been lied to, cheated, and robbed.
It was a matter of principle to him. He wanted justice. Antonucci
was convicted of stealing a $38,000 check from Dad and went to jail.
Released on parole after eighteen months, he immediately went back
to selling bogus Ted Williams memorabilia around the country. Dad
actually went on *America's Most Wanted* in 1995 to help in track-
ing Antonucci down. He was arrested the next day and went back
to jail. Dad had spent seven years and more than $1 million in legal
fees to put him there. In the end, though, Antonucci was just one of
many crooks and scam artists in the memorabilia business, which
was effectively unregulated until the mid-1990s.

With that mess behind him, Dad didn't want to worry about
another person in his life taking advantage of him. He was literally sick and tired, and he needed someone he could trust. In college
John-Henry had studied business and marketing. Our mother had
often been without enough money to buy anything other than the

bare necessities, and after a childhood of being denied certain luxu-ries, it became clear that making money was a motivational factor for John-Henry. Money seemed to be the answer to all of our family problems. Mom never had enough, and Dad was always giving all his money away to take care of other people, housing them, paying for their educations and medical bills, and buying them cars. Our father was constantly complaining about all the money he was spending on others.

John-Henry had set himself a goal: by the time he was twenty years of age, he wanted to have $1 million in the bank. He didn't accomplish that goal, but I believe it is a reflection of how driven he was to be successful and always have enough money for his family. He wanted his parents to never worry again about a bill or to go without something because they desired to help someone else, even an animal.

John-Henry was very successful in coming up with ideas to gen-erate money. He was more of an entrepreneur than a businessman, but despite being a greenhorn, he caught on very quickly. He was clever and learned fast. He was often criticized as a businessman, *at the age of twenty-two,* when he'd barely had any time to gain experience. Then, the smarter and more business-savvy he became, the more associates of his exhibited jealousy and envy. John-Henry picked up things that took others years of experience to learn. His critics took offense at that. He was successful. The son of Ted Wil-liams, six-five, with dark brown eyes and jet-black hair, John-Henry was in total charge, and Hollywood-handsome to boot. He was per-fectly ripe for punishment and criticism.

Dad trusted John-Henry and his business acumen. He admired his son's enthusiasm for and knowledge of the Internet and the digi-tal age that was fast approaching. He wanted John-Henry to "run the whole show" and "take over" when it came to the business of Ted Williams.

In many ways, John-Henry had been training for this job for

years. Dealing with the demand for our father's autograph had always been a way of life for him.

Over Dad's many years of being a celebrity, probably through trial and error, he had developed his rehearsed go-to remarks in restaurants and other public places, his own ways for handling gung-ho fans when they crossed the line. One of his tried-and-true methods was double-edged. As well as it worked for Dad, it came at a cost to his friends and especially his son. It worked this way:

Imagine you're visiting Ted Williams for an evening. You've been chatting about everything you've ever wanted to talk with him about, and it comes time for dinner. Then he says, "Let's go get something to eat." In the car on the way to the local restaurant (usually a dive with good home-cooked food), Ted Williams sets the stage. He says, "Now, listen. Let's not be bothered tonight. If anyone comes up tonight for an autograph, just tell them I'm under contract. I'd like to eat my food with a little peace and quiet. Is that too much to ask?"

Of course you agree. Ted Williams just asked you for a seemingly simple favor that makes a lot of sense. This is your time together, and nobody should be interrupting your time with him or Ted's meal. "No problem," you say.

As soon as you're seated, the heads at the other tables begin to turn. Someone recognizes Ted Williams and points him out. Within minutes, word spreads throughout the restaurant. Eventually someone finds the nerve to walk over and speak to Ted. Carrying a pen and paper or napkin, that person asks him for his autograph. Ted is very nice and charming to the fan, while glancing at you and with only his eyes says, *This is it. This is what we talked about. This is where you're supposed to step in and help.*

Remembering your commitment, you easily find the courage to protect your friend. You stand up boldly, pressing toward the sports fan, and kindly ask him not to disturb Mr. Williams while he's eating dinner. That doesn't work so well, though, because you're dealing with a sports fan who has already made the decision to disturb

Mr. Williams and is thinking, *Who the hell are you to get between me and Mr. Williams?* So you become more forceful, explaining that Mr. Williams is under an exclusive contract and really cannot be signing autographs publicly. It seems to work—but then Ted Williams undermines your work just a bit. He folds under the pressure and says, "Just this once." He takes the pen and paper, signs his name, shakes hands, and thanks the intruder for being a fan.

Now the gates have been opened and a line starts forming. Staying on the job, you proceed to turn them all away as Ted smiles at the fans and shrugs at the dilemma. Everyone goes back to their seats, while you and Ted have your dinner.

The story told over and over in the following days goes something like this: "I saw Ted Williams at Stumpknocker's restaurant last night."

"Really? How was he? Was he nice? Did you get his autograph?"

"He was great. Nice guy. He had a big smile on his face. I was going to get his autograph, but the guy who was with him was a jerk and wouldn't let Ted sign anything."

"Oh man, what a bummer."

Ted Williams 1, Protector of Ted 0.

But hey, it's no big deal. Nobody knows that guest of Ted's. He was just a nameless "jerk" who stood between Ted Williams and his fans.

It was a different story, however, when John-Henry was asked by his father to do the same thing. John-Henry protected Dad from autograph-seekers more than anyone else over the years because they dined in public so often. Dad didn't need to ask John-Henry to protect their time together; it was instinctual for my brother, and Dad welcomed his help. In addition, John-Henry didn't care what others thought of him. He was protecting his father, and he was protecting their precious time together. But the people who thought they had a right to Ted Williams's attention resented John-Henry and blamed him for coming between them and their hero. Ted Williams was a public figure. As fans, they had played a part in making him famous. They felt they had a right to ask for his autograph and never considered that perhaps Ted Williams wanted his son to intervene; they believed it could only be that a greedy son was keeping a number-one fan away. On the street, John-Henry was considered the bad guy who stood between Ted Williams and his fans. Mom and Dad were right about that name "John-Henry." It was a strong name for a damn strong man. John-Henry didn't mind being the "villain." Dad and I were the only ones frustrated and hurt when someone didn't understand or appreciate John-Henry for the many roles he served in our family.

While John-Henry was certainly well trained and well positioned to help Dad make money off of his signature, Dad's desire to have John-Henry manage the business of Ted Williams was more than just pragmatic. There was also an emotional component to it: Dad didn't want to be alone. He loved having his son around and was eager to spend time with him to watch his business ideas and endeavors unfold. The level of care that Dad needed and wanted cost a lot of money. Dad knew that John-Henry could be relied upon to make that happen.

From the start, John-Henry did just that, immediately making significant strides to clean up the market when it came to my father's memorabilia. He restricted free access to his father's signature, thereby making it that much more valuable. John-Henry and Dad knew what the expenses were going to be, plus they wanted to help finance John-Henry's own expanding Internet company.

It was a relationship that benefited both of them: Dad shared his livelihood with his son, and John-Henry protected his father's legacy and the value of his signature by not flooding the market with his autograph and by stopping the forgeries. The more successful John-Henry was, the prouder Dad became. John-Henry represented his father and flourished and reveled in that role. Who wouldn't?

I didn't. With Dad's blessing, John-Henry respectfully took full advantage of the privilege of being the son of Ted Williams and the opportunities that came with it. Like many fathers, Dad would do anything he could to help his son be successful. So he was motivated to help his only son in the memorabilia business and any other venture my brother thought would be successful. John-Henry, meanwhile, was determined to protect his father's name, likeness, and image. By contrast, I remained steadfast in my resolve to prove myself to my father by not relying on him for anything.

I have wondered if perhaps I made a mistake and failed to pick up on the subtle way my father was trying to tell me he loved me and wanted to help me. I was too stubborn, almost obstinate, desperately wanting to prove to my dad I could do things on my own and didn't need to ride his coattail of fame. Like the time he got me into Middlebury College, my dream choice. When Dad found out that I had been rejected twice, he called his friend Governor John Sununu. I was immediately accepted, but now I didn't want to go. I was accepted because of my dad and not based on my own merits. Maybe I should have graciously accepted the favor and been happy to have gotten into my dream school.

Another time Dad arranged a wonderful opportunity for me to work for Elizabeth Dole in the Red Cross, but I politely declined. I had already made a commitment to a company in Europe to be an international sales representative for a publishing company. Speaking French and German gave me the opportunity to practice my language skills and also promote sales in these two countries. I had worked hard to get the position, and I had done it on my own—no one in Europe knew who Ted Williams was. Getting that job was personal affirmation that I was liked and wanted because of *me* and not because of who my father was.

Though I needed to feel like I was independent and self-sufficient and could survive on my own, I fear I missed the only way my dad knew how to show me he cared and wanted to help me fulfill my dreams and aspirations. He did not hesitate to use every contact he had to help us, and yet I could never accept his help. He loved my independence, but I hated feeling like I couldn't accomplish anything without using him. It seemed to me that every single person who ever came in contact with my dad was looking for a way to profit off him or use their acquaintance as leverage in another situation. I just wanted to appreciate him.

For his part, John-Henry helped Dad to see how valuable he was on many levels. Suddenly Dad started to understand what a powerful potential lay in their future. It was a loving father-son business relationship. Each of them knew what to expect of the other, but in the end it was Dad who said:

"Let's keep the money in the family."

FULLY IN CHARGE OF OUR FATHER'S BUSINESS AFFAIRS, JOHN-Henry committed himself to improving the value of Dad's likeness and signature. There would be no more Antonuccis, no more household thieves. Taking advantage of Ted Williams ceased, and a lot of people were cut away from the financial teat. People had gotten used to taking advantage of Dad, and John-Henry was determined to stop that. Times were changing.

In the memorabilia business, John-Henry was on the leading edge of change. He got the FBI to pursue the crooks and helped convince states to pass legislation to curb the forgeries and frauds. This, of course, made him a lot of enemies in the business, and he quickly became the target and enemy of those who opposed the changes. It was easy for freeloaders to accuse John-Henry of being greedy as he took away their access to the free signatures they had sold or traded. It was easy for them to rationalize that John-Henry was doing this to harm them, without ever considering the inappropriateness of their own actions. John-Henry never stood in the way of his dad sending an autograph to anyone, just as he never stood in the way of Dad making or receiving a phone call or a visitor. The only people denied access were the ones of whom Dad himself said, "I don't want them around," or, "I don't trust them."

I think those who have claimed otherwise rationalize to feel good about themselves. They don't want to consider the possibility that they were anything less than Ted Williams's closest friend. Think about this: There are many reports from Dad's true friends—such as Dom DiMaggio, Al Cassidy, Bobby Doerr, and John Glenn—indicating that they spoke to him daily, weekly, or whenever they called. There are reports from the nurses and aides who assisted Dad in phoning his friends. Even in the last weeks of his life he reportedly made phone calls to friends and family. Yet somehow, it has been alleged, Dad was a prisoner in his own home and not allowed to talk to anyone because his son was now in charge. To me, that claim seems inconsistent.

In actuality, John-Henry was doing for Dad what the attorney Morris Engelberg was doing for Joe DiMaggio. Like my brother, Engelberg had seen the booming memorabilia market and helped DiMaggio take full advantage of the value of his signature and appearances. Engelberg was also highly criticized by outsiders, even though attorneys' actions are generally a reflection of what their clients want. Obviously, after sixteen years of service, one has to believe that Engelberg was doing something right and that DiMaggio was not completely oblivious to what was going on. It appears that Engelberg was willing to take the criticism to achieve his client's wishes.

John-Henry was more than willing to do the same. But this was a different relationship. This wasn't *just* business. It was a father and his son, and John-Henry's only objective was giving Dad and himself the best life together. Regardless, that goal put John-Henry in a position where he was subjected to a ton of unwarranted and unfair criticism.

Applying his business and marketing knowledge, John-Henry showed that by using the right advertising, clamping down on forgeries, and limiting production of signed items, the value of Dad's coveted signature would only go up. John-Henry was right. With smart input from advisers and marketing experts, John-Henry started offering signed photographs of Ted Williams that had never been seen before. He spent a lot of time and money researching and going through archives of photos to find special and rare images of his father. John-Henry's girlfriend Anita suggested offering limited editions and personalized items. After a while, business was booming. John-Henry worked more efficiently, Dad worked less, and they were both successful. Soon Dad didn't even need to sign a check. Everything went through the office. Dad's financial worries disappeared, and he relinquished control to his son with pleasure. He didn't want to see another bill. He didn't want to hear about another person asking for money, or money being sent for unattended colleges, overdue credit card bills, brand-new cars, or liens on houses. It was ultimately Dad's choice to whom he wanted to send money. He only needed to give word to the office. Dad loved this arrangement. He was finally free of the constant worry and grind of having to make money to pay for his own living and support everyone to whom he felt an obligation.

With the money that the memorabilia brought, John-Henry was able to get his father anything he wanted or needed. He bought Dad the biggest TV available, with satellite service, so that Dad could watch any baseball game anywhere in the world. Dad had the best medical help and nutritional advice. He had a professional chef. He had regular exercise and constant health monitoring. John-Henry made sure his father was taken care of by only the best or by those people Dad wanted to have around him or thought he could trust. Dad had a full-time butler of sorts who cooked and drove him wherever he wanted or needed to go. There were also regular maid services and a physical trainer. There were contractual obligations, insurance premiums, medical bills, lawn services, and twenty-four-hour caretakers, as well as the costs of home maintenance and utilities. John-Henry's goal was to make Dad's life as comfortable, healthy, and stress-free as possible.

This all came at a cost. It required a lot of marketing and sales work by John-Henry and, of course, a lot of signatures by Dad. It was an effective arrangement. Dad loved to be involved in John-Henry's business and liked to contribute. Especially after his stroke, it was therapeutic for Dad to be active. Signing was easy. It made him feel important and whole despite his new physical limitations. It was a good regimen for father and son.

Dad did sign a lot. At one time the inventory of signed memorabilia exceeded five thousand signatures. It was the height of the sports memorabilia boom, and Dad's signature was competitive with only the best. Mantle and DiMaggio were his biggest competitors in the business, with DiMaggio edging him out from time to time in retail value because he had married the sexy beauty Marilyn Monroe. Also, DiMaggio had a reputation for not signing for the public as much as Dad did.

There were many times when Dad couldn't wait to stop by the office and see the latest 1940s photos that John-Henry had discovered and purchased. John-Henry reproduced the photographs in the highest quality available, generally in a 16" × 20" format, and presented them in pristine condition for Dad's signature. Dad would always marvel at the quality of the photograph. He'd tell stories about the photo and what was going on in it, as well as every other story that surrounded the captured moment. John-Henry knew that if he could impress Dad, he could impress the buyers. It was a walk down memory lane, a baseball fan's dream come true, to hear Ted Williams recall these moments in history with such detail. It also kept Dad's brain engaged, stimulated conversation, and exercised his long-term memory. Reminiscing was great therapy for Dad.

Of course, there were challenges for him. With his tunnel vision, Dad constantly had to be reminded to look to his left to see the rest of the food on his plate or the hand extended for a shake, and sometimes he would sign too far to the right of a photo or item, ruining an expensive photograph or other item. Buyers would not accept these substandard signatures. He was also picky about the process of signing. When I tried to be the one feeding him the photos, I could never do it right. Either I didn't have the timing and technique down or I couldn't sustain the baseball conversation that accompanied each picture, so Dad would get annoyed and quit. The longest Dad could talk and sign before getting too tired was probably an hour or two. He'd stick around the office, though, and talk to folks or try to get John-Henry to commit to coming to the house with Anita for dinner.

Dad enjoyed it very much when John-Henry and Anita came to dinner, as it was his chance to hear how their day was and what was going on. He adored Anita, who had the special gift of being able to soothe Dad and keep things very simple and nonirritating when it came to business or family affairs. I don't think he ever yelled at Anita. My brother and I actually joked that Dad might have loved Anita more than he loved the two of us. Dad always tried to be on his best behavior around her. I think he didn't want to scare Anita off with his outbursts. He thought she was perfect for his son.

It's hard to admit, but I was jealous of her. She was very difficult for me to accept. She had completely captured my brother's attention, and John-Henry and I were spending less time together. On top of that, she had won Dad's affection easily. She had been Miss Massachusetts USA in 1988 and was every bit as smart as she was beautiful. She was a key component to my brother's business success, excellent with public relations and marketing, and a perfect complement to the father-son duo. They made a great team. But John-Henry and Anita could not separate their private lives from their business life, and it slowly ate away at their relationship. They were together for close to ten years. It took a while for her to be accepted by the females in the Williams family, not just me but my mom too. I think Mom compared Anita to herself, especially with their common backgrounds. I too had to make a conscious decision to accept her. She was very important to my brother and my father, and it would have been my loss if I didn't embrace her. I had to give her a chance. It didn't take long, though, before I absolutely loved her like a sister. She was a lovely addition to our family. I started wishing she would hang out with me too.

I remember a phone call from my father, who was very excited about something.

"Claudia? We got some wonderful news."

There was only one thought that came to my mind. "John-Henry and Anita are getting married," I said. I immediately thought it was a wedding announcement just by the sound in my dad's voice. Dad was so thrilled by the prospect of their getting married that he had jumped the gun. It wasn't exactly an engagement ring that John-Henry had given Anita, but a beautiful promise ring. Nonetheless, Dad and I both were actually squealing on the phone with delight.

"I know, damn it—it's great! Hold on! I'll let her tell you all about it!"

I could hear Anita's happiness come over the line like a burst of energy. I believe she wanted to get married more than anything. And I honestly think that if it hadn't been for the stress of the business and my brother's devotion and care for his father, they would have stayed together.

Unfortunately, the whole Williams family seems always short on time. There is no doubt in my mind that Anita and John-Henry loved each other very much, but when Dad got sick John-Henry made his father his first priority. Adding to the pressures of family life, dogs, business, and John-Henry's frequent absence from home, it took the final toll on their relationship, and she moved back home to Massachusetts.

I grieved the loss of Anita. I hated every woman who even got near John-Henry after Anita, and I kept trying to encourage him to reconnect with her.

JUST BECAUSE JOHN-HENRY AND DAD WERE WORKING TOGETHER didn't mean everything always went smoothly. While my father appreciated what John-Henry was doing for him (Dad couldn't believe how much a signed item could bring), there were times when he got frustrated signing autographs. It could be monotonous and exhausting, and when Dad had to sign a particular mass order within a certain amount of time, it was clearly a strain. It could seem like a daunting workload. I was not included at all in the memorabilia affairs—and quite frankly, I didn't want to be. I found the business to be loaded with smarmy and slimy people. So, when I rode my bicycle up to see Dad on the weekend, it was not unusual to find him signing hundreds of copies of the same photo. I'd sit at the table and chat with him as he signed. I could tell that he was annoyed at the repetitive chore, but also that he appreciated the support of his many fans, understood the value of the job, and knew that it needed to be done.

However, some of Dad's caretakers didn't usually see it that way. They thought it was awful that he had to sign so much, and when Dad complained, they were quick to condemn both the job and John-Henry. The moment they got any hint of unhappiness from Dad, they dissociated themselves from John-Henry and became self-appointed champions and defenders of Ted Williams. How dare John-Henry make his father do these chores? Instead of encouraging Dad and facilitating the work, they found it easier to apologize to him and claim that they "had to get his signature on these items." It made them feel more important to Ted Williams when they could point a finger at John-Henry for "making" them (and Dad) do this "terrible" task. I thought it was inappropriate and out of line for an employee to verbalize those kinds of feelings of dissatisfaction. It was not their place to criticize John-Henry and the relationship he had established with his father.

In addition, we had problems with some of the caretakers themselves. At one point the Florida Department of Law Enforcement sought and received permission to tap Dad's phones to gather evidence on a caretaker who turned out to be a known drug dealer. Under the cloak of working as a caretaker for Ted Williams, he was doing drug deals on the side. We couldn't believe it when the FDLE informed us of the trafficking that was going on. Another caretaker couldn't handle alcohol. They drank on the job and did not maintain the professional, polite, and courteous behavior that Dad expected when friends and guests came to visit. John-Henry, with no tolerance for that kind of behavior, had no trouble terminating them on the spot. From then on, he hired each caretaker to provide specified services, all in Dad's best interests. Dad trusted John-Henry, and John-Henry hired the caretakers to do nothing but assist Dad. But the more time they spent with Dad the more they would begin to believe they had been hired by Ted Williams himself—or worse yet, that they had become "Ted's best friend."

Frequently, these aides did not even know what they were defending Dad against. All they saw was signature after signature. Acting annoyed that they had to sit there and pass each photo under Dad's pen, they would announce dramatically that he had to repeat a signature, because "surely this isn't going to be good enough (or clear enough, or legible enough) for Mr. John-Henry Williams." The implication was clear: *Who the hell does John-Henry think he is?* Meanwhile, Dad knew exactly what was going on. He knew that it cost his son a lot of money to get access to the old negatives, and that each photo cost money to reproduce—some of them as much as $75 each. If a signature was not of the quality the buyer expected, he might not buy the photo. John-Henry's policy was all about customer service. Signatures are graded in the memorabilia market—the higher the grade the better the price. Collectors can be extremely picky, and during the Sharpie Era signatures were closely scrutinized.

When Dad's employees criticized my brother for "making" his father sign so much, what they failed to mention was that they too benefited from every autograph signed. When John-Henry was working in other business ventures and taking care of Dad's affairs, he didn't always have the time to sit by his father and feed the photos to him one after another. Caretakers could do it, though, and they got paid a bonus. Most of the caretakers couldn't understand the complexity of the father-son relationship, but years later, when it came time for interviews and the media, they couldn't wait to stand in the spotlight and explain how awful Ted Williams's son was, how he forced his father to sign until he was exhausted and his hand bled. That seemed to be the popular thing to say, but it was not truthful . . . not even close.

In the end, the complaints of his caretakers only annoyed Dad more. And inevitably, Dad would say, "I'm not signing another syphilitic thing as long as I have a hair in my ass!" With that, photos would go flying across the table and the Sharpie would be flicked away in inimitable Williams fashion. The signing session was over. The only reason Dad would threaten "never to sign another damned thing" was because he knew he could speak this freely in the privacy of his home and that John-Henry would know exactly what he meant.

In the criticism of John-Henry—criticism that continues to this day—there is a vital point that still gets lost in translation: *no one ever made Ted Williams do anything*. Ever. This was true when he was young, and just as true when he was old. If he didn't want to sign, he didn't sign. There was a clear understanding between father and son. Dad remained aware of the bills that needed to be paid. And there was no duping him. Dad exercised his control in every situation by either agreeing to a deal or not. Ultimately, it was Dad's choice and he knew it.

He expressed frustration and boredom because at times it *was* frustrating and boring. And most importantly, if he got mad and refused to sign, his decision was honored. The caretakers looking after Dad didn't know him and weren't familiar with his outbursts. From their perspective, they were paid to work with Ted Williams and his occasional outbursts seemed very passionate and real. As he yelled and cursed the sky over this "atrocity," they would get the impression that something incredibly harmful had occurred. In truth, the real source of his anger usually had nothing to do with the signing. He might have been having a bad day or heard some bad news, he might not have felt well, or he might just have been feeling like exercising his independence and control.

Dad's outbursts never affected the agreement or relationship he had with John-Henry; that was already proven and built on love. If Dad had blown up and refused to sign for people from the major memorabilia companies, like Upper Deck or Steiner Sports, it would have been a completely different situation. It could have permanently damaged a business relationship. Dad knew his son would understand his emotional outbursts and take his comments in context. But the unseasoned aides would misconstrue it all and blame John-Henry for Dad's discontent.

Despite the frustration of signing hundreds of items, Dad always managed to let John-Henry know how much he appreciated him—usually in quiet ways that people didn't see. Knowing that John-Henry would check all his signatures to make sure they were quality autographs, Dad would slip a personalized one, *just for his son,* into the pile of photos. Attempting to impart a father's wisdom, Dad would always say something nice and meaningful. Handwritten boldly in thick blue Sharpie, across a beautiful photograph taken long before his son was ever born, Dad would inscribe something he wanted his son to always remember. It didn't matter that there would now be one less photograph in the inventory. Dad was using the signing session to send a loving message to his son, and John-Henry received some of his greatest treasures in those personalized messages from his dad.

Chapter Twenty

WHILE MY BROTHER AND FATHER WERE WORKING DILI-
gently at the memorabilia business, I was in the middle of
training—hard. During my three years in Germany I had decided
to pursue my dream of competing as a triathlete. For the first time
the triathlon was going to be an event at the Summer Olympics in
2000. I was twenty-six at the time, and determined to try out for the
US team, so I'd moved back to the States, to St. Petersburg, Florida,
because one of the biggest triathlon clubs and training facilities in
the country was there.

Being in the middle of training, I didn't need or want the
reminder that my parents thought I wouldn't succeed at it and was
wasting my time, so I took advantage of the memorabilia distraction
and Dad's public appearances to work as hard and as fast as I could
to make up the time I had "lost" getting my college education. I had
tried to convince my parents, especially my father, that college could
wait. I really wanted a chance to become a professional athlete. I
would argue, "I can always go to school, but I will not always be

young and be able to train as hard as this requires. This is something I really want to do."

"You will never be able to do anything with it," my father had insisted. "And you are sure as hell not going to make any money doing it."

When I tried to get my mother interested by sharing my results, she would reply, "Now, how long are you going to do this?"

I persisted, however, and was even more determined not to burden my father in any way with my *foolish* pursuit of athletic dreams. I never asked my father for anything. I bought my own car, a Geo Metro, because it was all that I could afford and it was good on gas mileage for all the traveling to triathlon races. I rented a room in a house in St. Petersburg to keep my expenses down. It was all paid for by my savings over the years, from working as a nanny in Europe, from gifts and grade money, as well as the interest I was making on the money I had invested along the way.

And I was also clever enough to take a page from my brother's marketing book. I covered my racing suit with any logo of anyone who would sponsor me, even if it was for just $40 a month. I didn't care. That was two tanks of gas for my Geo. I can confidently say that I was never a financial burden to my father. I was determined to be completely the opposite of every other female in his life, to be the one exception to his often-stated belief that "every damn broad is a money-hungry, draining bitch." I was not *ever* going to be one of them.

I did accept one form of support, knowing that my dad had covertly orchestrated it. One of my bigger sponsors was an orange grove owned by a friend of my father's, Joe Davis, of Davis Groves. My father understood that I would not accept his financial support if he did not support my dreams. So he went around my stubborn and obstinate personality and got his buddy to sponsor me. I was the only competitor with oranges all over her suit, but I liked it, and I graciously accepted this subtle and indirect support from my father. It was discreet, and it felt good. My brother also supported me with his up-and-coming Internet company. The logo for Hitter.net was proudly and prominently displayed on my suit. Along with my numerous small sponsors, this support all added up and let me chase my dreams. In no way was I advertising that I was the daughter of Ted Williams, and I certainly wasn't getting any special privileges on the circuit. No one knew who my father was.

All I did was eat, sleep, and train. On the weekends I would bike home to see my father and visit with my brother. My racing results were dependent on nothing but me, my training, and my performance. What I was doing certainly wasn't easy or by any means celebrated by my family. I always felt like I was just amusing them. As long as I didn't cost them too much money, however, and was not a threat or a bother to my brother's business and his marketing world with Dad, no one seemed to mind. I didn't nag my father to support my "silly" dreams.

Dad seemed to enjoy the respite from needy people and loved to watch me swim in the pool near my brother's place. The first time he saw me swim, he exclaimed, "Jesus Christ, you look just like Johnny Weissmuller swimming."

"Who's that?" I asked as I rested by the wall.

"It's the actor who played Tarzan!" my father yelled, shocked at my ignorance. "He was a very strong swimmer."

"Me Tarzan," I joked, pounding my chest, and jumped back into the water. When I turned back to look at his response, he was shaking his head with his Kermit smirk.

I smiled at the compliment and went back to my intervals. He could not get over the fact that I would swim three to five thousand yards at a time. He kept converting it into miles and bragging to his friends how far his daughter could swim. He would often tease John-Henry, "Can *YOU* swim two miles? Do you know that your little sister swam five thousand yards today? Can *YOU* do that, John-Henry?"

After the swim, I would get John-Henry, and sometimes my dad too, to ride behind me in the golf cart as I ran for over an hour around the undeveloped roads of Citrus Hills. They were in charge of hydration and lighting the road. It was certainly clear that I took my training seriously, but they thought I was crazy in my work ethic.

"Jesus, don't you need a rest?" my father would ask. "Just jump on the back of the damned cart and we'll take you home."

It wasn't for lack of effort that I did not succeed at the highest level. By the end of 1998, however, I realized that my parents were right: I wasn't going to make it professionally as a triathlete. I had suffered a couple of injuries, and by the time I qualified to participate in the National Championships I was not in top form. The girls who were beating me were all younger and had been racing a lot longer than I had. I knew it was time to "get serious," as my dad would say, and commit full-time to a *real* job. I was very grateful that I'd had the opportunity to try for my dream. I gave it the best effort I could. My father and brother and Anita all came to watch me at the National Championships in Clermont, Florida. John-Henry took pictures, and Dad was able to see me fly by on my bike. That was my last triathlon race.

I can't help but wonder what would have happened if I'd been a boy and wanted to pursue an athletic career. I truly believe that if my parents had supported me and blessed my dedication from the start, it might have turned out differently. Dealing with them, however, ended up being a constant struggle. I wouldn't tell them how much time I was spending trying to become competitive because neither of them seemed to understand, and they sure didn't seem to appreciate all my training. Ironically, my father understood the hard work and the strain on my body. He'd give me recovery tips, such as getting into a hot steam bath and getting regular rubdowns, and he even encouraged me to eat plenty of protein.

"There's nothing wrong with a thick milk shake with a little added Tiger's Milk. Get yourself a good rubdown and make sure you get your rest. All great athletes get to bed early."

My mother simply thought it was a waste of time and told me that I didn't look very attractive running or struggling during hard training sessions. It was disappointing to me that I did not have the support of my family, but I have no one to blame except myself for finally ending my triathlon career. In the end, I decided, it wasn't worth it to go against my father's wishes and risk estranging him.

OF ALL THE CRITICISMS JOHN-HENRY TOOK FOR THE SAKE OF Dad's public image, the flack he took over the All-Star Game in Fenway Park on July 13, 1999, was the most ironic—though admittedly it was easy to understand from a fan's perspective. Dad's appearance at the game that year was historically memorable for baseball fans, past and present major league players, and our family. However, Dad's appearance at the game almost didn't happen. He was about to be eighty-one years old, he was tired, and he didn't want to be bothered. He had started to hate flying, and if he had to, he'd work himself into an anxious frenzy that bordered on being too stressful for him. The benefits often did not outweigh the risks to his health.

Dad preferred the safety of seclusion; there was comfort in his privacy. The older he got the more it seemed that public appearances were "big productions" and "hassles." Without John-Henry or me to excite and encourage him, he would have become a recluse. It wasn't that the actual performance was difficult, but a whirlwind of emotions that would encircle the upcoming trip and consume him. The buildup was too unnerving, and Dad would throw a tantrum. Telling him far in advance of any upcoming trip was not a good strategy: it gave him too much time. The anticipation was worse than the event. Dad would become consumed by the stress of it and want to throw in the towel on the whole deal. It got to the point that my brother would not tell him about a trip or a public appearance until the day before. Otherwise, the hassles of the event Dad would imagine would outweigh any benefits he could perceive, and he would refuse to attend. In the end, however, Dad was glad that he had been persuaded to go to the 1999 All-Star Game. Baseball loved him, and he still needed his fans' attention.

John-Henry worked with Major League Baseball and the Red Sox to set the plans. Timing was important, as Dad had just traveled with John-Henry in June to Shea Stadium for a "Ted Williams Night." The last thing Dad wanted to do was hop on a plane and travel again. John-Henry waited until just the right moment to tell Dad about the All-Star Game. Motive was important too. John-Henry was ultimately able to coax Dad into going, but not without an incentive. It wasn't until Dad realized that he could help John-Henry and his Internet company, Hitter.net, that he finally committed to attending.

It was tough for the fans to swallow when Ted Williams was driven out onto the field in a golf cart. Ted Williams looked old. It was difficult to see their hero looking so frail. Perhaps worse, though, was that they didn't understand why the Splendid Splinter wasn't wearing his team cap. What was that white hat? Why isn't he wearing a Red Sox cap? Something was wrong.

It's easy to see how this hat could have been misconstrued. It appeared to be an advertising stunt—and it was. Dad was in the last years of his life. He had learned about and stayed apprised of all modern technology because of his son's explanations and business ventures. Hitter.net, named to honor his father, was the first Internet service offered in the town where Dad was now living, Hernando, Florida. My brother wanted to offer his customers the best web access possible. By endorsing Hitter.net, Ted Williams was going to forever be associated with Internet access. So long as the company existed, it was another way Dad would be remembered.

In the end everyone got what they wanted: baseball fans everywhere were treated to the best pregame show ever; John-Henry got his wish for Dad to be celebrated as never before; and Dad got his wish to do anything he could for John-Henry's business. Yet there were critics who wanted to take their swipes at John-Henry for "forcing" his father to wear a Hitter.net shirt and hat. Unfortunately, not only did they never know the whole story, but it seemed as though they never wanted to know the whole story. They never took the time to do the research that would have revealed that Ted Williams spent that *entire* trip in New England promoting Hitter.net. Four days before the All-Star Game, Dad wore a Hitter.net cap and shirt when he visited the Dana-Farber Cancer Institute, met Einar Gustafson (the original "Jimmy" of the Jimmy Fund), and signed many items to benefit the Jimmy Fund. Two days before the All-Star Game, Dad wore a Hitter.net cap and shirt to the New Hampshire International Speedway in Loudon, where he served as grand marshal for the NASCAR Winston Cup Series' Jiffy Lube 300, announcing to the drivers when it was time to "start your engines." It was easier, however, to shame John-Henry for "demeaning" his father by making him wear that Hitter.net cap to the ball game.

In spite of all this controversy, Dad still loved the All-Star Game and the chance to meet the young players. My father still watched a lot of ball games on the huge TV that John-Henry had bought for him. It filled up Dad's room and reached the ceiling against one wall, and during a game it felt like you were standing right next to the batter. Dad loved it. After his stroke left him with tunnel vision, he needed a lot more light and loved things big and bold. With the satellite dish that John-Henry set up, Dad could watch any ball game playing in the world. I think Dad even watched some Japanese baseball at one point. He loved watching the new talent.

"I see more talent today than I ever have in my life."

One of the players I remember my dad talking about was Ken Griffey Jr. Dad thought the young man, first and foremost, conducted himself very well on the field. He described him as being tremendously talented, even a little better than his "ol' dad." What

Dad really loved and remarked about every time Griffey Jr. came to bat was how disciplined his approach seemed to be.

"Now there's a kid who knows how to wait on a good ball to hit. Rogers Hornsby told me in 1938 what to do to be a great hitter, and I sure as hell listened. Somebody must have told this kid the same thing."

Dad started following a couple of players in particular. Paul Molitor had captured his attention big time. He actually was so excited about Molitor that he called him.

"I think you are one of the best hitters I've ever seen. You are absolutely great. You know what? I don't know if anybody has said this, but every time you come to the plate and swing, all I see is Joe DiMaggio."

Dad seemed to know and recognize all the best hitters. He would compare the young players to some of the old-timers. Sometimes he would yell at the batter on the TV when he thought he didn't "wait for a good ball to hit." It frustrated Dad that the players didn't seem to have studied the game as much as he had. One comment he made frequently was how big and strong the players seemed—which, with the steroid era of baseball now in full view, seems particularly astute.

"I don't know what they're eating, but they sure are big and strong. Boy oh boy . . . must be something in the water."

There was Juan Gonzalez. Dad was impressed by how aggressive he seemed at the plate. Dad would describe Gonzalez as "muscles on top of muscles."

"I can't help it, that kid reminds me of Frank Robinson."

Then there was the duel between Barry Bonds and Mark McGwire. Dad was stunned at how big and strong these guys were too.

"Jesus, they hit the ball a TON!"

He would get mad at the pitchers and call them stupid when they tried to "throw by them, especially on the inside. Just dumb—these guys are only going to crush 'em."

At the '99 All-Star Game he couldn't wait to meet McGwire. He wanted to ask him if he could smell wood burning after he hit a foul ball. You can actually see Dad in clips of the 1999 All-Star Game tapping McGwire's elbow to emphasize nicking the ball. McGwire responded, "Every time, Ted."

Still, Dad was in his late seventies and didn't really have the energy anymore to keep track of all the young players. When someone mentioned a young talent, Dad would watch a game or two, but he was more interested now in enjoying a game or even just the noise of it in the background as he slept or talked with company. A few young players, however, were special to Dad. He really took a liking to them, believed in their ability, and was pulling for them to break .400. Between you and me, I don't want anyone to break my dad's average, but I know Dad would love to see it happen.

Dad thought that two players in particular might break his average. One of them was Tony Gwynn of the San Diego Padres, and the other was Nomar Garciaparra of the Red Sox. He always pulled for Tony and thought he was a great guy. He'd met Tony at the 1992 All-Star Game. At thirty-two, Tony was halfway into his excellent twenty-year career in the major leagues. Tony was a player, Dad said, who just might hit .400.

"If I had to bet, I'd put my money on that kid. I bet on Tony."

Tony has said he was scared to meet the great Ted Williams, but that it was also "like being a kid in the candy store. Imagine sitting next to the man who knew more about hitting a baseball than anyone who ever played the game. If you had any questions about hitting, here was the man who had all the answers." Of course they started talking about hitting right away. As good as Tony was, Dad saw some specific weaknesses in his swing and began schooling him on correcting them. In 1995 they appeared together on Bob Costas's radio show and had what's considered the best conversation about hitting ever recorded. Tony loved how freely my father shared his vast knowledge of hitting with him, and he would always say that he hit better in his second ten years in the majors because he listened to Dad's advice. He never hit .400, but he was among the small number of those who have come close, batting .394 two years after meeting Dad.

Dad made Tony laugh when he referred to him as a "strong little guy," even though Tony weighed well over two hundred pounds. He told Tony that he needed to develop a fear factor and never forget that the pitchers are "the dumbest guys in the ballpark." To which Tony replied, "You can think that, but you can't say it, Ted." To which Dad replied, "That's what makes you so special. You're so nice. You got a helluva chance to be a politician." Dad had an immediate connection with the player from San Diego and loved that his hometown team had someone they could adore and pull for.

He also really felt a connection with Nomar. They shared a similar background. Both were from southern California and of Mexican-American descent, and both had entered the major leagues with the Red Sox. Dad really admired Nomar's focus. He described Nomar's swing as one of the most natural he had ever seen, but still with so much easy power.

"He can hit anything he likes. I wish he'd wait a bit more on some of his pitches, but boy can he hit."

Dad wasn't so sure about all of Nomar's preparations in the batter's box and sometimes got a little impatient watching his rituals, but he understood. He believed Nomar was just "settling himself down and getting focused."

"What the hell. It works for him, and it probably drives the pitcher crazy."

Dad and Nomar evidently talked a couple of times, and Dad was always encouraging him. Dad had him over for breakfast once, and Nomar came to one of the Ted Williams Museum inductions. They seemed to have a lot of respect for each other.

Three months after the 1999 All-Star Game at Fenway Park, before the second World Series game between the Atlanta Braves and the New York Yankees, Major League Baseball held a ceremony for its All-Century Team. The nominees had been announced at the All-Star Game, then more than two million fans around the world voted for their favorite players in all positions. Thirty players were chosen. My dad, Babe Ruth, and Hank Aaron were the top three outfielders, each with over a million votes. Now every living player on the team gathered in Atlanta for this ceremony.

People have attested that the only reason Dad wore a Red Sox cap *that day* was because John-Henry wasn't there to "strong-arm" his father into wearing the Hitter.net hat. In fact, not only was John-Henry present, but they had flown there together and my brother escorted Dad onto the field and to the stage, arm in arm wearing his Red Sox cap.

Chapter Twenty-One

Guests, like fish, begin to smell after three days.
— BENJAMIN FRANKLIN

AFTER DAD'S STROKE, JOHN-HENRY AND I BECAME ACUTELY aware that our remaining time with him was limited and we began more and more to cherish every minute the three of us had together—*just* the three of us. Much as Dad loved to see his friends, and much as we loved to see him happy, it was also a struggle for him and for us.

Even when he was healthy he had seen guests—whether they were invited or not—as a disruption. There was always a honeymoon period when visiting with Ted Williams, and it lasted about three days. For three days he was able to contain the worst of his swears, avoid emotional outbursts, and genuinely make anyone feel like they had made a special connection with him. It was a very endearing and charming quality. This was Dad being nice, being respectful and disciplined, maintaining his best behavior. But it lasted only about three days. After that, anything could set him off and blast him into orbit with irritation and annoyance. *Here's who I really am, and if you don't like it, get the hell out of my house.* Meanwhile, the guests were just warming up to the idea that they were forming a meaningful bond and a lasting friendship with the great hitter.

Even Dad's childhood friends would annoy him after three days. His high school buddy Bob Breitbard, a successful businessman who ultimately dedicated the San Diego Hall of Champions in large part to Ted Williams, would eventually get under our father's skin. After three days, the sharp, sarcastic tongue came slashing out.

"You're just like an old woman—ya know that?"

Dad sounded like he was just being sarcastic, but deep down he was already fed up with you. In joke lies the truth.

As soon as Dad could get John-Henry's ear, he would beg, "Get that pain in the ass outta here."

It was not always easy being in the middle of that emotional stress, but John-Henry knew how to soothe Dad at times like this. Dad would almost inevitably follow John-Henry's lead, and in the end he was always glad he did. When John-Henry couldn't fix the family dynamics, though, I was called in. I was the "fixer," a skill I'd developed over the years by observing and disciplining myself to understand and figure out what made Dad mad. I could tell a mile away what was brewing and why. John-Henry often got lost in the details, trying to calm the storm, whereas I could pick up instantly on what was going on and show my brother why something was frustrating Dad.

John-Henry had put his whole life, his career, and his dreams on hold to take care of Dad and his personal affairs. When there was an argument, it was very disruptive, because naturally after everything John-Henry had sacrificed, why was Dad complaining? I couldn't have done it, and I'm glad I never tried. I was too much like Dad to be good at it. I was impatient. I was sensitive to criticism. I would not have had the resilience that John-Henry showed. I had to find a different way to connect with my father. It wasn't going to be through baseball; that time was over. There were moments when John-Henry took a lot of criticism from Dad, even when he was really just frustrated with life, but still my brother was always there to help his father. And Dad would not have wanted him anywhere else. This was acceptable and expected behavior from his son, but for a woman or, God forbid, a daughter to have attempted this role—I would have been crucified on day one. He would have had no tolerance for it. All women could be "dumb broads," and I had only barely moved beyond that line. Thanks to my half-sister's hardships and poor decisions, not to mention Dad's poor parenting skills, I was forever on the verge of striking out. I still had a lot to prove, and taking over Dad's affairs was not the way to do it.

I just quietly did my thing and kept smiling. I soothed when I could, counseled when asked, and became a mediator when verbal battles arose. I never asked for anything, and I loved them both. Despite their flaws, I recognized their love and respect for each other and felt good for them. Neither one could live without the other. John-Henry and Dad needed each other. I lived vicariously through John-Henry and his relationship with our father. I was not entwined with Dad as much as my brother was, and that slight separation between us was exactly what Dad liked about having me around. I was still a bit of a mystery. He had to respect that and treat me accordingly. I never had anything to complain about, and even if I did, I wasn't about to do so. So long as Dad never asked, I never felt the need to express discontent over anything. It just wasn't worth the risk. I wasn't about to be labeled a "whiny bitch." I was independent and could survive on my own. I was not needy. I enjoyed my visits enormously, but only as long as I felt like Dad enjoyed having me there. I knew to exit.

That is how I learned to enjoy and love my father—by taking him in a lot of small doses. That was the perfect prescription for a healthy and loving relationship. I would do as much as I could to calm the Beast and show him affection, but I also knew my place.

My father was two generations removed from me, and his opinion of women could not be changed. Only when he saw how determined and different I strived to be did he start to question his perception of women. Not all women, he finally came to see, were alike. When he did ask my opinion about something, I knew I would be heard even if he was asking just out of pure curiosity. I always tried to choose my words carefully because it wasn't often that I had his undivided attention.

Something wonderful evolved out of these limited encounters: I gained the respect of my father and my brother. I was a key component to the three of us getting along and enjoying each other. Mostly, I was a caring listener. When I spoke, they both listened. I could ease Dad's worries over John-Henry, and John-Henry could vent his frustrations with me. I had become a needed asset in the family and found my purpose; I felt valued. Finally, the two most important men in my life needed me and wanted me to be around more often. It had taken years, but that was okay. I discovered that I understood my difficult father better than anyone because I'd had to navigate the same complexities in myself. I am my father's daughter, and I am proud to admit that he is my hero, as is my brother.

It was on my graduation trip that my brother and I started to realize that Dad was tolerating our company and including us in his life for longer than three days—much longer. That probably came about as our growing understanding of his frustrations combined with his deepening trust in us. He knew he could be himself around us. Our love was unconditional and consistent. We were used to his outbursts and sometimes hardly noticed them. His swearing was just a cue that perhaps he was escalating and needed some attention. He knew we got him, and he knew he could rely on our allegiance. Just as you do when training an animal or raising a child, I learned to be direct and clear in my communication with him. I was selective in what I wanted to say and very thoughtful in how I said it. Most of all, I simply showed understanding.

"Dad, I'm right here and I'm not going anywhere. What's bothering you? You seem like you're angry about something."

"You bet your ass I'm angry. Where the hell is your brother?"

"He's probably at the office. You want me to call him?"

"Get him on the goddamned phone."

Instead of saying what he wanted, he seemed to think you should be able to read his mind. I think I actually got pretty close to doing just that. Lots of times, though, he simply needed permission to vent. I didn't take his venting personally as he let go, exhaled, and released the tension that was building up. If I confronted his frustration calmly and showed understanding, it was quickly defused and the conflict was resolved. Dad was simply looking for someone to listen and relate to him.

As soon as I got John-Henry on the phone, Dad would start to relax.

"What are you doing?" Dad would ask, just like a kid would.

My brother would say he was working or ask if there was something Dad needed.

"When are you coming up? Are you coming for dinner?"

It was apparent that Dad wanted our company. He was bored, lonely, or maybe felt like doing something. He wanted his kids to be around him. We were entertaining and enthusiastic; everything was conquerable and no big deal. We would smother him with hugs and kisses, and just a touch made him smile. He needed a distraction and escape from whatever conflict from the past was still unresolved. I think that between his failed marriages and his estranged daughter, he felt a lot of guilt. He knew he had made a lot of mistakes, but now, pushing eighty, he didn't feel like he could do anything about them. If Ted Williams couldn't be successful at something or if he failed at something, he abandoned it, just as he'd learned from his parents. Being around his son, Anita, and me made Dad feel worthy of love and proud to be our father. He could tell we adored him, Beast and all. He knew he was important to us. We all had our own unique ability to soothe, calm, energize, and entertain him, making him relax, smile, and laugh. I believe my brother and I did this better than anyone in our father's life, including Louise. Even with her commitment and stead-fastness, Louise would still battle him, sedate him with alcohol, and irritate him with complaints about his children, ultimately escalating the situation and his emotions. Instead of deflecting his moods and distracting him, she was just as moody and whiny as he was. Unlike my brother and me, she did not have the sensitivity to recognize when a storm was coming or when he needed a break and peace and calm. Perhaps over time, after numerous scoldings and with deep familiar-ity, she'd lost that ability. Or perhaps she had lost touch with her own inner kid, while Dad never did. His kids, however, matched him and complemented the person he truly was, on many levels.

After Louise died, Dad reached out to Lynette Simon, a woman about Louise's age, for company. Dad would get lonely, especially at night, and wanted someone around. Lynette and Louise had not been friends. Dad invited her over once for a visit. Lynette showed up for the weekend with two suitcases and some food. Dad had told John-Henry that she was going to visit for just a few days. Days turned into weeks, and tension started building. Lynette overstayed her welcome and thought she was practically entitled to move in. She took no time to set up house. It was about three weeks into her stay that I came home from Europe. John-Henry had called and begged me to come home. He was exhausted and frustrated trying to make Dad happy with his new female housemate and still care for his father. Dad was in a foul mood and wasn't getting his rest because his temporary bed partner snored and stank of cigarettes. John-Henry was trying to please his father by welcoming this Louise clone into the house, but she had clearly overstepped her boundaries and irri-tated our father to no end. Now Dad wanted her gone and was try-ing to get John-Henry to do the dirty work. When I walked into the house and saw my brother and father, I knew something had to be done. You could feel the tension and exhaustion in the air.

I found Lynette on the back patio, smoking. Something inside me snapped. From that day forward I think my tolerance forever changed toward the many leeches who latched onto my father and assumed they were his chosen one and his champion. I'd had enough. My brother had enough. It was time to dismiss the bloodsuckers. For the first time I drew my sword and took a strong stance. It was *our* time to be in our father's life. It was our time, and we weren't sharing him any longer with anyone who irritated him or was bad for his health. We could stand the criticism from others but could not stand to see Dad suffer.

"What are you doing?" I could feel my heart quicken and the adrenaline rush as I stepped out on to the patio, closing the door tightly behind me. "You, of all people, should know Dad doesn't like smoking."

"Don't you talk to me like that, young lady. Your father *wants* me here. I'll smoke if I want to."

"I'll talk to you any way I want. Put your goddamned cigarette out and get the hell out of this house." I was standing in front of her and could feel my horns coming out.

"No—I'm not going anywhere."

"Oh yes you are, you old cow." My words surprised me, but I went on. "I didn't come all the way from Europe to put up with you, your smoking, or the irritation you're causing my father. And you snore. Dad isn't getting his rest. Now get out. Get out of here!"

It was finally our time to have our father in our lives, even if it was through sickness. We were tired of being the only ones who were caring for our father while being criticized and undermined the whole time. No one offered help, but many helped themselves, and even more offered opinions. Some even passed judgment and spread vicious lies.

DURING HIS TIME IN THE KOREAN WAR DAD FLEW THIRTY-NINE combat missions. He often served as the wingman for John H. Glenn

Jr., the future astronaut and US senator. Dad admired John Glenn on many levels and described his "ol' buddy" as "my idol." So, on January 15, 1998, when it was announced that the first American to orbit the earth would be returning to space, Dad was captivated. He insisted that John-Henry search that "world wide web" and "find out everything you can on that computer of yours about *this*."

This became the latest obsession in the Williams family. Senator Glenn was only three years younger than Dad, and this motivated John-Henry to start following the coverage with immense interest. One of the goals of the space mission was to investigate the physiology of the human aging process. John Glenn was going to take part in numerous bioscientific experiments in space to discover what they might reveal about life and aging on earth. This caught our attention big time. The Williams family was all about slowing down the aging process. This became another influential moment in our family's desire to add to our longevity and enjoy our time together as long as possible. The same man who orbited the earth in 1962 was now seventy-seven years old, and he was going to spend nine days in space. Dad had just visited with Glenn in January, about two weeks prior to the announcement that he would be rejoining the astronaut corps. His new adventure became a family affair, and we followed the coverage attentively. Quite frankly, when you're talking with a man who was the first American to orbit the earth and is about to be the oldest person to fly into space, at the age of seventy-seven, the scientific future seems to be without limits.

When Dad was invited to the space shuttle launch, we all decided to go; this was not something we were going to miss. Designated Mission STS-95, it was scheduled for launch on October 29, 1998. Our father couldn't wait for the day to arrive. He made sure we were all prepared with our cameras and armed with binoculars. Dad wasn't always up for traveling by this time, because he would tire very quickly. He normally preferred to rest in bed and watch things unfold on television. He also didn't like to be in a wheelchair. But this was different. "Bring the damned wheelchair and the walker," he said, "and make sure I have my good binoculars!" Dad loved it that his two kids and his son's lovely girlfriend, Anita, were coming along to watch his old friend being launched into space.

We all piled into the Suburban to go to the Kennedy Space Center to watch the launch of the space shuttle *Discovery*. It was one of the most popular launches in NASA's history. More than four thousand journalists had asked for credentials to attend. There were members of Congress, President Clinton and Hillary were there, as well as former astronauts, celebrities, rock stars, and athletes. The place was buzzing. We were very grateful to be invited along on this memorable family outing.

Dad was scheduled for an interview with Tom Brokaw shortly after we arrived, and when the two met it was as if Mr. Brokaw had forgotten why we were all there. He seemed very excited to meet Ted Williams—but not because he was a famous baseball player or the former wingman and pal of astronaut John Glenn. Within minutes of meeting each other, Tom Brokaw reached into his jacket pocket and pulled out several fishing flies. Dad eyed them, and they started talking fishing. Before you knew it, Dad was quizzing Brokaw on every aspect of his fishing equipment, tackle, and gear. Dad wanted to know what Brokaw liked to fish for, where he fished, the tackle he used and how he chose his materials, how he tied the different flies, and the effectiveness of each one of them. Then he asked Brokaw to show him how he cast. *Uh oh*, I thought. *This ought to be funny.* The crowd that had gathered found the humor in Dad's turning the tables on the interviewer. The scene was surreal: in the middle of the "interview," with the space shuttle *Discovery* in the background, on a tiny stage, our eighty-year-old dad was giving Tom Brokaw fly-casting lessons. Dad told him his back cast was weak and short, and his technique didn't allow the rod to do its work or the line to travel its course. Like so many times before, all we could do was observe and smile.

This was the first launch from Kennedy Space Center that Dad had ever seen in person. The closest you can get to see a launch is about three miles from the launch pad. Kennedy Space Center does have a viewing area at its Saturn V Center, where it hosts VIPs (guests of Congress, guests of NASA, celebrities, et al.). I believe we were offered the opportunity to view the launch from there because we were guests of Senator Glenn's.

We drove to the NASA complex and were picked up by a friendly and informative driver in a wheelchair-accessible touring bus, which took us to the Center. On our way, we saw James Cameron, the director and producer of the movie *Titanic*. Dad had recently seen the movie and was impressed by the production. He wanted to meet Cameron. So I rolled Dad over in his wheelchair to Cameron's tour bus while John-Henry got the director's attention. We did not know why Dad wanted to meet the director, but we were about to find out. As we approached the movie director Dad boomed, "That was a *grrreat* movie! What a production! I'd like to share an idea with you that I think would make another great movie."

I'm not sure if Mr. Cameron knew who my dad was, or if he was even a fan of baseball, or if he just thought Dad was an arrogant old man in a wheelchair, but no sooner had Dad said those words than Cameron seemed to stop listening. He probably gets numerous suggestions from fans on what his next movie should be about. It didn't matter to us, though, because John-Henry and I wanted to hear what Dad thought was a great movie idea.

Dad continued: "Have you ever heard of the giant squid they presume lives in the depths of the ocean? Now, THAT would be a great movie! Don't you think? Make a movie on the mystery of the giant squid!"

My brother and I smiled at Dad's enthusiasm as he attempted to tell this great movie director, producer, and writer what to base his next movie on. Dad must have sensed Cameron's lack of interest, or maybe it was just time to go and we were holding up the bus traffic. "I think it would be a great idea," Dad mumbled to himself.

"It was nice meeting you, Mr. Cameron, thank you for your time," my brother and I said as he turned and got on his bus.

As we loaded back onto our own bus Dad said, "Well, I don't think he liked my idea too much."

"It's a great idea, Dad," John-Henry said, frowning in the direction of the celebrity bus.

When we arrived at the Saturn V Center, we had to walk through the building to get outside to the area where bleachers were set up. As we rolled through the building, admiring everything, Anita and I spotted Steven Tyler of Aerosmith. I was too shy to approach him, so I sent Anita to go tell him that Ted Williams wanted to meet him. It really was a secret ploy to impress my brother and to get to meet the rock star myself. It turned out that Steven Tyler was a big fan of baseball and had spent a lot of time in New England. He seemed genuinely happy to meet Dad. I smiled to myself as I followed the rock legend walking toward my father. Dad wasn't going to have a clue who this man was, and I only hoped he wouldn't say anything about his hair or the way he dressed. Dad hated long hair on females and *especially* on males. Knowing Dad, I thought he just might tell Tyler he needed a haircut.

When John-Henry saw us approaching, he couldn't believe his eyes. A big grin spread across his face. He bent over and must have explained to Dad that a music great was coming his way. Dad looked around for the likes of Herbie Hancock, or maybe Frank Sinatra or Count Basie. With his tunnel vision, Dad had trouble seeing if the light wasn't just right. He reached out his hand to find Steven Tyler and smiled big.

"Geez, you must be pretty great, my kids are sure all excited to meet you."

Mr. Tyler was a true gentleman, gracious and respectful. He told

Dad he was a big fan and was nice enough to take some pictures with us. But Dad wasn't going to let him off the hook that easily. He could sense the younger crowd in the group was thrilled to be meeting *this guy*.

"Now tell me, what kind of music do you play?"

"Oh, you probably haven't heard too much of my stuff, Ted," Tyler replied almost sheepishly. "I play rock and roll."

"Well . . . nope, I can't say I listen to that too much," Dad said, as friendly as possible. "But you must be pretty damned good. It sure is nice of you to meet me and my kids. I can see they're big fans. Thank you."

Dad's limited vision prevented him from realizing that there was a pretty woman accompanying Steven Tyler. But when she leaned in to shake his hand, she had his full attention.

"Who are you?" he asked as if he had just discovered a mystical forest creature. As he squeezed her hand his other hand also took hold of her hand, as if to capture the pretty thing and pull her right onto his lap in the wheelchair. There were giggles and laughs in response to the obvious come-on. Steven Tyler never missed a beat. He smiled at the compliment Dad was paying his lady friend and introduced her, but Dad never let go of her or his eye contact.

"I bet you keep *him* in line!" he said as he gestured with his head and eyes in the direction of Tyler.

Dad . . . stop hitting on Tyler's lady, I thought, but everyone loved the show of attention and Dad's obvious charm. My brother and I just shook our heads and smiled.

"Would it be all right if I got my picture taken with you?" she asked.

"Of course!" boomed Dad. "Let me stand up."

As soon as he attempted to stand everyone rushed to his side and crouched down beside him. The two of them insisted that Dad stay seated. Steven Tyler was so nice. He bent down and put his arm around Dad as if to give him a side-hug. John-Henry insisted on being the one to take the pictures. Out of all the VIP guests, my brother was probably carrying the latest and best camera money could buy. He took some great pictures.

I wanted to give Steven Tyler a hug, not because I was a huge fan, but to thank him for just being so nice. There were flocks of people approaching, and they weren't for Dad. Tyler still took the time to take pictures with us and even exchanged mailing info so that we could send him copies. Later, after we sent him a picture of the meeting, he sent John-Henry a thank-you note and a drum cover signed by the entire band. It was an unexpected surprise and very much appreciated.

The crowd took over after we met Tyler, and we were pressed to get outside to watch the shuttle launch. It was fast approaching lift-off time. There were only about a hundred people outside. Among them were numerous astronauts and other celebrities I didn't even recognize. Dad was only interested in the astronauts. He grabbed one and started asking questions regarding the launch and the setup and what all was going on. I'm sure that was why they had so many astronauts in this area—so that people could ask questions.

At eighty years old, our father had done and seen a lot, but he was about to have one of his most memorable life experiences. As the countdown started at T minus two minutes the crowd became quiet. We watched our father. He was so focused. He looked like he was holding his breath. There was angst in him, a nervousness you could see as he fiddled just a bit with his binoculars.

He turned and looked up at his son from his wheelchair. My brother must have read his mind. Before Dad even had a chance to say anything, John-Henry was right there to help his father to his feet.

"T minus one minute. All systems go."

We were all together, the four of us huddled in our own little pod, waiting for a four-million-pound space shuttle to lift from the ground and fly into space. We listened to the voice broadcasting from the Control Center. It came through the speakers:

"Ten, nine, eight—we have a go—five, four, three, two, one, and liftoff."

From three miles away, you *see* everything before you experience anything. The launch appears to unfold in the slowest of motions. We saw smoke starting to rise above the treetops. It quickly turned to enormous white billowing clouds mixed with fire that looked like storm clouds that had come down from the sky and mixed with a forest fire. In seconds that passed like minutes, the enormous vessel spit fire and began to levitate from the earth. It made its own bright light, which illuminated the sky. You wondered whether looking at it would hurt your eyes, but we were mesmerized; we did not turn away. Then we felt it. The heat reached across the water to where we stood and warmed our skin. But it scorched the sky, leaving a cone of fire behind it as the craft escaped into the blue sky. Then came the sound. It raced across the water, filling every quiet space, moving the water and shoving the air out of the way as it headed straight toward us. The reverberating boom passed right through us, and as it did our bones shuddered and the sound resonated in every body cavity. It grabbed us and shook us as if an earthquake had started right under our feet. One massive cannon had gone off, accompanied by billions of M-80s crackling and Wolfpack firecrackers popping all around it.

Every person was cheering and clapping in concert. You could feel the pride and awe as we all watched a spacecraft carry seven astronauts to a place few people will ever go. There was excitement and pure wonder as everyone stood with their heads lifted, watching it rip through the sky at more than two thousand miles per hour. Then, as if the rock star in the crowd had subliminally influenced him, Dad clenched his fist and shot it to the sky yelling, "Godspeed, John Glenn! Good luck, friend."

I did not expect to feel the emotions that wrapped around us, but there they were. We never looked away until we couldn't follow the shine in the sky any longer, and when we turned to look at each other in amazement, we all had tears in our eyes. We all looked a bit disheveled too. We were literally blown away. Dad spoke first.

"Wow."

I can't find accurate words to describe this experience, but Dad said it best. *Wow.* It was an exceptional moment in our father's life, and in our lives together. For months afterward he would attempt to describe it over and over to anybody who would listen. Dad and John-Henry vowed, from that moment on, that they would attend every launch.

That proved to be a bit too ambitious. We attended the next scheduled launch with big expectations. It was to be a night launch, scheduled thirty-five days later, on December 3, at 3:58 A.M. At T minus nineteen seconds, the launch attempt was scrubbed. We drove home, disappointed at the lost opportunity. The next launch window was the very next night (December 4) at 3:35 A.M. Unfortunately, Dad was too tired from the trip the night before to attend this one. That space shuttle did lift off on time, and the launch was no less impressive than the Glenn launch. John-Henry remained completely interested and would not miss it. He took many photos and enjoyed sharing every one of them with Dad.

Chapter Twenty-Two

Take a look at the back of your driver's license. According to the 2012 National Donor Designation Report Card, 42.7 percent of individuals in the United States age eighteen and older are registered organ donors. Some 101.4 million people have potentially given the gift of life. When you're declared dead, medical professionals will take your body to an operating room and begin harvesting the organs that a transplant coordinator deems suitable for donation. These organs will then be flushed of their blood and placed in an aqueous solution in the hope of preserving them for as long as it takes to transport them to their recipients. Sometime later your family will receive letters about the various patients who received your organs and the lives that were saved because of the courage you had to make an anatomical donation in the name of science.

The science of organ preservation and of making anatomical gifts is progressing every day. The decision of one person to become an organ donor has the potential to save many lives. Even with the risk of organ rejection, every donation advances the science, which in turn increases the chance of saving a life. Organ donation leaves a legacy in your name that far exceeds the impact of any foundation, will, or trust. The life-saving potential, however, of that donation is destroyed when cremation or embalming is chosen instead. Every living thing in the body, right down to the molecular level, is destroyed.

In the late 1990s we had a subscription at the house to a magazine called *Life Extension*. The publisher was an affiliate of a progressive vitamin and mineral manufacturing company. Dad, John-Henry, and I were always into good health and taking care of our bodies, so the Williams family was always on a vitamin kick. I believe my brother first learned of the science of cryonics from an article in that magazine.

But while that article might have planted the seed, there was more to it than just that. For much of our lives—dating back to our care for and nurturing of the animals on the farm—John-Henry and I had always thought a bit differently about death. During the '90s, we'd witnessed death in our own ways, and John-Henry in particular had been changed by it.

In early 1995 my mother had started taking care of her mother more. Because my mother had built her parents a home on our property, my grandmother conveniently lived less than four hundred yards away. Typical of firstborns, Mom had been the family caretaker for years—ever since she was a model sending checks back home to the family. In that time she'd helped her mother through all manner of emotional, financial, and health problems, even my grandfather's death on Memorial Day 1986. At the time I was fourteen and my brother was seventeen. Grumpa hadn't been feeling very well. I came home after school and went to visit him. I found him sitting on the doorstep to his house holding a shotgun. He looked ashen and was breathing heavily.

"Grumpa, what's the matter? You need to go to the doctor."

He did not respond. I ran and got my mother. She came over, took one look at her father, and went to call the ambulance. My grandfather grabbed her wrist before she walked into the house and said, "I'm not going anywhere."

Grumpa was intent on dying at home. It took his son Joseph and John-Henry to convince him to go to the hospital. Grumpa came home only a few days later and seemed fine. He had lunch with his son and my grandmother and decided to go take a nap. Later on that afternoon I came over to visit. My grandmother was outside in the garden.

"Where's Grumpa?"

"Oh, he's napping. Don't you go wake him up now. He's very tired."

I didn't listen. I wanted to see my grandfather. I opened the front door, careful to close it securely behind me. I tiptoed up the stairs to his bedroom. Grumpa was lying on his bed with his hands interlaced across his chest. He looked very peaceful . . . too peaceful. I stood at the foot of the bed staring at his chest. I wanted to see his chest move. *Please move.* I walked a little closer. When I touched him, he was still warm, but I knew he was gone. I raced down the stairs and screamed to my grandmother.

"Grandma! Grumpa is dead!"

"Don't be silly. He's just napping."

She started toward me and worked her way up the stairs. I screamed across the way to my mother's house. She heard me and came running.

I raced back up the stairs. My grandmother was trying to rouse my grandfather. She was speaking Swedish, her mother tongue. She was crying and calling my grandfather by his first name.

Mom finally got to the top of the stairs and knew instantly that Grumpa was dead. I thought we should try to do CPR, but she told me it wouldn't work. I had just learned it in school and insisted we try. Mom held me tightly and told me it was too late.

John-Henry took Grumpa's death very hard and came home from Vermont Academy to mourn. He hated it when they cremated Grumpa. He hated to think of his grandfather being burned down to nothing but ashes. He found it disrespectful and was angry with his aunts and uncle for choosing this method. When Grumpa's urn was placed on our grandmother's shelf, John-Henry put it away in the cupboard. He couldn't even look at it. It was the beginning of many difficult and heartbreaking family losses my brother and I would experience.

My father was very fond of Mom's parents. Knowing the important role our grandfather played as a surrogate father when he wasn't around, Dad would thank Grumpa, in his own way, for filling in during his absence. Dad brought Grumpa smoked salmon or some spicy sausage when he came through town. My father always remembered our grandparents at Christmas and would send them a check for a couple hundred bucks. Dad knew from what my brother and I shared with him how much we loved and leaned on Grumpa. We learned loyalty and honesty from our grandfather. He taught us hard work and discipline, but also patience.

In the aftermath of Grumpa's passing, Grandma became a vital part of our household, and she and Mom spent more time than ever together. Mom's brother Joseph and her youngest sister Paulette lived in New Hampshire, and her other younger sister Heidi lived in Massachusetts, so Mom became her mother's primary caretaker. Adored by everyone, Grandma was quite charming and could make every one of us feel like we were her favorite. She was enchanting and soft. You could always find her in her garden or among her tall hollyhocks. Her rhythmic voice and slight Swedish accent had a lulling effect, and she often hummed while she kept herself busy cooking, weaving on her loom, or worshipping the sun. My father described her as the sweetest lady, always remarking on her soft hands and comparing my own hands to my grandmother's.

Grandma and Mom grew incredibly close. I think the firstborn is always a little bit more special. One of their favorite pastimes was playing chess together. They could play all day sometimes. Mom would teach Dad the game and the special reward for winning—wishes. Our family tradition was that if you won a game of chess, you were granted a wish by your opponent. You could wish for a movie night or to go to a friend's house, get out of a chore or be helped with one, get something you desire, or even be taken for a drive somewhere. Without wishes, my brother and I might have never been able to go to a friend's house or get a toy we really wanted, so we got very good at chess. My brother won the Vermont State Junior Championship. It was tough to beat John-Henry. Games would end with someone flipping the board and pieces flying, especially if Mom was playing.

Mom was always keeping an eye on her mother. She took Grandma to the doctors and grocery shopping. Mom ensured that Grandma took her medicine, put on her compression stockings first thing in the morning to keep the fluid out of her ankles, and kept eating healthy. Mom took Grandma everywhere. There was always an adventure going on with Mom, and I think Grandma enjoyed the entertainment. Grandma liked to be dramatic and mysterious herself. She was flirtatious with her doctors and seemed to bat her eyes at young, attractive men. When Mom and Grandma had squabbles, it always revolved around Mom and her siblings and the complaints that each had about the others. Grandma attempted to defend and protect all of them, which usually left one of them angry at her for not taking their side. This was a common occurrence, but in the end Grandma often turned to her firstborn, Dolores, or Whoawa. (As a child, Mom's brother Joseph couldn't pronounce "Dolores," and instead it came out "Woe-wah.")

As Mom recalls, somewhere around September 1995, Paulette visited Grandma. Her youngest daughter was unhappy with how Grandma was living and decided it was time for her to come live with her in New Hampshire. Mom resisted the change and looked to her mother to back her up and say that she preferred to stay with her oldest daughter. But characteristically, Grandma was not assertive. She rationalized that perhaps a break was the right thing to do.

"I'll go stay with Paulette for a while. You're getting tired of me anyway, and you need a rest. I'll be fine."

There really was no arguing with Grandma. She was so passive. She just shrugged her shoulders, smiled, and said everything would be all right. She didn't like conflict and arguments. Paulette and Dolores, however, were veterans at it, and an argument ensued. As Mom recalls, it was one of the worst. Somebody pushed somebody else, and the word "bitch" was thrown around.

Grandma willingly went to stay with Paulette in Keene. Only a few weeks later she was on the phone calling Mom.

"Whoawa, come get me, *get me outta here.* Paulette keeps me locked up in the second-floor guest bedroom all day."

I don't believe this was actually happening to my grandmother, but it was what my mom heard and the way she still describes it today. I tend to believe that dramatic family license was at play. It is more likely that Grandma just wanted to get out of the house for a while and visit with Dolores. It was all Mom needed to hear, though, and she raced her dump truck toward Keene to rescue her mother, with a twelve-foot ladder in the back.

When Mom arrived it was dusk, but still light enough outside to see the house. Mom propped the ladder up against the house under the window of the second-floor guest bedroom. It took quite a few taps on the glass for Grandma to hear her. When she opened the window, according to Mom, she was very happy to see her firstborn. Mom said it didn't take much to convince Grandma to crawl out the window and climb down the ladder. Just as she got to the bottom two rungs she lost her footing and stumbled to the ground. She was unharmed, landing on the soft grass, but the commotion of the ladder sliding against the wall was enough to alert Paulette and her husband, Charlie. Another argument ensued, and a police officer arrived to ask Mom to leave the property. Grandma may have wanted to go with her eldest daughter, but the scene was too much for the officer and Grandma had to stay.

About a month after the ladder incident Mom found out that her mother was in the hospital. She headed over to New Hampshire to see her. According to Mom, when she arrived she discovered that her name was listed as a potential visitor who was not allowed to see Mrs. Wettach. Mom kept her cool, but inside she was livid. She left the hospital but decided she would come back later. Being a nurse, she knew that after-hours visitations would not be so strictly enforced. As she waited for the evening she contacted my cousin Zoey, who was living in Keene, and shared with her how (with Zoey's help) she was going to sneak in to visit her mother. Zoey was game. The plan worked, and Grandma was so pleased to see both of them. It was clear, however, that Grandma was beginning to fail, and it pained Mom to leave her side.

As all this was occurring, my brother was in the middle of moving down to Florida to be with Dad. When he heard of Grandma's failing health, he decided to go visit her. By now she was out of the hospital and back at Paulette's house. When John-Henry pulled into the driveway, Paulette came out to greet him and, according to John-Henry, supervise the visitation. John-Henry asked his grandmother if she would like to go for a ride in his new BMW. Grandma was eager to go for a ride, but as John-Henry remembers, Paulette said she would rather he did not leave the premises with *her* mother. John-Henry recalls that Grandma was clearly disappointed, but in her usual fashion she smiled at John-Henry and said, "She thinks you're going to take me away and bring me back to Dolores."

She was right. At the end of their long paved and groomed driveway, my mom stood by the side of the road, hoping to see her mother. When John-Henry returned with no Grandma, she was very disappointed.

It was very hard to understand how any of this could be happening. John-Henry called me in Germany and told me I should call Grandma. He warned me that she had taken a turn for the worse. Paulette answered, and the reception felt icy to me. I hadn't seen my aunt in probably over ten years, and I certainly had nothing to do with the present situation. I just wanted to talk to my grandmother. It was a difficult conversation. She was so hard of hearing. She assumed she knew everything I was saying and asking. I held the phone to my ear as I just listened to her recite things that were going on and how she was. I tried to ask her how she was feeling and if we should try to take some legal action so that she could see Mom. She responded that the weather was nice and asked me what I wanted for Christmas. At every pause I tried telling her that I loved her. If she heard only one thing I wanted her to hear that. Finally she caught it.

"Grandma loves you too, sweetheart."

Mom called to wish her mother a Merry Christmas and remembers being told that "Mother" was resting comfortably and wasn't to be disturbed. Mom accepted this and didn't argue. She would try again the next day. December 26 is my mom's birthday. She recalls that growing up with three other siblings, her birthday, coming right after Christmas, was often forgotten.

The next morning, on Mom's sixty-first birthday, the phone rang, and Mom answered.

"Whoawa? It's Joe. Mother died this morning."

I don't know what Mom said, but I can only imagine. She still cries when she recalls this moment. She called me next, and when I answered the phone I couldn't believe what I heard. My mother was hysterical. She was sobbing and inconsolable. Between wails of emotion she kept repeating herself.

"I have to find her. I have to find her."

"Where is she? Where is Grandma?"

"They won't tell me! They're afraid I'm going to cause a scene."

"Mom, try and calm down. I'm so sorry, Mom."

"I have to find her before they *burn her.*"

"Mom, call John-Henry. He'll find her."

"I have to see her! I have to save her!"

"Oh Mom, I'm sorry. I love you."

"I'm going to steal her from the morgue and bring her home."

I started getting concerned at this point. Mom was so upset, and her voice was filled with panic and anxiety.

"Mom, don't talk like that. You can't do that."

"I'm gonna find her and bring her home and hide her in the snow. She'll freeze, and the ice will keep her safe and preserved until I can bury her at home and keep her with me. I have to find her."

I got off the phone and called John-Henry right away. My mom can be very emotional. She can be dramatic. She can be hysterical, and she did cause many a scene. But this was different. Mom *needed* to see her mother. She *needed* to say good-bye.

"John-Henry, you have to go home. You'd better call Mom. She is very, very upset. I'm very worried about her. Please call her."

My brother didn't believe it was as bad as I had explained it, but when he heard Mom tell him exactly what she had told me, he was very concerned. He was on a plane the next day. It is hard to admit, but we both believed that our mother had an emotional breakdown. She was forever changed after that traumatic experience. She truly had a break of some sort.

As it turned out, Mom wasn't the only one affected. I believe that somewhere in the recesses of my brother's mind my mother's words took root, and that this very emotional experience may have also influenced him later in his investigation into how to handle Dad's mortality.

WHILE THE DEATHS OF GRUMPA AND GRANDMA CLEARLY HAD A major impact on how John-Henry thought about death, another catalyst for his learning about cryonics was a dog.

It all began a few years earlier when John-Henry and Anita were still together and she was grieving the loss of her beloved dog. He had never seen her so upset and badly wanted to take her pain away. In 1996 there was a lot of media coverage of Dolly, the cloned sheep, and in 1998 a group of Japanese scientists cloned twin cows as well. My brother thought maybe he could get the dog, Tara, cloned. It was

through his research on "how to bring your dog back" that he ultimately discovered the Alcor Life Extension Foundation.

Robert Ettinger, a University of Michigan professor of physics
and mathematics, had launched modern cryonics with his 1964 book
The Prospect of Immortality. He theorized that continuing advances
in medical science will eventually cure all known diseases and halt
aging, in effect making all humans immortal. He further posited that
bodies might be preserved in a state of *suspended biological activity*
until such time as they could be revived and healed. The book was
translated into many languages and was covered in all the media,
making Ettinger something of a celebrity.

In 1967 the first human, a psychology professor, was cryonically
preserved. The cryonics facility Alcor Life Extension Foundation
was established in 1972. Ettinger founded the Cryonics Institute
in 1976; when he himself died in 2011 at the age of ninety-two, he
became the Institute's 106th preserved human. The privacy of medical records makes exact figures unobtainable, but at the time of this
writing the estimated total number of people who have been preserved is around 270, mostly in the United States at Alcor or the
Cryonics Institute and a few in Russia. Privacy issues also make it
difficult to estimate how many living people have made arrange-
ments to be preserved in the future. Those who choose this option
are simply betting that *possibly* at some point in the future—fifty
years, a hundred, five hundred—medicine will have progressed to
the point where they can be revived to live healthy new lives. They
know it's a very long shot, but since cryonics is based on scientific
research, the possibility improves with every medical, scientific, and
technological advancement. Patients are pronounced legally dead
when the heart stops beating—but they are not *biologically* dead at
that point. Most of the body's cells are still alive. At normal temperatures, the cells of the body die slowly over the next few hours.
Cryonicists seek to minimize the deterioration of cells and organs,
including the brain, by immediately cooling the body to very low

temperatures. Contrary to popular misconceptions, the body is not "frozen," which would cause the formation of organ-damaging ice. Cryonicists drain the body of fluids and replace them with a biological solution that prevents freezing and hardens like glass rather than like ice. This is called vitrification. The body is cooled to below −200 degrees Fahrenheit, the temperature at which all cellular and molecular activities cease. At facilities like Alcor, the body is kept at that temperature in a large steel cylinder that is cooled by liquid nitrogen.

Many members of Alcor choose to have only their heads preserved, a process called neurosuspension. Although the popular media have run all sorts of horror stories about frozen heads and Frankenstein science, the reasons are quite practical. The brain, obviously, is the most important of all the organs. It is the seat of our intelligence and personality and memory. Alcor preserves the whole head to avoid the damage that could come from removing the brain. People who choose this option are betting that by the time medical science can revive their brain, it will also be able to grow or build them a whole new body. The hope is not to have the former body reanimated, but instead to have a whole new body created from the same DNA. Original memories and knowledge are preserved while a person inhabits a brand-new body.

Cryonics is not wild-eyed science fiction but is in fact extrapolation from current medicine and technology. Artificial organs are old news now, and "test tube babies" are a fact of life. Advances in robots and robotic limbs make the news pretty much every day. Cloning is a reality, and genetic engineering can change the DNA of a cell. Nanotechnology, which cryonicists believe will play a big role in the medicine of the future, is still in its infancy but making rapid advances.

In fact, although cryonics has largely been lampooned in the press as laughable or even freakish "fringe science," the medical establishment has been using similar methods for decades. It's now routine for human embryos that have been preserved by cooling to grow into healthy children. Patients are cooled on beds of ice to slow down body functions after a heart attack or during neurosurgical operations. And of course, organs removed for transplant are cooled for preservation. Through the science of cryonics, organs could be preserved for longer periods of time in order to make it to their designated recipients with less cell death. Vitrification (not freezing) allows the biological structure of an organ to be preserved, creating more time for recipients to receive their vital organs, with less damage to the organ itself. These are all now accepted applications of some of the science behind cryonics. This same science has the goal of suspending life, if only on the molecular level.

My parents believed that everything was manageable and conquerable through science. I found it an incredible coincidence that they found each other. They were both, during a time of strong religious faith in the United States, agnostic. They were not atheists. They did not hate religion—just the contrary. They both chose not to believe because they were not yet convinced or because they had their doubts owing to painful life experiences. I don't apologize for that. Despite their similarities, my parents had significant differences as well, but they were always united on how my brother and I should be raised. My father admired my mother's allegiance to her children and always described her as a great mother. She taught us right from wrong, good family values, kindness, and respect. She never mentioned God, and there was no Bible in the house. But we did not have a problem with religion. In fact, when we were kids and moved to Florida to be around our father, John-Henry and I went to the Island Christian School, where we respectfully took part in the morning prayer. Still, the first time I walked into a church was to sing for a wedding when I was eleven or twelve.

Our parents taught us that we needed only our own hearts and brains to determine our morality. Dad and Mom left it up to my brother and me to decide what direction we wanted to go regarding religion. They themselves relied on science to explain the challenges of life. I have to believe it is difficult to rely on luck or miracles if you're a scientist or a person driven by perfection. Dad depended on hard work. Sometime near the year I was born, he wrote his book, *The Science of Hitting*. You can see it in there. He did not believe in anything that could not be reliably proven. Unfortunately, God's existence cannot be proven scientifically. Faith in a higher being is a choice we make. Dad and Mom put their faith in science. Every day Mom worked as a nurse she learned to rely more and more on the "miracles" of science and the future of the medical field. I recall three magazines in our parents' homes: *Science, Discover,* and *National Geographic.* Our father gave us a *National Geographic* subscription one year for Christmas, and our appreciation of the world broadened because of it.

When my brother first approached me on cryonics, he was testing me to see how much I knew.

"Isn't that what they did to Walt Disney?" I asked.

"No, that's a myth. But do you know what it is?"

"Isn't it where they freeze people?"

Disgusted, my brother sat me down to explain what he had learned. Very much like our father, John-Henry would not quiz you on a subject unless he had already researched the answers. My brother had done his research and presented cryonics to me as something we as a family should consider.

You never know what will happen in your life that will reside somewhere in your memory, ultimately influencing your decisions. You may remember it consciously, or its impact may be more elusive. My brother remained pensive and thoughtful for quite some time about what I believe were a few pivotal moments in his life. To me it seems obvious that they influenced his interest in cryonics.

John-Henry's first significant girlfriend was Kelly, a very good friend of mine. I stayed with her and her family over a summer once, and John-Henry became infatuated with her. She was a star gymnast and had beautiful deep red curly hair. My brother described her as a vixen and thought she was cool. Their relationship ended poorly, with Kelly ultimately leaving him. My brother was often unavailable when she wanted him, and he could be moody and, as she would describe him, "cold." She wrote him a poem during their relationship called "The Ice Man," in which she described him as distant, as often aloof and far away. It was a fair description. My brother was very cerebral and preferred the undivided attention and interaction of one versus a few. He seldom enjoyed parties or crowds.

When Kelly broke up with him he was very upset, and he was determined to somehow win her back. He wrote her a poem attempting to explain why he was the way he was. He referenced "The Ice Man" and promised that he could change his ways and be warmer toward her. He placed the poem in a Ziploc bag and sealed it. Then he went into our cellar and emptied our deep freezer. He proceeded to fill the freezer with water, then placed the encased poem in the middle among some old chains so that he could pull the large ice block out when it was solid. It took two days for the ice block to form, but my brother didn't mind the wait because he wanted to be sure his ex-girlfriend had some time and space to think about her recent decision.

On the night of the second day John-Henry loaded the back of his Pontiac with the large block of ice and headed over to Kelly's house. He placed the ice on the cement path leading to her front door and left. He didn't know how long it would take for the ice to melt, and wondered if she would try to break the ice to get to the message or simply wait for it to melt. Either way, it was supposed to be a challenge and a waiting game to test her resolve about rekindling the relationship. He was patiently hoping that she would be moved enough to question her final verdict, especially when she read the poem that ended with the words: "the Ice Man has melted."

They never rekindled their relationship.

When Kelly broke up with John-Henry, he tried to "preserve" the relationship by promising he would change. When our grandfather died, John-Henry thought it was awful that he was burned, cremated. When our grandmother died, our mom wanted to hide her in the snow, letting the ice and cold preserve her. When Anita's dog died, he searched for a way to preserve the animal, harvest the DNA, and bring her back. John Glenn went into space so that scientists could use him to conduct numerous tests on the aging process in hopes of gaining new insights into how to prolong life.

So my brother had been thinking about all of this for a long time, and I believe that several events in his life had stoked his enthusiasm for this cutting-edge science. Many scientists regard their colleagues who explore outside the established order as mavericks; most will agree, however, that mavericks are often the drivers of huge scientific change.

Chapter Twenty-Three

By 2000 John-Henry was caring for Dad every day, witnessing our father's decline and his struggle to breathe given his heart failure. John-Henry was exploring every option *possible* to keep his father alive—every option.

We pursued specialized diets to enhance the nutrient absorption that is lost in older people. Dad's vitamin supplements were of the highest quality, sometimes costing over $30 per pill. Equipment to provide oxygen-rich air in Dad's room helped with cell regeneration and tissue healing. We used alternative medicine techniques to combat the MRSA infection that Dad developed in the hospital after heart surgery; it was essentially eradicated with the use of bee pollen. We tried Chinese acupuncture while Dad recovered in the hospital to help relieve his stress and anxiety. We researched the latest drugs, including their off-label uses. We even asked a psychiatrist to assess Dad and see if he needed some therapy to manage his mood swings. The psychiatrist diagnosed Dad with Sundowner's Syndrome. As the name implies, when the sun goes down, a person with this condition may become confused, agitated, or depressed.

So we bought Dad a light box that emitted full-spectrum light to mimic natural daylight. We also started taking him outside more often in the Florida sun.

When John-Henry read new research that showed patients live longer when they receive dialysis at night rather than in the daytime, he bought Dad his own dialysis machine. It was through this pursuit of life extension that John-Henry started to focus on cryonics as an answer. We were running out of options to treat our father; just when our relationship with him seemed to be at its best, time was doing its worst. Watching our father slowly die was killing my brother and me.

"I think we should all be cryonically preserved as a family."

I looked at my brother and could see this was something in which he had placed a lot of *faith*.

"John-Henry, we can't do that."

"Why?"

"Because . . . no one would like that."

"So?"

"We would be crucified by the media."

"We can keep it confidential. Doesn't it make you feel better knowing that there might be a chance to bring Dad back someday? A chance for us to be together again?"

"It's a wonderful thought, yes, but I don't know. . . . What does Dad think?"

"He thinks it's kooky. But he is interested, I can tell."

I smiled. My brother had no fear. He didn't care what others thought about him. He was going to do what he thought was right. He was going to do everything he could to help our family endure the pain of death. He was looking for comfort in a time of great despair and anxiety.

Interestingly enough, after the astounding 1941 season a reporter had asked Dad: What's next for the Splendid Splinter?

"I wanna be an immortal."

Even though I'd retired from racing, I still maintained the part of my workout schedule that included biking home on the Withlacoochee State Trail. I would drive my car to the beginning of the trail and then cycle the rest of the way home. It was about a forty-five-mile ride, a perfect supplement to my fitness regime. Dad would sit at the kitchen table and look out the window, watching to see me come up the long road to his Citrus Hills home, which had been built on one of the highest elevations in Florida. I was easy to spot because Dad insisted that I wear the "brightest goddamned colors" that existed. He even wanted to attach a high red flag on the back of my $3,000 racing bike just so cars would see me from afar. I finally convinced him that a flag was just not cool and that I was safe from cars on the trail.

"If you're going to be on the road, you wear the brightest colors you can find, you hear me?" I was usually the rider in neon yellow or orange with reflector tape down her back.

He would be waiting for me at the kitchen table with a big glass of juice and water. He was always happy to see me. He'd shake his head at me as I clicked across the linoleum floor in hard clip-on shoes, wearing full bright biking gear with a helmet that looked like it belonged in outer space. I would walk toward him smiling because he knew by now what was coming. I'd wrap my sweaty stinky body around him in a big hug and give him a salty kiss right on the cheek. Every time he would laugh and say, "All right, all right, that's enough. . . . Jesus, you smell a little gamey—maybe you should take a shower."

When I'd come back from cleaning up, there would be a hot dog ready for me. Dad believed I needed the sodium. To humor him I'd eat it every time.

I would spend a long weekend with him. I usually had Fridays off from work, so I rode up in the morning and headed back on Sunday afternoon. Every weekend I shared the latest in my training and my part-time job, all while I massaged his feet. He loved to have his feet massaged. I'd give him a homemade pedicure, which he thoroughly enjoyed. Every three weeks he would get the deluxe treatment, which included getting his nails clipped and filed. He was very sensitive in his feet. Even though I always approached him carefully but not too tentatively, inevitably I tickled him. He'd laugh and pull his feet away as if bothered. I'd shoot him a frustrated look—doing my own Kermit impression—and give him the same line he'd given us when we were giggling and laughing over something silly as children: "Get a little serious, Dad. Come on, I'm trying to do a good job here."

He'd be amused hearing me turn his own lines around on him.

After pedicures and massages, I read to him. We never got past chapter 1 of *Satchel Paige* because he always wanted to explain a blue zinger, darts, a grapefruit pitch, and all the other old-time baseball expressions. One of those times he told me that one of the things he was most proud of in his baseball career and life was standing up for Paige and other black players in his 1966 Hall of Fame speech.

"I was very proud of that move," Dad said.

By the time the next weekend came around, he'd want me to start reading the book from the beginning again because he'd forgotten where we left off, and every time I would hear a little bit more about Satchel Paige.

"Oh boy, he was something else. No one knew how old he was because he lied about his age. But he had the most rhythmic, mesmerizing body motions I ever saw. Once he got to the big leagues, I couldn't hit him at first. I went 0-4 in my first couple of games against him. When I finally did get a hit off him, it was only a little single to right."

Every weekend I came home I would see a change. He'd look a little bit more tired, a little thinner and shorter of breath. He went from waiting for me at the kitchen table to resting in his recliner to being propped up in his bed. I would come into the house and still go through our rituals as if nothing had changed and everything was all right, smiling at his same old comments and questions.

One result of Dad's heart failure was not being able to sleep at night. The only way he could get sufficient oxygen was to sit up, a position that allowed the accumulating fluid to stay below his heart and out of his lungs. Dad had always been an "early to bed, early to rise" man. Now we noticed that he would stay up late many a night, sitting at the kitchen table with us discussing what was new, what we felt passionate about, where we saw ourselves in five or ten years. They were some of the best conversations my brother and I had with our father.

One time as we sat there late into the evening, we decided to play a game. We put a tall glass at the end of the table. We all took our napkins and crumpled them up as tightly as we could. We sat beside each other at the other end of the ten-foot table trying to be the first to toss the napkin into the glass. John-Henry got close, but I couldn't even hit the table. Incredibly, not only was our father the first to dunk it, but he dunked it *every single damned time*. At eighty-one years old, after two strokes, with tunnel vision, and fatigued from being up so late not to mention from heart failure, he *still* beat us.

"Jesus, Dad, you are freaking amazing!" my brother exclaimed, a bit frustrated.

Dad smiled and shrugged with his palms up. "I'm just an old ballplayer."

Every so often during our evening talks Dad would inquire about the latest news on "the cryonics." He was interested in it, even if it was just because of the enthusiasm his son showed toward it. He looked over at me one late evening after John-Henry had gone on and on about the miracles of science and the unforeseen possibilities and said, "Are you in on this too?"

I didn't want to see Dad die. I didn't want to see my brother lose his father—the man he'd worked his whole life to make proud and to protect. My brother had sacrificed so much to be with and to care for his father, on every dimension.

"Who knows what the future will bring?" I replied. "How many people in the 1900s do you think believed we would walk on the moon one day?"

I could tell my brother liked my answer. "Yeah, and breaking the sound barrier and artificial hearts and penicillin and decoding the human DNA!"

Dad hung his head in fatigue. He was so tired. Though he could barely keep his eyes open, he smiled and half-laughed.

John-Henry helped Dad to the recliner where he now slept. Looking back, I think that was probably the night we made the most progress in opening Dad's mind to the idea that cryonics could be a good thing for all of us. This could become our hope and our faith, even our solace—the belief that maybe someday in the future we could be reunited as a family . . . maybe, even if it was just the smallest of chances. It was like a religion, something we could have faith in.

When John-Henry sat back down at the kitchen table, I drew a deep breath.

"There are very few people in the world who create ripples," I said. "If anyone finds out about this, it will create a tidal wave." After a long pause I asked:

"What about Bobby-Jo?"

He looked at me. I may have been three years younger, but there were a couple of times over the years when his little sister made some good points.

"I know. . . ."

In the following months John-Henry tried to find a doctor who would perform open-heart surgery on Dad. The mitral valve of his heart was very weak, and his ejection fraction (the amount of blood coming out of his heart and traveling to his organs) was about 15 percent—normal is between 60 and 70 percent. It was time to do something. We had to determine if we could buy more time with at least a pacemaker or heart surgery. At the University of Florida, Dr. Rick Kerensky explained the procedure of a diagnostic Swan-Ganz catheterization, also known as a pulmonary artery catheter, used to detect heart failure. It all seemed standard. Unbeknownst to me at the time, even this simple test posed a great risk for Dad in his condition. John-Henry would later explain to me that he had talked to the doctor in private and the doctor had informed him of the grave risks that Dad faced in the coming months.

It was heartbreaking to hear. But it was impressive to see how brave Dad was as the doctor explained his options, including valve replacement surgery. At eighty-two years of age, Dad was not a good candidate for heart surgery, but we were going to find him the best doctor. We were at the very least going to give Dad the best of every option.

Dad was clear in his mind and spoke with conviction.

"Doc, if you can give me any extra time with these guys, let's do it. I've had a great life, and what the hell, if I die, maybe I'll die on the table. I'd like to have some more time with my two kids. They are the only things that mean a damn thing to me right now. They're the only reason for me to stick around."

Dr. Kerensky had heard enough and scheduled the procedure.

We stood there in silence for a while. I couldn't fight back the tears. I couldn't be strong any longer.

"I'll be all right. . . ." Dad's voice broke when he saw me crying.

John-Henry saw an opportunity. He looked at Dad, got in close, and said, "Let's do it. Let's promise right here and now we're all going to do it."

After a long silence and a heavy exhale, Dad responded, "If it means that much to you kids, fine."

"Shake on it," John-Henry said. "Let's make it official."

DAD HAD ALWAYS TOLD US THAT OUR ESTRANGED HALF-SISTER was likely to contest his will. He warned us of this numerous times and did everything he could to prepare for it. In 1996 lawyers prepared a will that clearly stated Bobby-Jo was to receive nothing from

his estate after his death. One of the first lines reads, "I have purposely and deliberately eliminated my daughter, Barbara Joyce Ferrell, from this Will. . . . [She] shall be deemed to have predeceased
me leaving no issue surviving." Their relationship was irrevocably
severed. Dad had done everything he could to take care of her for
the rest of her life. She was a spendthrift, and he knew it. Though his
sense of obligation as her father had made him continue to provide
care, he'd done so cautiously. Years earlier he had set up an irrevo-
cable insurance trust to benefit all three of his children. The trust
contained an insurance policy worth $645,000 and 110 autographed
bats, all of which were to be divided equally. He directed the trustees
to distribute Bobby-Jo's proceeds in a manner that would take care
of her for life, by providing only the money necessary for food and
clothing.

Although our father never wavered in the scorn he expressed for
his first daughter, my brother and I wanted to give her the benefit of
the doubt. We were fearful that on his deathbed Dad might regret
the relationship he'd had with her and want to reconcile on some
level. We did not want him to die knowing his daughter might cause
problems even after his death. Despite our attempts to include her in
family decisions or to facilitate conversations between her and Dad
to inform her of what Dad wanted, he refused to have her around or
even to talk and try to reason with her. It was obvious to him that
she did not want to care for him as John-Henry and I were doing.
My brother and I and the hired nurses were the only ones caring for
our father. Dad could see this and he could also see how much we
were trying to keep him around as long as possible. Bobby-Jo was
the first one to say that we should not try to prolong our father's life,
that he was suffering and should be allowed to die in peace. Dad was
the last to say he was ready to die.

John-Henry still wanted to try for an alliance with Bobby-Jo.
He thought that including her in the family discussion of cryonics
might make her less likely to contest it later. He wanted to try to

make her feel part of the family and explain to her why this option had become important to us.

I wasn't so sure.

IN OCTOBER 2000, DR. KERENSKY AT THE UNIVERSITY OF FLOR-ida's Shands Hospital in Gainesville determined that one of the valves in Dad's heart was leaking. If Dad had been a younger man, they might have gone directly to valve replacement surgery. But given that Dad was eighty-two, Dr. Kerensky advised moving forward cautiously. He felt we should try a pacemaker first and in November performed a Swan-Ganz catheterization to check whether Dad's heart could handle one.

As I mentioned earlier, even catheterization on a man Dad's age was risky. I was in the operating room for the procedure, and Dad was partially sedated. "Just reassure him, comfort him," Dr. Kerensky instructed me. I stood at the top of the operating table, stroking Dad's hair, telling him softly, "You're doing great, Dad. Just stay relaxed." John-Henry and I watched on the monitor as the scope entered Dad's heart. It was maybe a twenty-, thirty-minute procedure.

After seeing the results, Dr. Kerensky spoke to John-Henry and advised trying the pacemaker. We went with his counsel.

The pacemaker didn't help, though, leaving us with one last option: valve replacement surgery. Dr. Kerensky had told John-Henry it would be difficult to find a surgeon who would operate on an eighty-two-year-old man. He suggested a surgeon in Ala-bama, but John-Henry did some research of his own and chose Dr. Wayne Isom, chief of cardiothoracic surgery at New York Presby-terian Hospital in Manhattan. Dr. Isom had performed open-heart surgery on Larry King, Walter Cronkite, and David Letterman, so John-Henry felt he'd be most sensitive to the issues that come with a famous patient.

Dr. Kerensky, John-Henry, and Anita flew up to New York

with Dad in January 2001. I arrived the day after the operation and went straight to see my dad in the recovery room. I felt weak in the knees seeing him lying there. After the heart surgery, his body retained fluids and swelled up. He was so puffy I barely recognized him. John-Henry had prepared me for the swelling, but it was still frightening.

Dad had a very tough time recovering. When he developed a MRSA (methicillin-resistant *Staphylococcus aureus*) infection, a bacterial infection that's very difficult to treat, we flew him to Sharp Memorial, a rehabilitation hospital in San Diego. There he'd wake up for short moments of lucidity, but mostly he slept, which was good, since your body recovers more quickly that way. For six months or so we'd only have him for twenty or thirty minutes at a time. Every time we did we encouraged him, told him he was getting better, and we love him enormously and tried to keep things as positive and optimistic as possible to motivate him. Unfortunately, some others around us did exactly the opposite. When his friend Bob Breitbard visited, he kept telling us we should shut off the machines and let our father go. John-Henry and I hadn't put Dad and ourselves through all that just to give up and switch the machines off.

It wasn't until we reached California that John-Henry made the phone call to Bobby-Jo. While in California, John-Henry did a lot more research on cryonics and visited the Alcor facility in Arizona. He became very invested in the procedure and wanted to understand everything about it. He asked if he could meet a patient who was to be cryonically suspended. He thanked that man for letting him observe, explaining that he was doing research to see if this was something we wanted to consider as a family. My brother then shared with the dying man that his father was Ted Williams, and the man thought it would be a great idea for the American hero. Shortly thereafter the man died, and John-Henry witnessed the whole cryonic suspension procedure.

When John-Henry called Bobby-Jo, I was on the line too. We

wanted her to feel how united we were and to understand that we were essentially reaching out *to her* to inform her about our thinking and trying to include her in our decision as a family.

When John-Henry asked her if she had ever heard of cryonics, we were surprised to learn that she actually knew quite a bit about it. She knew the role of cryonics in the preservation of sperm and ova. The conversation was going a lot better than expected until she asked, "What, are you guys planning on cloning Dad?" Her voice dripped with sarcasm.

I looked at John-Henry.

"No," John-Henry said. "That's illegal—but it would be neat to have a little Dad running around."

He explained that Dad had agreed to do what we wanted and that we were trying to include her in the decision.

"That's all I have ever wanted," she replied. "I just want to know what is going on in my daddy's life."

John-Henry and I thought it was an important gesture to show Bobby-Jo that we were willing to discuss this with her despite her feelings about it. Frankly, we were surprised by her response.

"Is it something you would consider?" he asked.

"Oh, I don't know. I'd have to ask my husband."

John-Henry was encouraged by the conversation. He was convinced that Bobby-Jo would support our decision and that she saw the rationale behind it. He thought maybe this was not something she would question or object to after all.

I wasn't holding my breath.

The next time we talked to Bobby-Jo she had completely changed her tune. Suddenly she was certain that she knew what our father wanted, that God would disapprove, and that it just wasn't right. John-Henry was sorely disappointed and told her so. She had yet to support any of our decisions or help us in our care of our father, and my brother could see only one reason: she was jealous and resentful of our relationship with him. At that moment we decided to stop trying to talk with her about our father, then braced ourselves for her wrath and envy.

When we were told Dad had improved enough to head home, he definitely brightened up. We flew him back to Shands in Gainesville that June. That was when we saw the biggest jump in his recovery. He was more alert, sat up more often, and was making some of his old sarcastic statements, even letting out a turkey call here and there.

Bobby-Jo had never visited him during his six months in San Diego, but now she did. And every time she kept asking questions like, "Is he going to make it? What are the chances he's going to die?"

"We need you to be positive with him," the doctor told her.

But she'd go into his room teary-eyed and say, "I love you, Daddy. It's okay, Daddy. You can go. Just let go. God loves you. It's okay to die."

It was then that the relationship between us turned adversarial. John-Henry had sacrificed his relationship with Anita, his business, his dreams, and his time, all to care for his father and keep him alive.

"You are not a team player," John-Henry told her. "You are not supportive. You don't care about Dad and you sure don't care about us. Every time you show up you just want to know if he's dying. You haven't had a relationship with your father for years. You haven't offered to help us care for Dad once, not one time."

The only times I ever saw Bobby-Jo were at Louise's funeral and when Dad was in the hospital.

Finally it was Dr. Kerensky who said he didn't want Bobby-Jo to come visit Dad anymore, that she was detrimental to his recovery. He wrote an order that Dad was to have no visitors other than me and John-Henry. No other visitors could even visit his wing, which was locked. Visitors had to call from outside the door, and if it wasn't me or John-Henry, the staff denied entry. From that point on, John-Henry and I effectively excluded Bobby-Jo from any family decisions.

I watched my brother take care of his father through all this and was so impressed with how careful and gentle and attentive he was. Many times John-Henry and I watched the nurses being careless or rough with Dad. Pretty soon John-Henry was inserting Dad's catheters, or adjusting his IV when a nurse had jabbed it into Dad's arm at a crooked angle. He knew before the nurses did when Dad was restless or needed suctioning. He just knew, instinctively. It reminded me of the way a parent instinctively knows when a child is sick or in pain. In this last stage of our relationship with our father, it was very much as though John-Henry and I had become the parents, caring for our father like a child. Our relationship had come full circle.

Chapter Twenty-Four

Jﬂﬂﬂ OHN-HENRY AND I BECAME FIERCELY PROTECTIVE OF OUR
father near the end. We immersed ourselves in the mission of caring for him. If you were not helping us, if you were not caring and
being positive, you were not with us. You were not a team player. It
felt like it was the three of us against the world. All the hired nurses
and assistants were just doing a job. They were not nearly as invested
as we were.

Still, it didn't take long before some of them became blinded by
the star and seemed to forget their place. When Dad had guests over
there were caretakers who would invite themselves to sit in the living room too, cocktail in hand, and enjoy the occasion as though the
celebrity guests had come to visit *them.* This was inappropriate and
unacceptable.

Dad had a soft heart, though. Even when John-Henry let caretakers go, for good reason, Dad worried about how they'd get by
now that they were out of a job. Though he'd belabor the decision
and struggle with feelings of guilt, in the next breath he'd complain
that they'd been an embarrassment.

This was where John-Henry was direct and efficient. He made the job description and expectations for caretakers clear and concise. There would be no tolerance for drinking, smoking, theft, or having personal friends or family coming over to visit—not to mention illegal behavior. Everyone who worked for Dad also signed a confidentiality agreement and was made aware of the security cameras in the kitchen and living room. Caretakers were not to share personal information about Ted Williams and his family with anyone else. We were allowing people into our home to help care for our father, and we expected this responsibility to be taken seriously. In the end, these agreements proved to be worth less than the paper on which they were written. If the fear of a lawsuit intimidated some of the caretakers, some members of the press must have assured them that they were protected if their comments were made anonymously. This was the green light that fired employees were looking for to make whatever allegations and accusations they wanted.

In 1998 one of Dad's caretakers was so upset with John-Henry for firing him that he sought retribution by calling the Florida Department of Children and Families, an agency that handles all types of domestic situations, including abuse. According to this disgruntled former employee's phoned-in report, Ted Williams was being abused by his son. He alleged that Dad was held captive in his own home; that he was isolated from the world, unable to receive guests or telephone calls; that he was forced to sign memorabilia items throughout the day; and that he was not receiving proper medical attention.

The department had to take the report seriously. It sent a female agent to the house, accompanied by a male deputy sheriff. Protocol required that the interview be conducted on a surprise visit and that Dad be interviewed by the agent without John-Henry present. The deputy was there to ensure that this protocol was followed. Dad was allowed to have our family attorney, Eric Abel, present for the interview. A tour of the five-thousand-square-foot house satisfied the agent that Dad's living conditions were excellent. Then Eric escorted the agent and deputy to Dad's bedroom, where he was resting that afternoon. Eric remembers Dad immediately turning on the charm for the female agent, flattering her and telling her how glad he was that she'd come to visit him.

"*You're here to see me?* Well, that's awful nice of you. Tell me a little bit 'bout yourself. Where do you live?"

Eric got the conversation back on track, describing the serious allegations and the purpose of the interview. The deputy stood near the foot of the bed while the agent proceeded to ask Dad a list of questions. She received her answers directly from Dad, without interference or influence from anyone.

"Do you feel isolated? Are you being held in this house against your will?"

Dad looked at the agent as though she had two heads, then at the deputy. "No, this is my house."

"Do you feel as though you can't have guests come to visit with you?"

Again, with his head cocked and an eye toward the deputy, "I can have guests anytime I want. This is my house."

"Do you feel as though you are not allowed to receive or place phone calls?"

Now Dad was realizing that she was sincere in asking these absurd questions.

"Of course I can receive calls and dial the telephone. The phone is here by my bed. Is there someone you'd like me to dial?"

"Do you feel you are receiving proper food and medical attention?"

"Yes, I think so."

"Do you feel you are being abused or threatened by your son in any way?"

"NO," Dad scoffed.

"Does your son make you do things you don't want to do, such as working or signing?"

"No. He doesn't make me do anything I do not want to do. He gives me a reason to get up in the morning."

"Is there anything your son is doing or not doing that bothers you or upsets you?"

I wasn't present for the interview—I was in the kitchen, following protocol—but if I know my father, he purposely let the gravity of his silence take hold at this point. He knew exactly what was going on and was feeling a bit more empowered by the situation.

Finally he said, "Yes."

Silence.

The agent bit. "What?"

"Well . . . he could keep me a little bit more informed about the family business. That would be nice. I'd like to know what's going on in that Internet business too. And he could come up to eat a few more dinners with me. I want to see him a little more."

Everybody exhaled.

The agent realized that Dad was doing fine and wound up the interview. As she departed with the deputy she said she had no real concerns but had to file the report with the department.

Still, the phoned-in allegations somehow got leaked to the press. And as usual, the press reported the allegations without corroborating them or mentioning the agent's findings. The media preferred simply to trade on the provocative allegations of abuse.

After the report and the interview, we often remarked on the fact that many seniors would have liked to receive the "abuse" Dad was getting: forced to live in a large beautiful home high on a hill in Florida, with full-time caretakers, maid services, a cook, and the best medical care. Anyone who knew Dad knew that no one ever told Ted Williams what he could or could not do. All John-Henry ever did was help Dad get his way.

MANY VISITORS WOULD TALK TO DAD ABOUT LETTING GO, TELLing him that it was okay to die, that God loved him. They failed to understand that this just irritated Ted Williams and was counter-productive to everything the three of us were working so hard to accomplish. He needed and wanted to be surrounded by optimism and encouragement. He was fighting every day. How dare these visitors question our father's quality of life or presume to know what our father would want? Every single day John-Henry was there caring for his father, trying to improve even the smallest aspect of his dad's life. John-Henry almost never left his father's side. He endured even longer than I could have done. He was relentless and determined to help his father get better. John-Henry took every day as it came. He lived each moment with his father as they both struggled on the road to recovery. They celebrated the smallest of improvements together.

Behind our backs, some of the caretakers criticized us for prolonging our father's life, for not letting him just die. This criticism fueled us even more. I started coming home on Thursdays and staying until Sunday evenings. We started doing our own therapy with our father. John-Henry would lift Dad out of bed and carry him into the pool, where he was weightless, and we performed range-of-motion exercises with him. John-Henry was always watching him and talking to him. John-Henry became a father, caring for his only son. I became John-Henry's helper, supporting him and loving Dad right alongside him. We stretched our father to prevent contractures, then we would massage him and let him know we loved him and were right there with him. John-Henry turned one of the wheelchairs into a shower chair. He cut a hole into the seat so that we could access every inch of our father. John-Henry fed his father like you would a small child. He was studying the best foods to give him and the easiest to digest. He got the best vitamins and had the most highly qualified nutritionists advising him.

When Dad became constipated and impacted to the point where we thought we might have to take him back to the hospital, John-Henry asked me for my help. We decided that the last thing our father needed was to think he was taking a step backward. We called Dr. Dorn, a friend, and he told us what we should do. John-Henry rolled his father into the walk-in shower and told him a nurse was coming by to help relieve his constipation. I put on a baseball hat and penciled in a mustache. I had to. My father would have never allowed me even to know what was ailing him, let alone see him naked. I lowered my voice and explained to Mr. Williams what needed to be done. He never questioned me or resisted. He trusted me. I gave my father a glycerin enema while my brother held him tilted back in the wheelchair. It worked like a charm, and Dad felt so much better. We gave him a vigorous shower that he thoroughly enjoyed, dried him, powdered him, and laid him back in bed. Our dad was relaxed and content. We were proud of ourselves. When we walked out of the bedroom, my brother gave me the biggest, warmest hug I ever received. He told me I would have been a great nurse.

As Dad's health continued to decline we remained steadfast. John-Henry studied the dialysis machine and wanted to know every level in Dad's blood. He would question the dialysis nurse and suggest possible tweaks. I admired my brother's unwavering attention to his father. He knew before the nurses did when his father was feeling uncomfortable or when he needed to go to the bathroom or when his tracheostomy needed to be suctioned. On good days we would bring Dad out on the patio and lay him on the massage table in the sun. Dad loved the warmth of the sun as we rubbed lotion on him, giving him a massage.

When our mother came down to help us, she convinced us that the sun was excellent at killing bacteria and persuaded us to let the sun reach every crevice and crack of Dad's body. She had obviously touched, loved, and cleaned every inch of his body and showed no hesitation returning to a familiar place. Dad put up no resistance. There were a few times when our American hero was sunbathing stark naked on the back porch of his Citrus Hills home. Mom was right. The skin rash he was developing disappeared.

Other times, when the weather was nice, John-Henry would roll his dad out under the large oak trees that surrounded his hitting cage and have his father watch him hit. Dad would watch intently as his son swung and swung. Dad wouldn't say much—he couldn't say much—but if you knew his body language you could see him twitch and see his hands grip as he watched John-Henry in the cage. John-Henry would stop every so often and talk to his father about what he thought he could improve on. Dad would give simple instructions that seemed to speak volumes to my brother. "Hit up. Quicker, hips, hands." Dad was watching and teaching.

The whole time we cared for Dad, my brother showed compassion, sensitivity, and thoughtfulness. We loved and respected our dad. John-Henry would look at him from time to time and say, "Do you know I love you?" This was not a son who was "just waiting for Ted to die so that he can get all his money." The fact is, John-Henry would have given every dollar he had just to spend more time with Dad. In 2002, shortly after Dad died, the *Boston Globe* ran an article called "The Kid's Only Son." It included this passage:

> "Ted needed John-Henry as much as he needed Ted," observes Dr. Jeffrey Borer, a New York cardiologist who began treating Ted Williams four years ago. Without John-Henry, Borer flatly asserts, Ted would not have made it through the last 18 months of his life. Perhaps not even the last eight years, following a stroke he suffered in 1994.
>
> "If I ever get that sick," says Borer, "I hope my own kids are that attentive."

That is so very true—and so very different from the way the press usually portrayed John-Henry in the weeks and months after Dad's death.

There were times we badly needed breaks—especially my

brother. So many people criticized him for playing computer games for hours. I admit I thought it was a bit excessive too, but I came to realize it was an escape for him. It was a distraction from all the worry and concern. For a while he could get lost in the fantasy of a game, forget about the impending pain and grief. I know this because, when my brother died, I sat for hours, lost in a trance, playing the same games we had played. So yes, for breaks we would play computer games. While Dad slept, we played games and watched tons of movies. Then we would start to talk.

We talked about our futures and what we wanted to do. John-Henry still wanted to make it in baseball. He spoke like he was determined and disciplined. He knew he might have only the slightest of chances, but he wanted to give it one last try with complete devotion. I understood him, but I believe another reason he wanted to play baseball, one he never verbalized, was to be forever near his father even after his death.

Baseball will always keep our father's legacy alive. No one can take away our father's performance on a green diamond, and regardless of everything else that transpired in his life and even in his death, our father will always sparkle. He will always be remembered as an American hero who fought for his country not once but twice and was considered by many to be the greatest hitter who ever lived.

Chapter Twenty-Five

I T WAS IN THE MIDDLE OF OUR CLOSE CARE FOR MY FATHER AT the end of his life that my brother and I got into the worst argument we'd ever had.

By that time I was twenty-seven, my triathlon dreams were over, and I was working full-time as an activities director at Fairwinds Treatment Center and helping to care for Dad. In the middle of all this, I felt ready to get out on my own and get my own place. My father had set up a trust in 1986 that contained a thousand bats for my brother and me. These bats had pristine signatures on them and had been locked away in storage ever since. I called my brother at the office to tell him I wanted to sell mine. I knew exactly to whom I was going to sell them. When my brother wasn't available, I asked his secretary for the number of Jerry Romolt. I knew my brother had done business with him, and I assumed I could too.

My brother was furious. He fired his secretary for giving me that number and was on the phone scolding me. He told me that I should have checked with him first because I had no idea how this business was run and did not know how to negotiate a proper price. He was very concerned that I was going to flood the market by selling all my bats and said I didn't know whom to trust. He had worked too hard to keep the value of Dad's signature high, and he was angry that I would potentially undermine all that he had done with one quick sale.

I had no intention of selling all my bats. I only wanted to sell enough to buy a house. When I explained that to John-Henry, we negotiated a deal that he could buy my bats from me for the same price that I had negotiated with Jerry Romolt. In the event of any future sales, he would also have first right of refusal. I had no problem with this contract, and for the time being it seemed to work out for both of us. John-Henry was controlling the market, especially the rare bats, and at the same time I was making enough money to make mortgage payments and live in my own place.

About three months into the contract, the money stopped coming. I waited and gave him reminders that he was behind. When there were still no payments and I had a mortgage payment due, I went ahead and contacted Romolt again. He was quick to step in and take the remaining bats.

Three days later I was served with an injunction to cease and desist. I couldn't believe my eyes when the sheriff showed up at the door and served me with the papers. I thought something terrible had happened. Instead, I opened the document to discover that my brother was suing me. He was trying to stop the sale of the bats. Jerry Romolt had already taken the bats. I already had his checks. I just had to deposit them. Now it was my turn to be furious.

I probably asked my father fewer than ten times in my life to sign something for me or anyone else. I had saved my money since I was ten and had never asked my father for anything. My father had left these bats to my brother and me, and I thought it was an appropriate time to sell *some* of them so that I could invest in a home. I called my brother and our attorney Eric Abel and gave them hell. I asked Eric how he could condone such behavior from my brother, especially since he knew our family so well and knew there were certainly other options to resolving this. I told my brother that I was so disappointed in him. I couldn't believe that he was suing his sister. "How could you do this?"

My brother yelled right back at me. He told me that Jerry would never pay me and should not be trusted. He told me I didn't know what I was doing. This was the only way he could protect me, the bats, and the market. It was business and I shouldn't take it personally. Angry and hurt, I did take it personally, and I didn't believe him. We'd never had a fight like that—ever. I didn't think we would ever come back from it.

I didn't always understand my brother. There were times when he seemed like a mad scientist so fixated on a belief that there was no getting through to him to ask a question. He didn't always have the patience to explain how he got to a certain conclusion and assumed that people, especially his little sister, would just believe him and trust him. He simply knew better. He would never take anything at face value and challenged almost everything. His mind raced forward, and it was hard to keep up sometimes.

The timing of this whole thing couldn't have been worse. I was served with the injunction in April 2002. By April 15, a judge had granted the injunction, and I was not allowed to sell the bats to Romolt. But I had already let Jerry take 175 bats with him when he left town. I called Jerry and told him I needed the bats back because the judge had granted the injunction. He refused, claiming that he'd already promised a buyer and couldn't back out of the deal now. If I cashed the checks, it would be the same as agreeing to the contract. Jerry then went on to tell me that I *couldn't* cash the checks because he didn't have the money yet, but as soon as he did he would pay me and then I could settle with my brother.

In the end, I never got paid, and I never got my bats back. By the time I'd obtained a judgment against Romolt for the $105,000 in bats, it was too late. Romolt had filed for bankruptcy. My brother was right. If I had listened to him from the start, I would never have been in such a mess. Now I was in legal battles with Jerry *and* my brother, with nowhere near enough money to pay attorneys. I gave up and just let the attorneys take over. They always ended up winning anyway.

Three months later Dad died, and my brother and I still were not speaking.

ON FATHER'S DAY BEFORE DAD DIED, HE WAS SITTING AT THE table looking out the window. He seemed very far away. I sat there thinking alongside him, and I thought of Bobby-Jo. Despite clear instructions from everyone, including my father, that no one wanted to hear of or speak to Bobby-Jo anymore, I picked up the phone and dialed her number. I was trying to eliminate any possible regrets. She was living in Citrus Hills at this time. She answered the phone.

"Hi, Bobby-Jo, it's Claudia. I thought you might want to talk to Dad. Would you like to wish him a Happy Father's Day?"

"Yes, I would."

That's all she said. I looked at Dad and tried to get his attention.

"Dad, Bobby-Jo is on the phone. She wants to wish you a Happy Father's Day."

I held the phone up to his ear. Dad didn't say much; he just listened. He pushed the phone away with his head and looked back out the window.

"Tell her I'll meet her at the ballpark."

I believe those were the last words he said to his first daughter.

On July 4, I spoke to my father for the last time. I was living in St. Petersburg, Florida. The phone call came early, around 6:00 A.M. One of the nurses told me that my father wanted to talk to me. I heard Dad breathing on the other end of the line. He didn't say anything.

"Hi, Dad," I said softly. "Happy Fourth of July."

"Claudia? Claudia, I love you." His voice was weak and raspy.

"I love you too, Dad, so much."

"I love you!" He said it louder now.

"I love you, Dad." I was standing in my bedroom looking out my window. I heard my father take a deep breath, and the air rattled as it passed by his tracheostomy. With one loud exhale, his words came out like a scream.

"I love you and don't you ever forget it!"

"I'll never forget it, Dad. I'll never forget you. I love you forever."

I should have gotten in my car and driven straight home. I didn't, though, and I regret it deeply. I wish I had rushed to his side so that he wasn't alone. I had flown to Boston that afternoon to visit some friends for the holiday weekend. I didn't hear of Dad's passing until around 10:00 A.M. the next day.

I've struggled with this regret for a long time. As in so many things, Dad died on his own terms. I don't think he would have let go unless my brother and I were *not* there. He fought to present his best side when we were with him, and I think he would have struggled with his passing if we had been there. It doesn't make me feel any better knowing he was alone, but I have to move on.

John-Henry picked me up at the airport, and I was frightened for him. He was very emotional. He kept apologizing to me that he wasn't there for Dad, and he was so sorry that he couldn't get ahold of me. I didn't say much.

"It's not your fault."

There was a mix of emotions flying all around. I was worried for my brother, and I was worried about the media tsunami coming our way.

John-Henry finally got to play professional baseball in 2002, at the age of thirty-three. He signed with the Gulf Coast League Red Sox. Dad "was proud of his son and glad he decided to take a shot at baseball," Bill Nowlin writes in *The Kid*. In the last weeks of his life Dad told one of his nursing staff, "You know, I'm really proud of

John-Henry playing pro ball. I never pushed him to it, but I'm real glad he's doing it now."

In only his second game John-Henry broke a rib chasing a foul ball into the stands. Dad died eight days later, on July 5, 2002. The next month John-Henry resigned from the Gulf Coast League team. He knew we had a war coming on, and he didn't want to bring any embarrassment to the Red Sox.

When Dad died, John-Henry arranged to have his body rushed to Alcor. Bobby-Jo was calling the papers the very next day, saying that John-Henry was having Dad "frozen" against his wishes and that my brother was going to sell DNA to make money. She cited the 1996 will, in which he stated that he was to be cremated and his ashes spread on the ocean where he'd fished. Ironically, this was the same will in which Dad removed her from his estate. She claimed that John-Henry was planning to have our father cloned. "I will rescue my father's body," she told the Associated Press. "Me and my attorney are working on that." She initiated court proceedings.

As I had predicted, the media had a field day with the story. An OJ-level news circus descended on the Citrus Hills house and the courthouse in nearby Inverness. John-Henry and I were devastated by the loss of our father, grieving, alone in the house, and besieged by news crews every time we set foot out the door. No one seemed to realize or care that we were two kids who had just lost their beloved dad. I couldn't help but wonder if this was how they would want to be treated when they lost a loved one.

Almost all the coverage was negative. "Ted on ice. Freeze-dried Ted. The Frozen Splinter. Could this be any worse?" a Boston sportswriter opined. An ESPN writer moaned, "I just hope and pray that we never see anything stranger or sicker than John-Henry Williams grabbing his dad's body and freezing it for God knows what reason. . . . Stop and think about that for a moment. Ted Williams. Frozen stiff. By his son. The whole thing is so bizarre, so ghoulish and so twisted." Television commentators followed suit. Connie

Chung called it "macabre." A CNN commentator said it was "grotesque" and "revolting." And on and on.

A lot of the critics the media were quoting were former caretakers or people from the memorabilia business who had a grudge against John-Henry. They were just waiting for their chance to jump on the bandwagon and bash him. It was a media frenzy further fueled by revenge.

Most of the press accepted as fact the hyped and half-truthful information offered by Bobby-Jo. She took a part of a conversation we had with her while in California and twisted and manipulated it so that it sounded like we would somehow benefit financially by cloning our father. That was completely fabricated. Clearly, most of these comments came from positions of nearly total ignorance about cryonics. As journalists piled on with knee-jerk exclamations of horror, it was obvious that very few had done any research into the science. The general public, most of whom probably knew even less about it, followed suit. It has been more than a decade since Dad and John-Henry died. The wild speculations made by Bobby-Jo and some members of the press have never occurred: my father's and brother's DNA has not been harvested; their bodies have not been cloned; and there is no "bunch of little Ted Williamses running around." Those things will never occur. This decision was made by a family who loved and respected each other. It is not a science fiction film.

I hate that I feel forced to explain and justify why we chose to preserve our family cryonically. Quite frankly, it is no one's damned business. It is a private family matter. It was a decision that came down to the three of us when my brother and I were the only ones caring for our father. We were the ones feeding him, bathing him, comforting him, and giving him the best care we could afford. Dad could see that. The media do not get to vote, or invite the public to vote, on such matters. It seems unimaginable to me that anyone should have any say in the disposition of a body in another family.

Instead of remaining private, our family moments and decisions were publicized and criticized. No one was supposed to know our personal family choices. We trusted people when we shouldn't have, and we were silent when perhaps we should have screamed. I convinced my brother and a team of lawyers not to dignify any of the awful accusations and comments of others with a response. I told my brother this was not a matter in which the public had any right to make a judgment. But judge us they did, criticize us they did, ridicule us they did, harass us they did, and finally, they crucified us for the entire world to see. Our character and our integrity were beaten to death.

Perhaps I was mistaken about maintaining our silence. Perhaps we should have unleashed a war of words and systematically dismantled each and every lie that was said about us. I'm not sure. I am sure of this, however: I cannot rest if I do not defend the two most important people in my life, my beloved father and my beloved brother.

One of the saddest things for John-Henry and me, which few people know, was that we wanted to offer a very special memorial service for Dad's fans. We wanted to give fans an opportunity to say good-bye to their hero. Unfortunately, when Bobby-Jo went to the press she robbed us of that gesture. Instead of grieving with the fans, we were protecting ourselves from the media. We were unable to offer closure, and that is something we did regret. That we did not hold a memorial service seemed to give critics permission to strike out even more against John-Henry and our family decision.

Privately, we had our supporters. Longtime friends of the family, those who truly knew our family, were always respectful and supportive. We were impressed by the friends and dignitaries who had the principles and courage to openly respect our decision as one to be made privately, as a family. Presidents called to express their respect for our father and the family's wishes. We received calls and cards and read statements from business leaders and friends—including

Jack Hillerich, whose company produced the Louisville Slugger bats, and members of the Red Sox organization—all of whom were always mindful and respectful of our grief and our family's wishes.

I was terribly hurt, however, when Anita did not come to us when Dad died. She had become part of our family. I couldn't understand why she did not come to be by our sides at that great time of need. She understood so much of what we all had to go through when dealing with our estranged sister, the media, and the disgruntled employees. She knew they had nothing nice to say about us and were only trying to profit from the Williams name. I couldn't understand why she wouldn't put aside whatever differences she had with my brother and just be there with us as we mourned our father. It was a terribly painful time. She had been in that foxhole with us and understood so many of the family dynamics we were going to have to cope with. We needed a friend with us while we were in hiding from the press, grieving, alone. She never came down, though, and when she finally called, I yelled at her. I told her that she should be here, be with us, and we could comfort each other even if it was just as friends. Dad would have wanted it—he would have expected it, because he loved Anita too.

The members of the press portrayed the post-death legal matters as a family battle. There was no battle. The only three who had any right to weigh in on the matter were Dad, John-Henry, and me, and we had already agreed. While the press raged on unilaterally, we the family kept silent. Many times people have asked me why John-Henry and I didn't set the press straight and fight back against all the terrible lies that were written. This was mostly my doing. John-Henry would probably have fought back. He and Mom were fearless that way. They didn't seem to care what people thought about them. They spoke their minds. I was more like my father. We did care what people thought. At the time I didn't think it was a war we could win. The press had made up their mind, and a mob had been formed.

John-Henry and I were not talking, we were grieving. So the press quoted anyone who would talk. If these persons wanted to remain anonymous while telling their lies, the press simply called them "a source close to the family." It seemed like anyone who claimed to know Ted Williams was presented as a credible, reliable, and worthy source. Apparently the press never checked these "sources" for honesty, validity, integrity, or, most importantly, credibility. The biggest headlines came from the most unreliable sources. They ranged from disgruntled former employees, known drug users, spurned lovers, and casual acquaintances to people with purely biased opinions. These were the worst of the people ever associated with our family, and they were invited onto the public stage, where they couldn't resist appearing on live television or providing quotes to national newspapers. They seemed better suited to *The Jerry Springer Show*. Speaking irresponsibly and without regard for anyone other than themselves, they showed the entire world how simple-minded and untrustworthy they could be. I can confidently say that most everything written about my brother was fabricated. There was only a splinter of truth in a pile of lies.

We made only two comments to the press. First, upon Dad's death, we released a brief statement confirming his passing, thanking many people for their support, requesting that donations be made to the Jimmy Fund, and reminding the world that Dad was a private man in life and that he had wished to remain private in death as well. Second, when Bobby-Jo breached that privacy by grabbing headlines with provocative falsehoods, we denied them as absurd and again requested that donations be made to the Jimmy Fund in lieu of flowers.

Later, in July, we also made public "the pact" that John-Henry, Dad, and I had all signed back in 2000. It was just a handwritten note that stated: "JHW, Claudia and Dad all agree to be put into biostasis after we die. This is what we want, to be able to be together in the future, even if it is only a chance."

The press placed a lot of importance on "the pact." However, the lawyers made it very clear to us that a signed document was *not* necessary for cryonic preservation. They explained that in Florida (and other states) the remains are the personal property of the estate and are passed on to the heirs for disposition. Since John-Henry and I were Dad's only heirs, we decided what was to happen with the remains. We knew what had been unanimously agreed upon. Even if Bobby-Jo had been an heir and objected, the majority of the heirs (in this case, two out of three) would have decided what was to happen with our father's body.

Despite the legal assurance, I am very thankful that we had that note. If it hadn't been for that little piece of paper, we could have been subjected to extended litigation by Bobby-Jo and even more public harassment over a matter that was never intended to be made public.

I can tell you that my family chose cryonics out of love. No one would spend over $100,000 and subject themselves to public outrage and ridicule for someone they don't dearly love. There was no ill intent or devious plan. Dad's loss of health and impending death was a time of terrible grief, and we had to deal with it on our own. It was during that moment in the hospital room that my brother and I realized our father would do anything for us. To him, we were worth living for despite the impaired quality of life that might ensue from further medical intervention. Our father knew we needed something to hold on to for hope and comfort when we missed him the most, and if cryonics was the answer, then the solution was simple. As far as he was concerned, he had lived his life. He was going on regardless, and he wanted to give his two children, especially his son, whatever they needed to keep going.

To best understand the decision, any father, mother, or child only needs to imagine being in the same situation. If you are on your deathbed and your loving family asks you only for this one thing, to give them a scintilla of hope in the future, would you agree? Whether you are a religious person or not, it should not matter that you would choose cryonic preservation over cremation or burial. That is, if you believe life on earth ends and the soul survives to be directed by God, then the disposition of the body would seem to be immaterial—whether it's cremated, buried, or cryonically preserved should not change God's course. From the other view, if you believe in the possibility of cryonic preservation and future scientific reanimation, then the disposition of the body is critical: it *must* be cryonically preserved.

Logically speaking, it would seem more appropriate to challenge cryonic preservation on the grounds of not being a good "investment." That is, you might rationalize that it is better not to spend your money on cryonic preservation and leave it for your children instead. But even that argument can fail if the children disagree, preferring to invest the money in the science of cryonics and the hope of its future. What if the cost was affordable and equal to the cost of cremation and burial? In that event, I imagine that participation in cryonic preservation would increase dramatically.

I don't think John-Henry, my dad, or I truly believed at the time, without a doubt, that one day we would all awake from suspension and be reunited. But we did take comfort from the idea that it was a possibility, however remote. It's no different from holding the belief that you might be reunited with your loved ones in heaven. Many people have taken comfort on their deathbed from the thought that they are going to see their loved ones once again. There are no atheists in foxholes.

Bobby-Jo stated that cryogenics was "very immoral," that she "was against it, and would stand against it." To me, it seemed like a desperate attempt to try to destroy the one last connection we had with our father. Bobby-Jo made it clear that she was going to make us lose our father all over again. I believe she resented the fact that we were able to have a good relationship with Dad despite his sometimes difficult personality. She hated John-Henry and vowed to "save Daddy" by "thawing Daddy" and "burning Daddy." Knowing the realities, we thought it likely that Bobby-Jo's efforts were less about "saving Daddy" and more about her own demons and anger. She was not driven by love for our father, but by her hate for us and her desire for money.

John-Henry was determined to stick to the terms of the note. No one was going to take away his hope and desire. He was so distraught over Bobby-Jo's self-righteousness and indignation that he wrote me a note because he could not even utter the words. On a napkin, it read, "This means so much to me, I would die for it." When I look back now and see that note, I can't help but wonder if he already knew at that point that he was ill.

Even the prospect of his imminent death could not tempt Dad to reunite with his eldest daughter. In the last months of his life, Dad made it perfectly clear that he did not want to see her. Bobby-Jo hired several local lawyers to try to sue for the right to visit with Dad at his house. She was convinced it was only John-Henry who wanted her excluded. It had to be John-Henry. When the attorneys learned that her father had made the decision—he told them himself, "colorfully" and directly—they refused to file for Bobby-Jo. Ultimately, Bobby-Jo found an out-of-state lawyer to represent her in her quixotic pursuit to see Dad, then "save" Dad, while grabbing some headlines and trying to remind the world that she was a daughter of Ted Williams.

John-Henry and I believed what really motivated Bobby-Jo was simply money and her self-important, self-righteous husband. She pursued politicians, former baseball players, and media centers and even created a website. She threatened John-Henry and me with continued media harassment, informing us that she would keep going until she got the money in full. She stated in mediation that she would stop all of her actions and promise to never speak of the matter again if we agreed to have the court break Dad's insurance trust and give her immediate access to all the money and bats in it.

We agreed. In December 2002, Bobby-Jo dropped her legal case.

But her husband Mark, despite the agreement, tried to keep up some public interest in the case until 2004, when finally a judge enjoined both of the Ferrells against any further objections or legal actions regarding Dad's remains.

As 2003 progressed the media circus moved on to new "scandals." Then, in August of that year, a man named Larry Johnson, who'd been employed briefly at Alcor, went to the media with accusations that Alcor had callously mistreated Dad's remains. He alleged that our father's neurosuspension had been botched and gruesomely mishandled. In an apparent attempt to profit from supposed photos of Dad's "frozen" head, Johnson posted them on his website and charged a fee of $20 to access them. Alcor sued Johnson and settled with him out of court. Johnson agreed to cease and desist and pulled down his website. We discovered during these proceedings that the same lawyer who represented Bobby-Jo in her claim to collect Dad's remains and have them cremated was also involved in this case.

The media eventually moved on again, and nothing more was heard of it until Alcor learned in 2009 that Johnson intended to publish a book on the subject. A judge in Arizona, where Alcor is located, enjoined Johnson against publishing the book. A few months later Alcor, having learned that Vanguard Press in New York intended to publish the book anyway, sought a temporary restraining order in New York State Supreme Court. Alcor argued that publishing the book would violate not only the prior court ruling in Arizona but also the patient confidentiality agreement Johnson had made as an Alcor employee. The suit also charged Johnson with defaming Alcor and Alcor personnel. Despite my appearance in court and public plea, Judge James Yates allowed the book to go ahead.

I issued a statement: "This book serves no public purpose and obliterates the innermost sanctuary of a family's privacy. I believe Larry Johnson violated the confidentiality of my family in the most vile manner. The privacy of my family and the resulting horror is of the highest degree and should never have been outweighed by the public's interest."

Alcor continued to pursue its case against Johnson into 2012, when he declared bankruptcy and issued a retraction and apology.

To this day I do not understand why Judge Yates allowed Johnson's book to appear. It could never have been published in Arizona, and I doubt it would have been published in Florida either. Publishing those photos was no different from releasing autopsy photos or private medical records or committing any other breach of patient confidentiality. Fortunately for my family, the photos in Johnson's book are not of Dad or John-Henry.

I started to wonder if this circus would ever end. I wanted to move on. I was tired of reading hurtful things and hearing about late-night talk-show hosts referencing our family as comedic material. I was approached a couple of times to write a book and give my account of my family and our choices, but I did not have the energy or the motivation. I could never defeat the biggest Beast of them all—the media.

ONE THING THAT I HAVE BECOME PASSIONATE ABOUT IS PROTECTing a family's right of privacy. If a family's private affairs are to be published, it should be by their choice, and not under the cloak of "freedom of the press." The state of Florida, for example, has already begun to curb the press and the media's access to private family affairs.

It's true that historically Florida courts and the state constitution tended to give more weight to guaranteeing public access to government records—which would include autopsy records and photos—than to the right of privacy of the deceased or the grieving family. That began to change in the 1990s when, for example, a judge sided with the family of the fashion designer Gianni Versace, who was shot to death in Miami, and ordered that releasing the autopsy

photos to the media would serve no public interest while only prolonging the family's grief.

The watershed came in 2001, when Dale Earnhardt died in a
crash in the final lap at the Daytona 500. The death of NASCAR's
most loved driver came at a time when there had been much discussion in the media and within NASCAR itself about the need to
improve driver safety. The press, particularly the *Orlando Sentinel,*
wanted access to Earnhardt's autopsy photos, with the stated purpose of having a paid expert examine them and make an independent
determination of the cause of death.

Earnhardt's widow, Teresa, went to court to have the photos
sealed. Grisly autopsy photos of NASCAR drivers Rodney Orr and
Neil Bonnet, who had also died in crashes, had been spread all over
the Internet, serving no public interest but morbid curiosity, while
brutally intensifying their families' agony. Teresa Earnhardt was
determined to protect her family and her husband's memory from
such callous treatment. "We can't believe and are saddened that anyone would invade our privacy during this time of grief," she said. "I
want to let you know that if access to the photos is allowed, others
will demand them, too. And make no mistake, sooner or later the
photos will end up unprotected and published . . . and most certainly
on the Internet."

A judge ruled in her favor, stating that the photos had no "bona
fide newsworthiness" and that making them public would only
bring the family "additional anguish and grief."

A bill was entered into the Florida State Senate to guarantee a
family's right to keep such records private. Dozens of news organi-
zations opposed the bill, arguing that it violated the freedom of the
press; tens of thousands of Earnhardt's fans made phone calls and
sent emails asking their legislators to support it. The State Senate
unanimously passed the Dale Earnhardt Family Protection Act, and
Governor Jeb Bush immediately signed it into law. When news orga-

nizations challenged the law in court on First Amendment grounds, the Florida Supreme Court turned them down, and the US Supreme Court refused to hear an appeal.

The Earnhardt Law has prompted other states to reconsider their policies on making autopsy records and photos public. North Carolina, Michigan, Delaware, Georgia, Iowa, North Dakota, South Carolina, and Tennessee have all enacted some form of restrictions. Some other states had already restricted access to these records. I see no reason why this law should not be enacted in all states. It's certainly not an issue I have put to rest.

Chapter Twenty-Six

I ONCE SAID—IN THAT CONVERSATION WITH MY BROTHER AND father years ago—that if I had one wish I would wish for world peace. I changed my mind. If I had one wish, I would wish to have my brother back.

John-Henry didn't tell me right away that he was sick. He didn't want me to know.

Fourteen months after our father died, my brother was diagnosed with myelodysplastic syndrome. I remember staring at the cursor on the computer screen reading the definition over and over. Precursor to leukemia. This wasn't happening. I couldn't move.

John-Henry had gone back to playing baseball in the 2003 season, for two independent league teams, the Selma Cloverleafs and the Baton Rouge River Bats. But he began to tire quickly, and one day he couldn't carry his bags in an airport without stopping for a rest. He left his baseball dream and came home to Dad's house in Citrus Hills. When I saw my brother, I hugged him as hard as I could. I didn't want to let go, ever.

"You are going to Dana-Farber—right?"

"No, I think I'm going to go to California. There's a really good doctor out there."

"Why? You have to go to Dana-Farber. They will take care of you. They will try everything. Please."

My brother was so strong, so fearless. I believe he went to California because he wanted the anonymity. I believe he knew he couldn't be strong and fearless and still fight cancer, especially if he didn't feel accepted. California represented escape and his best chance of focusing just on himself and fighting this horrible battle.

John-Henry didn't tell our mom until he was officially diagnosed with acute myelogenous leukemia. He was trying to remain optimistic and confident that he could beat this. He kept discouraging anyone close to him from coming out to California to visit him. He did not want anyone to see him.

I bought a ticket and flew out. He was angry with me at first. I just wanted to be near him. I slept on a cot by his hospital bed. Sometime in the middle of the night he reached down and tapped my head.

"I'm glad you're here."

"Me too."

He was silent, and I kept swallowing hard, keeping my tears at bay. I wanted to say so much, but didn't know what to say. John-Henry couldn't die. Please don't die.

"You know what?" His voice came through the dark. "I am so glad Dad died before he knew I was sick."

"It would have killed him, John-Henry."

"I know. . . ."

Despite our attempts to keep it quiet, word got out, and before we knew it the media and newspapers were running stories.

I was tested as a possible peripheral blood stem cell donor. I was a perfect match. The doctor told my brother that only if I'd been his twin could I have been a closer match. I underwent a procedure called apheresis to harvest circulating stem cells, but not enough could be collected. Harvesting my bone marrow was our next option.

All through John-Henry's treatment he continued to monitor the media coverage and the reports written about his father and himself and his family. He kept in contact with many people via email, but turned them all down for visits.

At the most difficult time of his treatment, when he was the sickest and vomiting constantly, he still kept his laptop on the bed with him. One day about a month before he died, he looked over at me and said, "Look at this."

An email was up on the screen. It was from Bobby-Jo.

"I hope you suffer. I hope you die slowly thinking of the pain you put Daddy through—you deserve it."

I was sick. I couldn't believe what I was reading.

"Don't even look at it. Delete it—forget it—forget her."

I think up until this point I still could have found a way to forgive Bobby-Jo. Dad was safe, and there was nothing she could do to take him away and, as she said, "make us lose him all over again."

My brother and I truly believed that Bobby-Jo's personality was largely explained by her being a victim of circumstances. She had her own demons to work through and probably never felt the love of her father. We also felt that she was often a puppet under the control of her husband. I think there was a moment when she really would have rejoined our family if she had not been so influenced by him, though the patterns in her behavior and her troubled relationship with Dad began long before Mark Ferrell came on the scene. When I read that email, though, I wanted to throw the laptop across the room and stomp on it. I really wanted to stomp on her. All the understanding I was trying to have for her, even despite the whole cryonic controversy, disintegrated.

MY BROTHER DIED ON MARCH 6, 2004. AS SOON AS HE WAS GONE, people started reaching out, apologizing for attacking our family. Some of my brother's worst critics called and emailed, stating that they'd had no business commenting on such a private family matter. They admitted to feeling guilty and apologized for getting involved. But the damage was already done.

Still others emerged, darker and more cynical, to try to get Ted Williams's daughter to accept offers that John-Henry, far from "buckling" under their pressure, wouldn't even consider. So many dealers saw this as an opportunity to profit and take advantage now that John-Henry was no longer there to keep a watchful eye on the family business. They knew I was the only one left.

One of my father's most prized possessions was a baseball autographed by Babe Ruth. It was signed "To my pal Ted Williams from Babe Ruth," and it was the only autograph Dad ever asked for. It showed up at a lower-end Internet auction site after John-Henry died. It had been stolen sometime in the late to mid-1980s from Dad's library/office in Islamorada, where it had sat on a little plastic holder among other memorabilia. Sadly, the fact that it had been displayed in that room, on the second floor of his house, meant that it had to have been someone very close to Dad who had stolen it.

Other items that had been entrusted to friends were suddenly offered on the Internet and described as given to them by their good friend Ted Williams. Dealers called to ask for clippings of Dad's hair, old canceled checks (highly prized among collectors because they cannot be forged), even prescription medication bottles. I couldn't believe what dealers wanted to buy. I hadn't realized how valuable the personal checks were, and I was shocked that the sharks were trying to take advantage of the fact that I was not savvy in the memorabilia business. Former employees also emerged, attempting to profit off my father by pitching marketing ideas, from dollar bills or T-shirts with Dad's image on them to coveted memorabilia. Personal memorabilia appeared on auction sites reportedly gifted to the consignor by his pal Ted Williams. I never recognized the name and wondered why Dad would have gifted away such a valuable piece of memorabilia. When Dad passed away, our family did not own one game-used baseball uniform, glove, or set of cleats.

I had a completely new battle to fight, and now I was alone on this wicked battlefield. I had to take over in an area in which I had no experience and was forced to deal with individuals for whom I had little respect. I was criticized by everyone from former dealers to my brother's closest coworkers. I couldn't win. I didn't do anything right, and the criticism was coming from all sides.

I felt more anger and hate in my life than I ever had. I innately understood my father's disdain for the sharks of the memorabilia world. You have to have a tough skin with these bottom-dwelling, bloodsucking slime-buckets. John-Henry was able to disregard the low-lifes until they disappeared or offered the proper prices on his terms. I needed help, though. I wanted to believe someone was going to defend me and protect me. I wasn't accustomed to being swindled or bamboozled and felt dirty just dealing with these people. It seemed they just wanted to put me over a barrel. My natural propensity to believe and trust people was obliterated. I couldn't believe my feeling of abandonment and their complete disregard for my well-being. Only eighteen months after losing my father, I had lost my brother, and these people *still* thought only of themselves and of how they could take advantage of the situation.

It's ironic that the very people who had leapt to the podium to blurt out their malicious and inaccurate descriptions of John-Henry and our family came back to apologize when they learned of his leukemia diagnosis and his untimely death.

Arthur W. "Buzz" Hamon, the former director of the Ted Williams Museum, joined forces with Bobby-Jo and Mark Ferrell to depict John-Henry as a heartless villain who was cryonically preserving his father against his wishes. Peter Sutton, our family attorney in Massachusetts, somehow was included in an email list and received copies of all "mass" emails updating everyone on their latest plans to slay John-Henry in the media.

Shortly before February 2004, we received an email from Buzz. He apologized for getting involved with our private family decision and regretted saying the things he did about John-Henry. He stated that he would never want someone to judge him for what should otherwise be a private family matter. On February 9, 2004, Buzz shot himself in the chest. Ironically, it was the tenth anniversary of the opening of the Ted Williams Museum.

Lewis Watkins was one of the original founders of the Ted Williams Museum and a local artist. He also became a foe of our family when it was discovered that he had taken advantage of Ted Williams's name and signature on several projects; he insisted that Dad wanted to sell these lithographs to raise money for his museum. Watkins demanded cash and pocketed it. He also was paying a poor local artist cash for creating artwork of Ted Williams, then claiming it was his own work. Some of the "anonymous" quotes in articles led us to believe that it was Watkins jumping into the fray to defame John-Henry. On August 26, 2004, my brother's thirty-sixth birthday, Lewis Watkins was reported missing by his family. On August 28, his body was found by police in his art studio, with a gunshot to the head.

George Carter, one of Dad's caretakers, insisted that he knew what Ted Williams wanted when he died. "I knew Ted Williams like a book," Carter said. "He wanted to be cremated and have his ashes spread over the Florida Keys. He told me that many times. I would bet my life he wouldn't approve of this." Just months after my brother died, George called me and personally apologized for speaking to the press. He said, "It wasn't my place to criticize you for what you chose to do with your father's dead body." He went on to say that he knew above anything else that John-Henry and I loved our father. He told me that he should have never talked about my mother and father the way he had for Leigh Montville's biography of Dad, because she was portrayed inaccurately in that book. He then told me that he was so sorry that I had lost my brother. He told me that he too had cancer and the doctors had told him it had metastasized to his brain. He told me that he didn't expect to live much longer but wanted to make sure I knew that he was sorry and that he considered me a friend. George died shortly thereafter.

Richard S. "Spike" Fitzpatrick was the attorney representing Bobby-Jo in her attempt to claim Dad's body. On his website he is described as "Ted Williams' attorney" and as the one who handled the dispute over Mr. Williams's frozen body. On March 20, 2006, Spike died of cancer. Ironically, Spike told our family attorney Eric Abel that Bobby-Jo was "pissed" that she was being described in the media as an estranged daughter and that if Eric would stop calling her that, she would agree to settle. She stated that she "didn't like that 'the media' was quoting what others were saying about her."

And finally, on July 28, 1953, Dad was relieved from active duty, never to fight again. On July 28, 2010, Ted Williams's estranged daughter Bobby-Jo died of liver disease.

I have discovered so much about people. I can't believe how easy lying has become, how commonplace it seems to be now for someone to say something cruel and sinister about another person without any evidence. It is sad what people will say to boost their importance and pad their ego.

Chapter Twenty-Seven

On March 6, 2014, it was ten years since my brother died. It doesn't seem possible. It feels like maybe three years. I miss my brother every day.

One of the last conversations I had with him motivates me to keep going.

"If I ever get out of this, I'm going to become a doctor," he said.

I watched my brother and so wished that would happen. *Please let that happen. Please.*

"And I'll be your nurse, Brother."

He smiled at me and closed his eyes.

"I think I'd be a good doctor. You could be a doctor too, you know."

"No . . . I'm not smart enough."

"What? Yes you are . . . Claudia, why aren't you more confident?"

"I'm confident, I just know my limitations."

"We'll go to med school together."

"I would love that. That would be awesome. We would be great study buddies."

When my brother died, I didn't even go to the hospital. I just sat in the hotel room and stared at the walls. I didn't even want to think.

It seemed to take forever to get out of my hole.

Eric Abel is the attorney who represented my dad and my family for more than twenty years. He was a trusted adviser and a friend to all of us. Dad was impressed with his youth and his competency right out of the University of Oklahoma College of Law and often referred to him as "that kid lawyer." From the day they met, Eric was a very close friend of John-Henry's. The two of them worked (and played) together. Eric helped John-Henry structure and build several businesses for our family, as well as defend attacks against all of us.

Eric is now most certainly my best friend. In 2006 we married on the ninth of January. He encourages me every day and supports my dreams and aspirations. Finally, with his support and belief in me, I found myself in front of another adviser, asking her what it would take to get into nursing school. It's taken me a long time to return to a promise I made my brother, but in May 2014 I will graduate as a registered nurse.

No one in my nursing program knows anything about me or my life. I'm just an adult student named Claudia. Some of the students think I'm a bit intense, but they can't ignore that I'm serious about what I am doing, I care for people, and do well in my work.

As part of my nursing education, I've been required to complete a certain number of clinical hours in patient care. In our community, where all student nurses work in order to gain experience, I chose to work in a rehabilitation clinic.

It's strange sometimes how the world works. Or perhaps there really is divine intervention.

He was one of my first patients, and he was scheduled for a hip replacement. I was nervous as I stood outside his door, thinking, *What am I doing . . . I'm too old for this. . . .* I knocked and poked my head in around the corner. The elderly gentleman was lying on the table and was clearly in pain. I approached him carefully and smiled at him. He was grumpy and didn't even want to acknowledge the student nurse. Grasping at straws and trying to break the ice, I looked for something I could talk about. He was wearing a New York Giants jacket.

"So, you're a Giants fan? You must be from New York."

He glanced over at me and just grunted.

"I'm a Patriots fan myself," I tried again, smiling.

He just stared at the ceiling, seemingly annoyed.

"I'm here to give you some therapy and ultrasound on your hip. Will you please roll onto your side?"

He complied.

I carefully exposed his backside and gently started rubbing his hip and thigh.

"So where are you from?" I asked.

"Vermont."

"Really? Me too."

"No wonder you are a Patriots fan. You must be a Red Sox fan too."

"Oh yes, I guess you could say I'm a big fan. It runs in the family; I guess you could say it's in my blood."

"I love the Red Sox," he said.

"Me too."

We were quiet for a while. Then the nearly eighty-year-old man said, "Well, I got a story to tell you."

I quietly listened to him as he started to tell me about one of his fondest memories.

"I was there at Fenway Park when Ted Williams hit his last home run."

He turned his head and looked for a reaction.

"Really? I wish I could have been there."

"It was 1958, and the stands were packed."

"You mean 1960, right?"

"Was it? Are you sure? Maybe it was 1960. . . . Anyway, it was a bright sunny day, and I was there."

"I was told it was a cold and overcast day."

He turned again and took a closer look at me.

"You must really be a fan. There's no way you were there," he said, eyeing me, trying to figure out how old I was.

I just smiled and continued to work on his hip as he continued.

"The Splendid Splinter. He was something else. He had the sweetest swing and was always so focused."

"He really was."

"But you know what the greatest thing about Ted Williams was? He served our country and fought in two wars. He is and always will be an American hero in my book."

"He's my hero too."

"Yup, he was pretty great. . . . And you know what made him a great man?"

"What's that?"

"His whole career he supported the Jimmy Fund—he really cared for those kids. And he never left the Red Sox. He stayed with his team his whole career—not like today's players."

We were both silent, alone with our own memories. Finally, and I'm still not sure why, I said something.

"Isn't life amazing?"

My patient was staring at the wall as I finished up.

"Mmm-hmm."

"Would you have ever thought that fifty years after that day you saw Ted Williams hit his last home run his *daughter* would be taking care of you?"

For a moment my patient didn't move, then he slowly turned and looked at me. He didn't say anything as I helped him pull up his pants. He just kept looking at me.

"His daughter?"

I nodded my head and smiled again.

"You are Ted Williams's daughter?"

I nodded again and realized I had to get going. I had already spent way too much time with my patient.

"Will I see you again?" he asked.

"I might be able to see you tomorrow. Take care now. I have to go."

He didn't say anything. He just watched me walk out of the room.

Actually, I left quickly because I suddenly feared that he might start asking me about the post-death controversy. I didn't want to feel judged.

The next day when I walked into work I saw my patient in the waiting room. He was about half an hour early. He was dressed from head to toe in Red Sox clothing. His hat, his jacket, his T-shirt, all Boston. He smiled broadly when he saw me and asked if he was going to get me as his therapist. I hadn't even looked at my schedule yet. It turned out I did get to work with him for the next couple of days. Every day he brought in a newspaper clipping or a book or another story that pertained to Ted Williams. Never once did he mention anything about Dad's passing.

What I remember most about the few days I got to spend with my patient was how much Ted Williams had impressed him. Despite my father's flaws, despite the post-death controversy, my patient seemed to remember only his finest qualities and attributes. It gave me hope that more fans out there in the world actually see what is really important in a person. Maybe I have a whole family of fans out there willing to understand and perhaps forgive my brother and me for not managing to give them a chance to say good-bye to their hero. It made me sorry all over again that we hadn't found a way to celebrate the wonderful life my father had, together.

On the last day of therapy, before he went back to Vermont to get his hip surgery, my patient found me in the clinic to say good-bye.

He shook my hand and held it for a while. Then he said, "I'm sorry your family had to go through all that you did when your dad and brother died. It wasn't fair. You should have been given the freedom to mourn your loved ones. It wasn't right how you were treated."

The idea of freedom.

I barely got out "Thank you." His words touched my heart. It felt so good to hear someone share some sympathy and compassion for what we had gone through. His words left me with the hope that maybe others like him had kept open minds and hearts as they watched our family's ordeal and never lost sight of the truth through that time. Like my father, he valued the sanctuary of a family's privacy and knew that no bond is more significant than a family's love.

Acknowledgments

Writing this book, remembering many precious times, has been the best part for me. I want to thank Dad, Mom, and John-Henry for so many of my best days. I have immense respect and appreciation for all they have given me—the genes, the moments, the opportunities, and the love. Though they are with me every day in spirit, I miss their hugs, their friendship, their understanding, and their love.

Thank you, John Strausbaugh, for your patience and guidance.